Chasing God

Chasing
GOD

One Woman's Magnificent
Journey of Spirit

S̲HIRLEY C̲UNNINGHAM

Amoranita Publishing Co.
Scottsdale, Arizona

Amoranita Publishing
Box 15563, Scottsdale, AZ 85267-5563
Phone: 480.998.3081
www.amoranita.com

Cover design: Lightbourne © 2002
Back cover photo: Dr. Jerry Smith
Editing: Shanti Einolander

Library of Congress Catalog Card Number: 2002091772

ISBN: 0-9720571-0-2

First Printing, USA, 2002

Printed on acid-free, recycled paper

Available through bookstores or directly from the publisher.

Contents

DEDICATION

To the God beyond our naming
Who kisses us gently and fiercely
Each moment of our lives

ACKNOWLEDGEMENTS

In gratitude,

My most profound thanks goes to the Spirit of God who first led me on the surprising adventure that is my life, and then invited me to share it in this book. My gratitude goes immediately to all those who have had roles in *Chasing God*: my parents, Ron Cunningham and Anita Eulberg Cunningham Keppler; my siblings, Jim Cunningham, Mary Jane Keppler and Betty Sands; my grandparents, Florence and Jim Cunningham and Henry and Elsie Eulberg; my large extended family of uncles and aunts, especially Jean Marie Eulberg, FSPA and Roy Eulberg; my father-in-law, Ben McCauley, my first husband, Bob McCauley, and to my son, Kelly Benedict McCauley. Multitudinous thanks to my second husband, Jerry Smith, who walked through the day-by-day work of writing with me, took photos of my art, and helped with countless research and business details.

My life-long friend, Judy Noehl Hooks, deserves more thanks than I can ever give for standing at my side since we were children, offering support, humor, and love. Her enthusiasm for my early vision of this book and the steps along the way has buoyed my own.

I would like to thank others who have been on stage here also: the religious men and women who have been my teachers and counselors, especially the Franciscan Sisters of Perpetual Adoration and Jim Bertrand, MC. My thanks go, too, to Joe Hanss, M.D, Sandra Indes, Bonnie Danowski, Jean Erwin, Mary Kelly, Sue Joyce Godwin, Beverly Davidson, Petrina Green, Marguerite Davis, Susan Boles, Doreen Virtue, Ph.D., Coral Quiet, M.D., Christine Bourne, M.D., the radiation therapists of Arizona Oncology Services, the friars and staff of the Franciscan Renewal Center, Father Brian Fenlon, Celestine Cepress, FSPA, Marlene Marschall, Mary Ann Liebert, Sue Ann Thompson, Teresa Wysocki, Alice (Cookie) Olson, Irene Simes, Gabrielle Lawrence, Ph.D., Mother Teresa, Jane Fielding, Father Ernie Larkin, Dianne Murphy, Molly Macchiaroli, and my companions on the Black Madonna pilgrimage, especially Kathleen Peterson, Lorna Roberts, China Galland, Jackie Wall, Kathleen King, Martha Cone, Ellen Zweben, and Megg Watterson. Thanks, too, to the Goddess Gate pilgrimage group, particularly Cecilia Corcoran, FSPA, and Jean Kasparbauer, FSPA.

My gratitude goes also to those from whom I have learned: Ellen Bader, Ph.D., Lonnie Barbach, Ph.D., Patrick Carnes, Ph.D., Frances Ferder, FSPA, Father John Heagle, Harville Hendricks, Ph.D., Harriet Lerner, Ph.D., Ralph Earle, Ph.D., Roz Meadow, Ph.D., David Schnarch, Ph.D., Joan Timmerman, Ph.D., Aviva Gold, Meinrad Craighead, Julia Cameron, the staff of the Shalem Institute, and my counseling and spiritual direction clients, retreatants and workshop participants.

My appreciation to friends who have read drafts or offered assistance in bringing *Chasing God* to print: Mickey and Rev. Larry Grooters, Kayleen Buck, Carla Woody, and Jeanne Taylor.

Last but not least, I am grateful to my editor, Shanti Einolander, and to Shannon Bodie, cover and interior designer of *Chasing God*. Their professional guidance and good humor were a blessing to me.

FOREWORD

Shirley and I met as third graders at St. Gabriel's Parochial School in Prairie du Chien, Wisconsin, when the world was new. We were two precocious little girls, filled with the promise of every tomorrow, and we have traveled a journey of friendship, which stretches over fifty-five years. In Shirley, I have been blessed to see the reflection of my best self, even as I celebrate the beauty and talent which is uniquely her own. I know I am not alone. Over the years of her work as a spiritual director and counselor, many others have also seen their higher selves reflected in her eyes.

What did we remember as we came together in delight all those years ago? I like to think we called each other to stand at a high bar of excellence. Each of us, as needed, was reminded by the other that, as Children of God, we can act no less than the God within who calls us. We searched diverse paths looking for Spirit to guide us, only to discover God laughing with us in the gentle whisper deep down inside.

Shirley's whisper has become the truth which is *Chasing God*. The meaning she has found in her life and discloses here has meaning for us all. It is my privilege to share the celebration of her journey, with dearest love.

Judith Noehl Hooks
Prairie du Sac, Wis.
April 20, 2002

Getting Started

C *hasing God* is the story of my spiritual adventure following the powerful pull of Divinity. The book has been a work of Spirit. Inspired writing, from start to finish. Every day I've quietly waited at the keyboard for each word in the same way I've journaled through thirty years of crises and crossroads, attending to guidance through my dreams and hunches.

From my Catholic girlhood, to entry and exit from the convent, marriage, motherhood, divorced "singledom" at age fifty, annulment, re-marriage, and breast cancer, it's been an amazing trip, on the chase, steadily lured by the Holy One out of my conventional ideas, even my identity. I've found God hovering at every turn as I've eagerly traveled the terrain of the Spirit with no map, always on new ground, going I knew not where.

This book is not a theological treatise or a psychological case study, but the living breath of my life. A story of Spirit, true in its essence, in its depths. Every dream and prayer has been reported as the gift that it is. However, for literary purposes, and to protect the innocent or the guilty, whichever the case may be, some identities and incidents have been changed. My descriptions of the convent I lived in and the jail where I worked are my perceptions alone. Others made their own judgements, perhaps quite different from mine. This book is not a history of either setting, but rather, conveys what I learned along the way.

Yet, inevitably, my life is intertwined with those I have loved. Its full meaning cannot be told without disclosing pieces of the stories of others. As a counselor, clients often ask me for help with their secrets or those of loved ones. We all struggle to balance the complexities of dealing with our own secrets and those of others. It can be difficult to decide when concealment is harmless and when it carries a price too high in lost trust not to be opened. In guiding others, the prescription that guides me is, at the least, to do no harm. That is my intent here as well.

Secrets can destroy marriages. My husband kept a secret from me for twenty years. I knew and loved the man who lived with me in my world, a world of family, faith and love. I did not know the man who existed in a sphere separate from mine. My goal in telling my story is to present the truth that is mine alone with respect and acceptance.

These tales are, of course, my personal perspective on events remembered. May they ultimately bless each person who has a part in them as they have finally blessed me.

A friend recently asked me how I started writing this book. On reflection, I realized I'd been prewriting it in journals I'd filled over the last thirty years, sometimes using exact quotes in these pages. That was the long-range preparation. Shorter term, I remember Kate, a companion on the Black Madonna pilgrimage who, in passing the time on a long van ride through France, asked me about myself. I "fessed up" to being an ex-nun on a shamanic pilgrimage. She was interested then. Why had I gone into the convent? Why had I left? After marrying and having a child, how could a good Catholic girl like me get divorced, and then to be single and marry again in her fifties? Annulment, which was part of my story, was something she'd never heard of. But she herself was single in her fifties. Kate, fascinated by my spiritual metamorphosis, said, "I can imagine each part of your life as a chapter in a book." Little did I realize then how many chapters still remained to unfold.

Another short-term impetus for writing this book developed for me during a powerful workshop on intuition development. When Marguerite, one of the leaders, invited me to surrender anything from my past that could block the new gifts God had for me in the present and future, to my amazement, the spirit of my long-dead father spoke: *Tell your truth; write your story.* Once I understood that my old resentments toward him had blocked my creativity, the birth of the book had truly begun. My tears that day, I know now, were the breaking of the waters.

Chasing God was born of an urging I could not resist.

You will find two movements here. The first eleven chapters, "The Tales of the Chase," tell my spiritual autobiography. The second movement in the last chapter, "If Only We Attend," answers the question, "What value does my story have for others?" My hope is that as I have found courage to move through my fears, others will see that they, too, are called to transformation by the crises and crossroads of their lives.

So, I have written here of what is most intensely personal, stories of freedom, surrender, giving, forgiving, and love, knowing that the meaning is larger than my life. What my life has meant to me may also have meaning for you, the reader.

My purpose in writing this book is to let the Divine light shine through the small window that is my life in this world and, perhaps, illumine the way for others.

Can we, each of us, attend to our lives and find the light? That is my passionate hope as I invite you to join me on a magnificent adventure—chasing God.

TALES OF
THE CHASE

1

Following the Call

FRANCIS

Hollowness of poverty,
Gaunt-framed friar,
Thou, now filled with fire,
Walk before me,
Brown-robed,
Barefoot,
Thong-waisted
'Mongst the bird-thronged boughs . . .
Bearing
Wounds of brackish poorness,
Wounds of burning love,
Wounds of bleeding joy.
I follow.

"**M**om, Mom, what is it?" October winds whistled through the heavy silence from the other end of the line, rattling the dorm window beside me, then sweeping across the already leafless Missouri landscape.

"Honey, I've got some bad news. Your grandpa died."

Grandpa Eulberg? My grandpa? That strong patriarch dead? He'd had a recent sick spell, I knew, but it hadn't seemed serious. I struggled to take in what was turning out to be very serious.

"Mom," I started, then choked on the words, on my tears. I could see his handsome face, intelligence sparkling from his smiling eyes.

"It's ok, Shirley. It's ok, honey." Her tearful voice belied her words. "Can you get here for the funeral?"

I desperately wanted to, but how? Home was five hundred miles away and I had six dollars in my wallet, not even enough for a bus ticket. But, wait. Peter was in town. He could drive me home. I'd call him yet tonight.

Next morning, it was still dark when he picked me up at school. We set out, shivering and sleepy, to cross the cold, gray fields of Missouri and Iowa. As the quiet hours stretched out, I fell into silence, thinking long thoughts of my grandfather.

Henry Eulberg had come from Germany as a boy of sixteen with no particular prospects. It was the turn of the century and trouble was brewing in Europe. I'd never clearly heard the story. Immigrant Germans in the war-weary forties and fifties didn't talk about life in the old country. All I knew was that Grandpa's family, worried about their son, had sent him out of the impending German crisis to America, a land of safety and opportunity.

He found his way to the Midwest and married a wife

whose family, only a few generations in the states, supported themselves brewing the good beer they knew from the old country. His bride, Elsie Bittner, had grown up in Prairie du Chien, Wisconsin, on the banks of the Mississippi. The young couple settled in Garnavillo, Iowa, a little village a few miles from her girlhood home, only a ferryboat ride across the river.

I looked at Peter in the seat beside me noticing, for the first time, gray strands threading through his thatch of dark hair. Nearly thirty years old, he'd just returned from California and a year studying photography. I didn't have to guess what Grandpa would have thought of that. By the time he was Peter's age, he'd had the first two of ten kids and was running a lumberyard to provide for them.

Peter's brand new, 1961 Oldsmobile rolled smoothly over the highway. I doubted my hardworking, frugal Grandpa ever had a new car in his life.

My thoughts drifted to summer vacations at Grandpa and Grandma's house when I was a little girl. My big uncles had indulged me, their only niece, but not Grandpa. If my plate wasn't clean at the end of a meal, he'd frown sternly. "Daughter, you stay there until you finish that food, or I'll put it in your pants and bounce you on it." It didn't take long alone there at the table before I'd downed the last of the runny eggs, not wanting to risk his threat. There was never a doubt about who was in charge or that the family stuck together.

Looking sideways at Peter, I wondered if we would stick together. For three tumultuous years we'd taken turns vacillating. Unlike Peter, Grandpa knew he wanted a wife and family, and faith was his strong bulwark. Peter, on the other hand, was a skeptic.

As the quiet hours of the seemingly endless gray day passed, something settled deep in my gut. At long last, after three years, I knew Peter and I didn't belong together. We didn't fit. It was time for me to end it.

The day of the funeral, Garnavillo's tiny church was crowded with family and friends. The whole town knew Henry at the lumberyard, his wife Elsie, and all the Eulberg kids. We stood as the lengthy funeral Mass finally ended. When the choir intoned, "In paradisum, deducant te Angeli . . . May the angels lead you into paradise,"[1] pallbearers slowly processed down the main aisle, through heavy incense, carrying the body of this man we loved to its final resting place.

In the cemetery, bleak, gray clouds hung low overhead,

Grandma and Grandpa Eulberg

snow clouds. I shivered a little, sitting in the funeral home's shiny white car behind the hearse. It was comforting to be crowded here, knee to knee and shoulder to shoulder with Mom and Grandma, my brother and sisters, protected from cold winds whistling through the fields of dead stubble just beyond the cemetery. The only sound was the occasional whoosh of wind against the car windows.

Shifting in my seat, I closed my eyes. I hadn't slept well the last nights and was tired from crying. In the restful stillness, I slipped into a quiet, inner place, a place of rest. Then, as if marching one by one, words slowly came into my mind: *What does it profit a man to gain the whole world and suffer the loss of his own soul?*[2] In the silence, I turned the words over and over, examining them from all sides, like facets of a gem. Loss of soul? Loss of one's true life? Suddenly, a rush of tears flooded me. Grandpa, Grandpa. I knew beyond doubt that my grandfather had lived his life faithfully. But what about me? In that moment, I recognized a terrible yearning for my own true life. Loss of soul? I could never, never allow that to happen. I must live the life I so intensely longed for, the life that was uniquely mine.

Wiping the tears from my face, I opened my eyes to a single ray of sun, breaking through the overcast afternoon sky.

I'd been thinking about entering the convent for a while. When I was a teenager in the fifties, I knew well that a girl was expected to be a wife and mother, or in the Catholic ghetto where I was raised, a nun. Careers were practically unknown. In my small hometown, Prairie du Chien, women could teach, nurse, waitress, clerk in stores, type in offices. My Aunt Florence, an artist, was curator at the Villa Louis, home of Louis Dousman, a fur trader who became Wisconsin's first millionaire. I watched her construct dioramas for the museum, but I knew she was an exception.

Educated women were rare, and nuns were among the few role models. They ran our all-girls school, St. Mary's Academy, with efficiency and high standards, letting us know, with no boys around, we could be as smart as we really were. I'd found plenty to admire in these women: the good they did, their dedication, their ideals. Their life was a special calling to serve.

Although I'd been educated by Notre Dame nuns through grade and high school, it was the Franciscan Sisters of Perpetual Adoration, my Aunt Jean's order, that attracted me. The FSPAs had a spirit all their own. Mom often remarked how happy the nuns were and I, too, had felt their peace and joy. I'd considered joining them but fought the idea, never telling Mom or my closest friends. I liked boys, clothes, and dances. I couldn't imagine giving them up. Until now.

But there were practical questions. The Franciscan sisters accepted new candidates in September. Would they accept me late, at mid-year, or would I have to wait another year? In that case, it would be more than one year before my chance to take this step would come again. My savings for school had run out. To stay in college, I'd have to get loans, loans that would take years for me to repay.

I fretted. Not only was I starting late, I didn't know if the nuns would think I was a likely candidate. Most girls joined the sisters right after high school, or even before. My timing was all off. With Sister Jean in Guam, there was no one to ask if exceptions were ever made behind those convent walls. I had to find out for myself. Soon I had an appointment at St. Rose.

To my surprise, the General Superior of the Order, a petite woman in her sixties, answered the door in person. Mother Joan welcomed me with a smile, asking about my drive along the river road to LaCrosse, as she led me to the convent's formal parlor. To my relief, we settled into comfortable easy chairs. Despite my admiration of the nuns, I'd always felt shy around them, but Mother Joan didn't expect me to stand on ceremony.

She offered me a Christmas cookie from a plate of homemade goodies, then set it down on the coffee table next to a file folder with my name on it. "Your application is here, Shirley, and I've read it. It looks good."

When she smiled, I took a deep breath. Although at twenty-one I'd interviewed for a handful of jobs, this was another matter.

The little nun tilted her head to one side. "Tell me why you'd like to join us."

I dusted the last cookie crumb from my fingers and began to unfold the story of my fleeting thoughts of religious life since childhood, and my resistances. Her kind, brown eyes never wavered from my face. Her quiet attention helped me to go on. "I was running away, Mother. I tried to forget, wanted to forget. I had boyfriends, went to school, worked at jobs. And I did manage to push the convent out of my mind pretty well, until recently."

She nodded and smiled. "So many of us run away from God."

Her words cued a poem that haunted me.

As if she'd read my thoughts, she asked, "Shirley, have you ever heard of Francis Thompson?"

She was about to go on, but I interrupted, reciting the

words that had run in my head like a refrain: "I fled him down the nights and down the days, down the labyrinthine ways . . ."[3]

Mother Joan's eyebrows raised slightly. We were both surprised. For a moment, we looked at each other, then I gathered courage to tell her about Peter, my grandfather's death, and the words that had come to me in the cemetery. "Mother, I'm here because God wants me."

She sat back in her chair, fingering the rosary beads hanging at her side, looking at me intently. After a moment, she leaned to softly touch my arm. "Shirley, I believe you do have a vocation. Since you are a little older than most of our new candidates, you will be able to adjust to entering now, mid-year. Would you like to come to St. Rose in January?"

At her words, an immense joy flooded over me in waves.

Mom and Dad

I tried to compose myself, to find my balance. I hadn't realized that in fighting this call for years, I'd blocked something I'd longed for but couldn't name. Now, it settled into my heart with gentle sweetness. I really was going to enter the convent!

In the weeks that followed, the most peaceful interlude of my young life began. I quietly said goodbye to surprised friends at school and went home, home to Mom. After Dad had died, two years earlier, she'd moved in with her bachelor brother, Roy, on his hog farm near Grandma's house. At the beginning of the school year, harvest time, Mom had explained her decision to move, to rent out our house in Prairie. "Doesn't make sense for me to be alone here with the kids, and Roy alone there with all that work," she said. So she'd left the house I'd grown up in to take the kids closer to her large, extended family.

I packed up and left college. Home was where Mom was. It didn't matter where. I soon decided it was good for all of us to be around Roy, my youngest uncle, not yet thirty years old. Laughter rang often in the rafters of his rickety old farmhouse, Roy's the loudest of all. He'd come into the kitchen out of the cold, Iowa winter, red-cheeked, stamping snow all over the floor, good-naturedly recounting some incident of Sophie, his favorite "piggy." A city girl, I didn't know what to make of Roy's hog stories. He teased me plenty for it, but the house was so cheerful, I didn't mind.

Meanwhile, every day the mailbox was stuffed with a fat letter from Peter.

I'd read his proclamations of love, his offers of marriage on any terms, but strangely, his pleas didn't touch me. After a while, I stopped reading the letters, letting them pile up under my bed.

One cold evening, he came to the farm in person. He shrugged off his jacket and started right off. "I want you back. We can get married. Tell me what to do."

I listened to him say over and over what he'd already written, but the feelings I once had for him were strangely absent. He sat across from me at the kitchen table, smoke curling up from his cigarette, resting among the many already smoked butts in the ashtray. Our romance was over. That there was no going back was very, very clear to me. "Peter, I've already explained. You know my plans to enter the convent. I don't want to hurt you, but this is something I have to do."

His black eyebrows came together in a worried "v" above his glasses. "I made a mistake by going off to school in California."

"No, Peter. It's not that. You needed to go to school." I tried again, tried to explain. "My decision came later, when Grandpa died. I told you about it."

How could I expect him to understand? He had so little faith, so many doubts. "Something really important happened to me, and I can't ignore it. It's about God."

He gave a short laugh. "Well, I can't compete with God." He avoided my eyes, stubbing out his cigarette in the overflowing ashtray. "So you won't change your mind?"

What else could I say? Peter glanced up, then sighed, and pushed himself out of the chair. He'd seen the finality in my face. I stood, too, as he turned away from me to pull on his jacket. "I hope you'll be ok. . . ."

"I'll have to be." He stepped off the porch into the winter night, turning to give me one last crooked grin and the stiff, two-fingered wave that was his characteristic salute.

I stood in the doorway watching as the taillights of his car blinked smaller and smaller in the moonlit lane, red lights in the white snow, gradually disappearing into darkness. I knew part of my life had ended.

More snow fell. Temperatures hovered at zero, but neither Peter's departure nor the harsh Iowa winter could break my joyful mood. The weather didn't bother Grandma either. Mom and I watched her anxiously those first weeks after Grandpa's death, wondering how she'd get along, but she went about her days as she always had in December. In the corner of the front parlor, her miniature tree faithfully reappeared, sparkling with its antique star and the old ornaments that had been carefully packed away since last year. It would soon be Christmas. That meant not only decorations, but also cookies and candies from Grandma's homey kitchen.

She called early one morning, enlisting me. "Shirley, take me grocery shopping. I want to start baking."

Still in my nightgown, I huddled over the phone, hugging myself for warmth.

The thermometer just outside the window read twenty degrees and clouds overhead looked threatening. Although there were only a few miles between Roy's farm and Grandma's house, I knew I'd be sliding on black ice to get to there. But she wasn't taking no for an answer.

I told her I'd hurry, downed a cup of hot coffee, and bundled up. The wheezing car was stiff as I steered it down the icy country lane. Flurries blew past the windshield. I shivered.

By the time I loaded her into the car, the heater had taken the edge off the cold dampness. "God, Grandma. I'm surprised you'd even want to go out in this weather." Ready for adventure, she just grinned at me, head and chin wrapped in a bright blue scarf. Apparently, it had never occurred to her to break her annual family rituals despite weather, arthritis, or loss.

"Got your grocery list?"

"Right here." She pulled a wrinkled yellow paper from her purse. "I make the same cookies every year. Your grandpa always took me shopping. Oh, Shirley, I do miss my Henry."

She absent-mindedly smoothed the list on her knee, gaze drifting to the flurries outside. That was as far as she would go. She turned back to me. "We'll be all right. We've got lots of work to do. We'll make cookies." In that moment, I felt her staunchness.

By late afternoon, we were safely parked in Grandma's driveway with our load of groceries. On the drive home, the snow shower had become a whiteout. Stepping gingerly on icy patches, I guided her slowly to dry sidewalk under the eaves next to the house and saw that she made it into the nearly darkened kitchen. It took me a few more trips in the wet snow until the last bag of groceries was on the table.

Grandma had been studying the snow squall outside the window. "You call your mom. You're staying here tonight." She read the weather right. By ten o'clock, we were snowed in.

Next morning, I stood cozily wrapped in Grandma's extra flannel nightgown, surveying the untouched whiteness outside the warm kitchen. On the window ledge, a cardinal landed in the snow to breakfast on breadcrumbs she'd scattered. I held my breath, motionless, until Grandma bustled into the kitchen. "That guy keeps me company all winter."

The jittery bird startled into flight. "Scared 'm!" Grandma's blue eyes crinkled. "But you're not going anywhere today,

Shirley girl. Radio says all the roads are closed 'til the snow-plow gets through. Lucky thing you're here. Lots of cooking to do."

An assortment of bags, boxes, and cans were lined up on the counter: cinnamon, walnuts, sugar, brown sugar, chocolate mints, candied cherries, chocolate chips. Grandma pulled her recipe box, already fingerprinted with flour, from its place in the cupboard. She spoke to me over her shoulder, "Go get some clothes on. I'll get started here."

I poured a cup of coffee from the speckled blue pot on the stove to take to the chilly bedroom with me. By the time I pulled on my jeans and got back to the kitchen, Grandma had boiled and stirred the first batch of candy. "It's cooling there, in the pan of cold water in the sink." Grandma's voice was cheerful as she stuck a finger into the taffy. "I think it's ready." Though nearly too hot to handle, we pulled, stretched, and twisted the sticky candy in our buttery hands.

I chattered about going to the convent. Grandma listened. A very short list had arrived in the mail from the nuns, suggesting items to bring when I came: black stockings, black oxford shoes, a long-sleeved nightgown, plain underwear, a few toiletries. Not much else. I got my first impression of what the vow of poverty might entail. My mother would inherit my glamorous red coat with its black fur collar. I wondered how Aunt Jean had parted with her prized possessions when she'd left home.

Grandma, peering through her bifocals at the brownie recipe, answered without looking up. "My Jeannie was only seventeen when she went to the convent. She didn't have any fancy clothes, but I don't think she minded. . . ." Her voice drifted off. My aunt, a missionary, had been teaching in

Guam these last few years. I knew Grandma missed her, especially now with Grandpa gone.

She measured flour into her big mixing bowl, then glanced at me. "Jean took the name, Sister Mary Richard, for your Uncle Dick, you know, after he was killed at Pearl Harbor."

I knew the story. Grandma'd been through many trials with her large family. First, the war years when her boys were in service, one in a prisoner camp, one killed, and now her daughter so far away when her husband had died. Grandma's eyes welled up, but she shook herself, turning from the brownie bowl.

"Oh, quick, Shirley. This taffy's ready for the pan."

Then the next task, testing drops of red and green anise candy in cold water. Was it hard yet? Yes, and once set, needed to be carefully scored into bite size squares to be gleefully broken apart by all the younger grandchildren later. Then more measuring, mixing, boiling, stirring, baking.

In between, I quizzed Grandma for more of Jean's convent stories and watched the red bird outside, happily flitting between the breadcrumbs on the windowsill to his birdhouse. As the day passed, I felt as free as the cardinal. I had all I needed, too. My red coat didn't matter.

Finally, Grandma eased herself into a chair by the table. I sat across from her, young legs tired. Flour was everywhere, all over the table, her apron front, my nose. She twinkled her blue eyes at me over the mess we'd made, then pushed a sugary bowl and spoon across the table for me to lick.

Chocolate fragrance wafted through the house. Our day's work was done. The kitchen was full of delectable Christmas sweets ready to be wrapped: brownies, taffy, anise candy, fudge, peanut brittle, fruitcake, hand-dipped chocolate covered cherries, divinity, starlight mint surprise cookies, cherry winks, and a hard, German honey cookie that could pull your teeth out.

I helped her carefully stack the boxes and tins on the unheated porch that stretched across the front of the house. That done, Grandma pulled her sweater around her; "I'll catch my death out here." She bustled into the warm house, pulling the door shut behind her, but I wasn't ready to go in. I stood admiring winter's etching on the frosty windows, glistening in the streetlight's glow. Although it was only four o'clock, it was already dark.

This year Christmas would be like always, a day of celebration with the many uncles, aunts, and cousins around the holiday table. Grandma always filled it with steaming bowls and platters—potatoes and gravy, dressing, corn and beans, cranberries, homemade bread, and the lovingly basted turkey done to a turn. Even now, the place seemed to echo with the voices and laughter of my uncles and aunts as they elbowed each other in the crowded dining room, arguing about politics and football. We'd all be together, Mom and my little brother and sisters, too.

I looked through the glass door at the big maple table covered with white lace. Grandpa's chair was empty. This time, he wouldn't be here to quiet us down, to lead grace. My heart ached knowing we'd all miss him so much this year, my last Christmas at home. Suddenly cold, I shivered and stepped back into the warm house, quietly closing the door behind me.

On Christmas Eve, new snow in the farm lane sparkled under a night sky full of stars. Mom and I wrapped the last gift package and added it to the pile under the tree. Dishes full of scalloped corn and special Christmas cherry and nut salad waited in the refrigerator for the trip to Grandma's house tomorrow. The kids were tucked in and sleeping long since, dreaming of the day to come. Even Roy had gone to bed early. Mom and I quietly let ourselves out of the darkened house. The car tires crunched on cold snow as I slowly drove down the narrow lane to the highway. We were quiet, each thinking our own thoughts as we wended our way past the white fields of rolling farmland and across the bridge over the frozen Mississippi on our way to Prairie du Chien and Midnight Mass.

The sandstone walls and copper steeple of St. Gabriel's glistened in the moonlight and snow, visible for blocks as we crossed town. Once inside our old parish church, the fragrance of pine boughs filled the air of this Christmas Eve, as always.

We had just settled into our seats when acolytes in red and white entered the dark church, their flaming candles casting shadows to the right and left of the aisle as the celebration began. Finally, the boys stood in rows in the sanctuary between the manger scene's bower and the red poinsettias banking the altar. The priest swung a golden censer, incensing the manger, the boys, and then all of us. I breathed deeply. Children's voices sang ancient chants in Latin. Their melody echoed against the vaulted ceiling like a visitation of angels.

So many memories in this church. When I was a girl, the nuns had lined us up to march here from the grade school across the street. I'd climbed the narrow wooden stairs to the choir loft many times to sing these same Gregorian chants with my classmates.

I remembered my confirmation. I was ten years old, proud of my new, green taffeta dress as I knelt at the communion rail. I still remembered the bishop's gentle slap on my cheek, meant to convince me I was a "soldier of Christ," ready to suffer for the faith.

I remembered the funerals: my grandparents', my father's. So much loss.

I glanced at Mom kneeling in the pew next to me. Her eyes were closed, but a tear was trickling down her cheek. She felt me look at her. Without turning, eyes still closed, she found my hand and squeezed it.

This was our last Christmas together. We both knew it. The closeness that had grown between us after Dad died would change when I left for the convent. I was excited to go, but I knew she felt she was losing me.

When Dad died, she had three kids to raise, all in grade school, and no money. I'd worried and felt helpless about my mother's life. When the attorney who'd sorted out the estate offered me work, I moved home to help with the kids. At least I could do that, now that Mom had her first job in twenty years. We were constant companions those days. Saturday nights with my bachelor uncles brightened the week for both of us. They made sure their pretty, newly widowed sister and nearly grown-up niece didn't work all the time. Money worries and death seemed far away when we danced wild polkas, drank beer, and laughed at Roy's jokes.

Soon, the day of my leave-taking arrived. On the trip to LaCrosse, Mom was unusually quiet. My one small suitcase sat on the back seat. I drove the winding road beneath the bluffs, looking out across the embankment to the frozen river. Ice fishermen walked between their shacks on the

Mississippi. It made me cold to look at them. I lit a cigarette, offering one to Mom. "You ok?" I asked.

She picked a piece of tobacco from the tip of her tongue, then smiled at me. "I was just thinking of when I was your age, remembering the man I wanted to marry. You know, before your dad came along. I've told you about it." She took a deep drag on the cigarette. "It really bothered me, Shirley, that your grandpa broke up my engagement."

A sudden pang twisted inside me. I looked at the bare elm trees lining the road, their brush overhanging the river. I didn't want to cry. "Mom, is this really hard for you? My going, I mean?"

She laughed. "Well, sure. But you have to live your life, do what makes you happy."

"You know we can have visits, Mom, and I'll write. . . ." My promises sounded so feeble. How could I show her how much I loved her, how much I appreciated her letting me go?

She lightly touched my arm. "I know you will, Shirl."

Then, somehow, we were there. I parked on the snowy street, then leaned to look up through the windshield at St. Rose Convent. It was an impressive red brick building of many stories and wings presided over by the cupola of its large chapel. The convent sat behind a high wall. The cloister was intended to shut out the world, I knew.

I swung my suitcase out of the car and stepped up to the convent door. Every bare twig of the towering trees surrounding St. Rose was delicately blanketed in beautiful snow. The air was crisp. I'd see my mother again, and soon. Visiting was scheduled monthly, a few hours on Sunday afternoon in the convent parlor. I grinned at Mom, ground out my last cigarette on the cement step, and entered a whole new world.

The washroom mirror was so small. I stretched to see what I could of the short veil riding sideways on my hair. Not sure how to anchor it, I poked around with a bobby pin for a while, then gave up. I straightened to peer into the mirror again. No lipstick. I clamped my pale lips together and watched them turn pink. Although it was January, I felt sweaty in my black serge uniform. Or maybe it was the layers of underwear. I'd never worn a T-shirt under a dress before, and the cotton half-slip covering my winter-weight stockings added even more layers. Well, the starchy white collar looked good, anyway. I stood on one foot and leaned closer to the mirror. My uniform was ankle-length. I could barely see the black suede oxfords below.

Thank God I only had to go to chapel and class in this get-up. Then a new worry struck me: What if on our permitted afternoon walks off campus, I ran into my old boss out on the streets of LaCrosse? Or—heaven help me—Peter?

The bell for chapel mercifully interrupted my ruminations. I hurried out of the washroom and down the wide hall. As a novice rushed past me, white veil and floor-length habit flying, gracefulness itself, my clunky crepe-sole caught on the edge of a floor tile. I stumbled, catching myself awkwardly on a wall. I had always hated flat shoes.

Rounding the corner into chapel, I caught my veil with one hand, sideways again. Just a few months, I consoled myself, and I'd feel better in the habit and veil.

At first, we, the new candidates, had few visits and no phone calls. Abruptly cut off from the cuddly breast of worldly life, we were being weaned. It helped that the food at St. Rose was plentiful and tasty.

The refectory, as our small basement dining room was

called, provided a revelation in the practice of silence during my first days in the convent. As we filed in without speaking, I watched my classmates for cues. Each found her assigned place at one of the long, empty tables. No tablecloths. Two novices I hadn't met moved quietly around the room, serving us steaming dishes, tantalizing with their savory aromas. I closed my eyes and imagined the tasty roast beef to come. Still standing, we recited meal prayers in hushed voices. When the sister in charge was seated, each of us slid her stool from under the table to sit. It was to be done quietly. Mine skidded.

Sister glanced my way. Silence was to be taken seriously indeed.

I eyed the creaky drawer in the table. It seldom opened easily but I needed the plain white plate and the flatware stowed there for my dinner. I gently pulled. It didn't move. My face felt hot. I pulled again. This time, the drawer let loose, contents clattering.

Sister glanced my way again.

Would I ever learn to be quiet? I imagined myself moving in slow motion, like swimming in deep water, as I carefully fished in the half-open drawer. The last spoon finally rested soundlessly on the table. Never so conscious of my every move, every sound, I took a deep breath, wondering how long the meal would last.

Across the table, my classmate Marlene loudly clinked a water glass against the edge of her plate. She peeked at the head table, as alert to the nun there as I had been.

Then, a convent ritual I hadn't heard about began.

Another classmate, Mary Ann, took her place at a lectern in the corner. It was time for spiritual reading. Our souls as well as our bodies were to be nourished. I was relieved, not for the inspiration, but for the sound. Any sound that might mask my noise!

Mary Ann carefully enunciated the title chosen for our edification, her voice loud and clear as it bounced off the bare walls and floor of the dining room: "Written by Father Raymond White, SOB."

I quickly brought my napkin up. The unintended insult to the Order of St. Benedict sent me into spasms of laughter. Across the table, Marlene silently grinned.

No flicker passed over Mary Ann's innocent face.

Oh, God, I prayed. *Don't let me spray this mouthful of soup all over the table.* I bit my lips, tensing my fanny muscles. *Don't let me strangle and die here, so early in my convent career, a martyr to soup and silence and SOBs. It's not that funny! It's not that funny!* I urgently lectured myself.

The dining room wasn't the only surprise. Two classmates who'd been aspirants during their high school years, Angelina and Anne Marie, were assigned to show me to the dorm. I was mildly irritated to notice how much they seemed to relish teaching convent routines to a green newcomer. They cheerfully led the way climbing many stairs to the third floor while I huffed and puffed along behind, trying to keep up.

Once there, Angie swung a door open. Metal beds painted with dark brown enamel stood in neat rows, each one made up perfectly with immaculate white cotton coverlets hanging evenly to the floor. The dormitory's uncovered windows and shiny hardwood floors were dazzlingly clean and austere.

Sheets hung like curtains between the beds, creating

space for a small wooden stand with basin and pitcher and enough room to get in and out of bed, to dress. I noticed a towel and washcloth on the pillow, a speckled blue basin near the large window leaking cold, wintry air.

"This cell is yours." Angie flung my suitcase on the bed. As I flipped it open, both dark heads bent over it. I shifted from foot to foot, not liking the inspection of my neatly folded undies and socks. Maybe I could distract my curious companions.

"Where are the bathrooms?"

Anne Marie straightened up. "We'll show you." She led the way down the hall to a small bathroom where five toilet stalls and sinks were partitioned off from three showers. There were no tubs in sight.

"Oh, the tubs are downstairs where the sisters live. We don't get to take baths until we're professed sisters." Suddenly, visions of a warm tub full of fragrant bubbles filled me with longing.

As we retraced the many steps back to study hall from the dorm, I started to calculate. Our class numbered more than thirty. How long would it take us to shower in that small bathroom three at a time for ten turns? And we weren't the only occupants of St. Rose. How many women were housed here? Maybe 250? How much time and hot water would they need? We all had the same hours for work, prayer, and sleep. The convent schedule clearly made daily tubs and showers impossible. Well, others had done it. I'd have to get acquainted with the little basin in my cell.

The basin I could deal with, but I keenly felt the lack of privacy as my gradual adjustment continued. With thirty ever-present sisters, community life meant we moved through the day together. The loss of my old independence was difficult. I needed some one-on-one time with a peer. The Postulant Mistress, Sister Maureen, noticed.

"Shirley, Marlene will show you around the college today." I was grateful for the break from the group, and grateful for Marlene. Like me, she was older than most of the class and had work experience.

After lunch, she led me through the corridors of the college. We laughed about the dining room episode of the night before, wondering what it was about silence that made little things seem so hilarious.

"Marlene, do you worry you'll strangle in the silence at meals?"

She gave a snort of a laugh as we turned a corner, entering the science lab. "I don't mind that so much as the Magnum Silentium." Neither of us had expected that centuries-old monastic practice of silence from the last "amen" of night prayer until after breakfast, not at St. Rose. She sighed. "I'm not sure I'll ever be able to stop talking and get to sleep at 9:00P.M."

Today, it felt good to laugh out loud, here, in school. The classrooms, the library, the lecture hall, even the science lab felt familiar, not like the atmosphere of the convent.

"Sister Maureen lets me putter around over here in the science lab when I can't sleep."

That surprised me. Marlene noticed my questioning glance.

"Feels like my old turf," she said. "I'm a nurse. I worked night shift for years."

"Oh, I wondered why I'd heard you slip into the dorm after lights out."

"Yeah," she said, "it's good to know some of these convent rules can be bent."

Marlene led me to a corner of the lab behind counters filled with microscopes to a cabinet full of small glass jars. She took a container from the shelf and shook it.

"So what are these? Specimen jars?"

She stepped around the counter between us, eyes twinkling, obviously enjoying having an audience. Satisfied that the small blue bottle had been sufficiently shaken, she handed it to me.

"Well, you're not supposed to know this yet, but when we finish our year as postulants and become novices, we won't be permitted to have deodorant. I'm supposed to make home-made deodorant for us."

Dumbfounded, I looked at the blue jar in my hand, then at her. I sniffed the small jar of baking soda, lotion and who-knew-what. It looked lumpy.

"So you're the class mad scientist?"

She laughed, but didn't deny it.

"Marlene, how can we wear that long, black habit in summer without deodorant? We'll smell like goats."

"Guess we'll find out. Actually, my concoction deodorizes pretty well if you can get it to stick to your armpits."

I handed it back to her, imagining chunks falling to the floor, leaving a white trail behind me as I crossed the dark tile floors of the convent. Was this about poverty, chastity, and obedience, or just about leaving civilization as I'd known it?

I didn't want to think about it.

Despite my new wardrobe, our nightly practice of Great Silence and my grooming concerns, the first weeks at St. Rose were peaceful. I did feel close to God in those days. The nuns told the story of Mother Amelianna, the founder of the community. She'd gathered the first sisters to pray before their humble convent tabernacle in the light of a small oil lamp. Together, they promised to keep an uninterrupted vigil of prayer before the Blessed Sacrament, day and night. Now, over a century later, I took my turn.

The St. Rose altar's façade glittered with marble and gold. Paintings and statues of life-size saints peeked from nooks and porticos. A huge oil painting above the adoration chapel altar, I learned, was St. Margaret Mary. I wondered what she saw as she gazed at the moon in the night sky. She seemed transfixed. I felt mesmerized, too, holding vigil in the chapel. I knelt for hours, losing track of time, hardly breathing, lost in the sacredness there. I knew from the writings of the great mystics, John of the Cross and Teresa of Avila, that the God who wanted to draw me close stood helpless as if outside a gate, waiting for me to open to Him. The handle was on the inside. How could I ever say no to the Holy One who had always been so good to me? I couldn't. That is what held me in the early days of my adjustment. That, and Mother Joan's words.

Mother Joan talked to our class frankly about the difficulties of religious life. "Yes, it can be hard. Just imagine that Jesus is asking if you can do this for Him."

I thought of her words as I silently rose in the pre-dawn hours to begin each day with prayer, meditation, and Mass, all before breakfast, before coffee.

I thought of them again one night as I sat hunched over my desk in study hall, squinting at the page of dense prose assigned for tomorrow's theology class. I wearily closed my eyes. Behind my burning eyelids, ponderous theology tomes boiled in a sea of red waves. The back of my neck and head throbbed.

Ten years of temporary vows stretched out ahead of me before I would finally be accepted by the order. This was boot camp. Yup, basic training.

I needed an aspirin.

Sister Maureen had her eye on me. "You're so intense about your work, Shirley. Do you get headaches often?"

I eyed the tin of aspirin she held, wishing I'd been allowed to keep my own supply. What was she getting at? Wasn't I supposed to work hard at my classes?

I watched in astonishment as she broke an aspirin in two and handed me half. "I think in a little while you won't need these."

I mumbled my thanks, hoping I didn't look as bewildered as I felt. Did she really expect me to somehow relax and not need even this tiny dab of aspirin? Before I could decide, the bell rang. Time for chapel. Damn. Not done reading yet, and after Compline it would be time for bed.

Head still pounding, I shut the theology book, pages unread, and dragged my way through the darkened halls to chapel. I knew the next day, like all the others, would be dictated by bells. Before dawn, a bell to rise, then a bell to pray, a bell to eat, a bell to study, and a bell to recreate. When would I ever finish my homework?

The next day between classes, I found Marlene in the empty, third floor science lab. Peering through a microscope, her face wore an expression of intense concentration, but she slid back from the table when I walked in.

"Have time for a break?" I asked.

She flashed me a quick smile, then wheeled her stool around, and pulled another from under the counter for me.

"Not really. I've got so much to do, I think I'll flunk. Feels like I never finish my assignments and projects. But we can take a few minutes. Sit."

I yawned, lowering myself to the stool, letting my arm-load of books slide to the floor. I hadn't slept well last night, although the quiet prayer in chapel just before bed usually relaxed me.

Marlene leaned back, stretching her arms overhead. "Thank God for a free period. I need the time." She gestured at the pile of books and papers surrounding her microscope. "It's hard to work on such a complicated project in short spurts, stopping and starting all the time."

I'd had a feeling Marlene would understand. Her fat chemistry text was open, staring up at me from the table between us. I leaned forward for a look. The symbols and equations were more daunting than the prose of my theology book. I shuddered.

"Marlene, how do you get anything done? This atmosphere—are you used to it by now? I mean, all these bells? Even when you're right in the middle of something?"

Marlene rubbed her chin. "Hmm . . . guess I've adjusted some since September. It wasn't so easy at the beginning of the school year." She straightened the pile of books, lining them up even with the edge of the table. "By the end of the term, my projects somehow got finished. I was surprised my grades were good."

"Really?" The muscles in the back of my neck relaxed. "Maybe I'll make it, too."

"Sure you will." She laughed, swiveling back to her microscope. Her throaty chortle reassured me.

"Well, for a while there, I thought I'd accidentally joined

the Benedictines, monastic schedule and all." She chuckled again, not looking up.

My eyes moved across the lab table to the window. On the campus below, clusters of tiny, black garbed nuns moved, graceful as birds, soundlessly skimming the icy pond, drifting from bank to bank, black against white. I studied them. I'd learn the rhythm, too, I promised myself. I'd learn the balance, the letting go, the trust that all will be well. I'd learn.

Our willingness was what Sister Maureen had to work with. It was her job to teach us about life inside the walls, not just to orient us to dorms and dining rooms and bells, but to what religious life meant.

In one of our first classes, she began to talk about why women came to the convent. Something in me hungrily reached out for her words. I glanced around the study hall. Everyone was intently focused on Sister Maureen, perhaps wondering if we'd hear her tell our own stories.

She began, soft voice lilting. "Do you remember the story of the young man who asked Jesus what he should do to be perfect?"

The nun paused, looking around the room at each of us, her face gentle. "He told the young man, 'Honor your father and mother. Speak the truth. Keep all the commandments.'"

I felt a lump rise in my throat. I knew I'd tried to do that, to keep the commandments. Sister Maureen brought her gaze back to me as she continued.

"The young man said, 'I have done this from my youth.' Jesus told him, 'Then sell all you have and follow me.'"

Her voice softened as she finished the story. "It was a magnificent invitation." The nun's eyes moved across the room again. She paused, looking directly at me. "Your invitation is the same."

The lump in my throat dissolved into something warm spreading through my chest. A tear rolled down my cheek. This *was* a story about my call. How had she known it?

She bowed her head slightly to me, smiling, then scanned the room. "It's important that you understand. The vows you are preparing to make will be of help to you. The vow of poverty brings great freedom, freedom from care, freedom from distractions. Perhaps some of you are already beginning to see."

My thoughts drifted to my struggles in college to balance my checkbook, to pay my bills. It was a relief not to have to do that. I felt taken-care-of in this simple life. I had very little, but my mind was easier, I could see that.

Sister Maureen stood and walked around her desk coming close to us. "Your vow of obedience means you are willing to serve. Jesus calls us to love and serve each other. This vow means you freely choose to serve others."

I wondered what work I would be assigned here. Would I be a teacher like Sister Maureen and my Aunt Jean?

As if she had heard my thoughts, she continued, "Each of you will find your work in the community, according to your gifts."

Maureen took a few steps, setting the rosary beads at her side swinging and quietly clicking with each move. She stopped at my desk, smiling at me.

The last vow was chastity. I thought of Peter, of passion, of turmoil . . . and I thought of my mother's wistful remark: "The nuns always seem so happy."

Sister Maureen's smooth voice broke my reverie.

"Chastity, too, brings freedom. It means you can be single-minded in your service, free from family responsibility. At the same time, it's a great sacrifice to give up a husband and children."

My mother's face floated before me. I remembered the day we said goodbye in the convent parlor. Giving up children was a great sacrifice, I knew, but giving up a husband? My mother's deep faith had seemed to comfort her more than her married life. Had she ever wished she'd entered the convent? I'd never asked.

Sister Maureen's voice brought me back again. "Human love is a great blessing, but if you've been truly called to a life of chastity, many people you serve will love you, and God's love will fill your heart for your generosity."

I sat back in my chair. I knew God couldn't be outdone in generosity. I'd felt it so often in chapel.

Just then, the bell rang. Time for prayer. Sister Maureen turned, gesturing us to follow her to chapel. As I moved silently down the convent hall, my steps fell in with my classmates, walking in a peaceful rhythm.

There was much to learn about these traditional vows, and much adjustment to the practicalities of everyday life. I was in boot camp, basic training, and I was willing, but was I able? That was the question.

One bright summer morning a week before first vow day, I swung my legs out of bed in my narrow cell, full of energy. The long-awaited vow day, the day to really become a nun, was almost here. I bounced out of bed creating a breeze. The curtain between my bed and the next one blew open, revealing a smooth pillow and an undisturbed white coverlet.

Where was my friend, Sharon? I hurried to chapel, worried about my missing classmate.

After Mass and breakfast, Sister Maureen called us to attention before we left the refectory. "All of you, please come to study hall. You can finish dishes and your household chores later."

Once in study hall, I looked around for Sharon. Her desk was empty. Had she become ill in the night?

Sister Maureen walked in, face somber. The rustling in the room quieted.

"Girls, please be seated. Before I begin, I want you to know the discussion here today is to stay in this room."

Her words scared me. What unspeakable thing had happened to Sharon?

"There's no reason to talk about any of this among yourselves or with anyone else." The nun turned her level gaze on me. "As you see, Sharon isn't here this morning. It's become clear this is not the life for her. Each of you is unique, so Sharon's situation shouldn't concern you."

I felt as if I'd taken a blow to the solar plexus. I blurted out, "But Sister, Sharon was one of my closest friends—"

Before I could say more, Sister Maureen stood, cheeks flushed. "It won't be helpful to discuss this further. Shirley, please come with me." The nun quickly dismissed the class, turned and wheeled into her small office just off the study hall.

It was clear I had offended her. I followed, glancing at the crucifix on the wall behind her desk, breathing a quick prayer. *Dear God, don't let me be sent home, too, just days before my vows.*

She pointed to a chair beside her desk. As I shakily seated myself, she cleared her throat. "Shirley, you've come here from a secular college where you've expressed your opinions freely. That's the way of the world. Now, you must learn to curb your opinions. Some questions are not raised here. You must learn humility."

My face burned. I'd tried to be a good novice, to turn to prayer with my questions, to follow the rule. I wanted to be accepted by the community, but so had Sharon. I found my voice. "Sister, I'm sorry. It's just that it was such a shock that Sharon—"

She cut me off. "Shirley, please. Take seriously what I said in class. You are not to discuss this matter. No good comes from it. Give me your word."

Her brown eyes told me that clearly I was on dangerous ground. I couldn't look at her as I swallowed my questions and mumbled assent.

"Go to chapel now, and say a prayer for Sharon, and for yourself."

I managed to hold back my tears until I got out of there, but by the time I reached chapel, I was sobbing.

Marlene, feather duster in hand, stepped out of the shadows behind a statue of Michael the Archangel guarding the chapel door. "You ok?"

Our eyes met. She'd been close to Sharon, too. We both knew we had to cope with the unexplained loss of our friend in silence. She hugged my shoulders and whispered, "Wherever she is, she'll be all right."

I looked up at Michael wanting to believe Marlene, hoping and praying Sharon's fate wouldn't be ours as well.

My anxious prayer to St. Michael was answered just a few days later.

On the Franciscan feast of St. Clare, Aug. 12, 1964, the sun shone brightly. I stood with my classmates outside St. Joseph's Cathedral ready to make my first vows in religion before the crowd of family and friends waiting inside.

An organ prelude signaled the beginning of our quickly moving procession across the churchyard. A rush of wind caught my veil as I ran to keep my place.

Once at the door of the church, I smoothed my new veil and habit and stood still. A soft, ethereal song filled the vaulting cathedral. It took my breath away.

The courts of heaven are paved with stars,
   glistening stars.
This is what love prepares for the bride,
   glistening stars.
Oh, hide my life within your arms, in your embrace.
Such love is God's mysterious gift, His love for me.[4]

With a full heart, I spoke my vows, yearning for the closeness with God they promised. Like a bride, I received a precious gold ring, engraved with the emblem of Francis. It glinted on my hand as I read the card with my new name on it, "Sister John Ann," the name I'd requested, honoring St. John of the Cross, and my own dear mother.

My new life had finally begun. I'd made it!

2

Free, and on the Road

After first vows, most of my classmates left the LaCrosse motherhouse for teaching and nursing assignments in schools and hospitals staffed by the community. But not me. I was left behind to study. Missing my buddies, I chipped away at the last few courses of my bachelor's degree, expecting to finish in spring. But before that day arrived, there was an unexpected turn of events.

Fall semester had just ended when Sister Maureen called me into her office. I wondered if I had unknowingly transgressed some rule and fallen into disfavor with her. I never could be too sure with Maureen. Her door was closed. When I tapped softly, she invited me in, looking up from an open file folder on her desk. In my anxious state, I was grateful not to be kept waiting. I sat gingerly on the edge of the wooden chair in front of her, suspecting she knew I was nervous.

Maureen smiled and got right to the point. "Sister John Ann, we need you to take over a seventh grade classroom after Christmas. The sister there is being transferred."

My expectations suddenly collided into one another, like a line of children following a leader who stops dead in his tracks.

She saw my reaction but, mercifully, dropped her gaze to the file folder again, making no comment.

"Since you finished student teaching last year, you are now prepared to do a good job."

Maureen looked at me again, tilting her head slightly, smiling. Was she encouraging my questions? I doubted it. Ever since the day Sharon left, Sister Maureen's unspoken rules always made me nervous.

I looked down at the gold ring on my hand, symbol of obedience. It wouldn't be safe to ask how and when I might finish my degree, or why a nun had to be moved in the middle of the year. I settled on a lesser question.

"Where will I be teaching, Sister?"

"Wisconsin Rapids."

Where was that? Somewhere in the frozen northland?

Maureen selected one sheet from her file and pushed it across the desk. It was a roster of faculty names at St. Stanislaus School. "You'll be with two of your classmates, Sister Mary Ann and Sister Aaron." Maureen knew I'd missed them when I'd been kept in LaCrosse, heading for graduate studies. While I loved books, I had mixed feelings about the separation from my friends and my status as a special case. I was on the academic fast track as a full-time student while they had to teach all year and slowly drudge toward their first-degree summer school after summer school.

Maureen straightened the papers in her file folder and closed it, sitting back to turn her piercing gaze on me again. I could almost hear the questions in her mind: Was I aware of the privilege I'd been given to finish studies this year? Was I able to detach from it now? Was my ego clamoring?

Trying to sound optimistic, obedient even, I heard

myself chirp, "I'm glad to know my classmates will be there, Sister."

It would be a relief to get to the frozen northland and away from those piercing eyes. If I just knew more about it! My immediate future felt like a black hole. But, questions were not welcome. I'd learned that lesson painfully.

Sister Maureen stood up, signaling the end of our conversation. I quickly stood, too, hoping my disappointment didn't show. Avoiding her eyes, I mumbled a thank you and turned to go.

Before I closed her door, she called out, "Oh, and Sister, we'll try to keep you in LaCrosse next year to finish your course work."

Later that night, I sat in chapel, distracted from night prayers by a snippet of conversation floating through my head. Months ago, Sister Ann, my art instructor, had casually asked me, "If you were to choose a major for grad school, what would it be? Art? Philosophy? English?"

The question had both pleased and disturbed me. The recognition of my talents was affirming, but I'd wondered if study would pull me off my path, distract me from the real reason I'd wanted to be a nun in the first place, which was to be close to God.

As the last chanted note of Compline faded into quiet, the soft movement of my companions leaving chapel brought me back from my worries. A white-veiled novice snuffed out tall, beeswax candles standing in the sanctuary. The marble and gold altar flanked by kneeling angels fell into semi-darkness, lit only by the red glow of the tabernacle lamp. Alone there in the silence, my heart knew I'd come to St. Rose with a generous spirit three years ago. I knew I was willing to do whatever work the community needed.

So what was going on? Why was I so unnerved by Sister Maureen's unexpected announcement today? Was it the sudden change of direction, the unknown of mission life in the hinterland? Or was my ego in revolt? Just how big was my ego anyway?

At twenty-five years old, I didn't know.

I leaned back in the hard, oak seat, closing my eyes. One point was clear, negotiation with Maureen was unthinkable. Yet, her message had a positive conclusion: "We'll try to keep you in LaCrosse next year to finish your course work."

Maybe I'd go to graduate school later. But did I even want that and the years of academic life that would follow?

Uneasy at the thought, I knelt down on the creaking kneeler.

The abrupt contact of my knees with the hard wood snapped me into visions of forty wriggling seventh graders. Yes, I'd student taught, but taking over a crowded classroom in January was like jumping on a moving train. Could I do it? I shifted my weight from knee to knee, eyes drifting to the golden monstrance on the high altar.

As I focused in the dimness, the monstrance reflected what light there was into a golden aura around it. I squinted, trying to decide if the glowing cloud was expanding. I wasn't sure. The silence grew deeper, stilling the moment into peace. Was it darkness? Was it light? My tired eyes couldn't decide. But the moment was gentle, reassuring. Something not seen or heard had comforted me like an embrace. All would be well.

Soon, I found myself in Wisconsin Rapids. The convent's housekeeper, Sister Agnes, picked me up at the train station.

"Just call me Aggie," she offered."

I grinned. Her breezy greeting and the wisp of red hair escaping the white linen at her hairline told me my new convent wouldn't be so bad after all.

Agnes carefully wheeled the station wagon through snow-packed streets. We made small talk as I peered through the frosty windshield, curious about my new hometown. Once at the convent, Sister Agnes led me through her antiseptically clean kitchen. At the end of the hall, I noticed a closed door.

"Is that the Superior's office?"

Agnes nodded and whispered, "Yes, she's either holed up in there or gone most of the time." I wondered when I'd meet her.

Agnes rounded the corner, easily hoisting my suitcase up the stairs to my room. Pale blue carpeting and walls were a welcome change from the unrelieved plainness of the motherhouse dorm at LaCrosse.

"Towels are here, soap there." She spoke over her shoulder as she pulled open cabinet doors beneath a porcelain sink.

I laughed. "A private room! What luxury!"

She laughed, too. "Yes, and no more pitchers and basins."

I took a closer look at the immaculate sink, then quickly backed away. "Oh, Aggie, what a smell. There must be a rat in here someplace."

Sister Agnes sat on the edge of my bed and let out a hoot of amusement. "Haven't you ever been to Wisconsin Rapids?"

I shook my head wondering what was so funny.

"This is paper mill country, Johnnie. That stink is no dead rat in your drain. You got a whiff of the chemicals used for making paper."

"Oh," I grinned weakly. "Guess I'll get used to it."

And so life in the Northwoods began.

In the classroom, the kids seemed to like me well enough and I liked them. They were energetic twelve-year-olds, cute and funny, smart and dumb, full of vinegar. But so many of them! I knew immediately if I didn't have a large bag of tricks, classroom control would be a wistful memory.

Every hour away from the kids, I planned and worked, planned and worked, dreaming up projects. Besides the planning, I was soon swamped in papers and projects to grade, night after night. Like the motherhouse, the mission convent followed a schedule of prayer and recreation, but blissfully, there were no bells and lights out time was more flexible. In my private room, I could work into the night.

My late night strategy for classroom survival worked pretty well until February. One Friday night at the end of a particularly grueling week of work, I sat at dinner, exhausted.

Aggie watched me as the Superior finished meal prayer and left the dining room followed by the rest of the household. "Johnnie, you didn't eat. Don't you like my tuna hotdish?"

I smiled at her, glad for her concern. "It's not your hotdish. I'm just too tired to lift my fork. I don't know what's wrong." It was the truth, though I felt silly admitting to Agnes how weak I felt.

She got up from her place, eyes widening. "Well, you just go to bed right now." She quickly stepped behind me, sliding my chair back from the table. "I'll clear up here. You'll feel better in the morning." Grateful for her kindness, I stumbled off to bed.

Next morning, a gentle tap on my door brought me back from uneasy dreams.

Sister Agnes poked her head in, smiling brightly, tray in hand. "I brought you some breakfast, Johnnie."

I tried to swim up through the fog of my heavy sleep. Agnes bustled to the window, opening the blinds to the morning sun, then turned to look at me. The sudden shaft of light burned my eyes but I leaned on my elbow, trying to sit up.

"What's the matter, hon?"

"Aggie, I don't know. I just feel so weak."

She crossed the room quickly to place her cool hand to my flushed cheek.

"You didn't sleep it off?"

I tried to sit up again. The effort was too much. I fell back in the bed. "No, I don't know what's happening!"

Agnes sat looking at me for a moment, a little line creasing her forehead. "Well, you just rest awhile." She quietly rose to lower the window shade again, then leaned down to pat my arm. "I'll be back later to check up on you."

I nodded and turned to the wall as she left, grateful to close my burning eyes, to sink into the undemanding darkness of sleep.

Days passed. I lost track of time, sleeping and waking fitfully.

Sister Agnes brought meals to my darkened bedroom, watching me anxiously as tray after tray was left untouched. I could hardly turn over in my small convent bed.

When next Agnes gently touched my cheek, it was hot and dry.

"Sister, you are burning up. Hasn't the Superior been in to see you yet?"

"No, no one's been here but you." I saw her alarm. In a rare moment of consciousness, I realized I was scared, too.

An errant wisp of red hair escaped the white headband under Agnes' veil. She poked it back under her coif. "I told her four days ago you were sick."

"All I know, Agnes, is that I'm sick, sicker than I've ever been." The words took all my energy.

"Put some clothes on." She reached into the pocket of her white kitchen apron and dangled the car keys in front of me. "I don't care if the Superior likes it or not, we're going to the doctor."

I had mononucleosis. It was weeks before I returned to the classroom, months before the slightest over-exertion didn't send me to bed. As I gradually regained strength, the illness didn't trouble me as much as a host of doubts about life in the community. They circled in my mind like black birds of prey. How could this episode have happened? Weren't we all dedicated to service, to care?

When the school year ended in May, I was glad to leave Wisconsin Rapids. On the train ride back to LaCrosse, a blooming spring landscape flew past our windows. My classmate, Sister Mary Ann, sat facing me. She wasn't blooming.

"This has been such a tough year," she said. "No matter how hard I tried, the kids were out of control. They say the first year of teaching is the worst, but all the tension at the convent was added to it. This one not talking to that one; somebody else cranky because of crumbs left on the kitchen counter; another unhappy about changing to a new habit." She poured out story after story of her struggles, her face tight.

I listened quietly, sad for the change I saw in my classmate. She had seemed so sweet and soft when we were postulants and novices together. Now she was tired and tense.

"So, . . . you, too?" Glad she had broken the silence about

our year, I sighed. "I was worried I was the only one."

She leaned across the narrow space between us, forehead furrowed. "Are we too idealistic, John? Have we expected too much? Is that what's wrong?"

I opened the lunch box Sister Agnes had packed for us and passed Mary Ann a carton of juice. "I don't know, but I'm glad we're talking. When I was sick this winter, I felt very alone."

Mary Ann thoughtfully sipped her juice before answering. "You know, the Superior never said a word about you while you were ill. We got the idea you weren't to be disturbed."

This was news to me. "Why wouldn't she tell you I was sick?"

Mary Ann shook her head. "I don't know. Maybe guilt? Agnes was really angry that she hadn't taken you to the doctor sooner."

I looked at Mary Ann, weighing her words. "Agnes would make a better Superior. She was so kind to me." In the weakness of mono, I felt I could have died without Aggie's help.

Mary Ann reached for the lunch box, found a green apple, and polished it on her knee. "What bothers me is: why is mission life so different from the motherhouse? I never saw indifference, bickering, and bad temper there, and it certainly would never have been tolerated in the novitiate. We'd have been sent home. Were we kept away from the professed sisters during our formation for a reason? Was our training all rhetoric?"

"I don't want to believe that." I found my own green apple and bit into it.

"Well, I don't either, but the year wasn't what I expected."

I dropped my apple core into a napkin and crumpled it.

"I don't know why the Superior was absent while I was sick, but one thing for sure, I'm going to talk to Sister Maureen about it. There must be some way the nuns keep track of how a Superior does her job."

As the months of summer school in LaCrosse passed, the breath of fresh air Pope John let into Catholicism with the Vatican Council became a windstorm. If Mary Ann and I thought we'd find respite from conflicts at the motherhouse, we were wrong.

The Council, a three-year meeting of bishops, was the first in almost one hundred years. Pope John's idea was to update the Church by decentralizing Rome's authority, sharing responsibility with national bishops and aligning with current social justice movements.

Catholics began to hear new definitions of the Church. No longer described as a depository of truth and guardian of faith, the bishops said it was not a structure, but rather, the Church was the people themselves, the believers, the faithful, and that all members were important, laity as well as priests and religious.[5] The implications were huge. The safe haven from the outside world that required only child-like acceptance of clearly defined answers to all questions and demolished all debate was gone, and with it, the certainty that refuge had provided. Lifelong Catholics, priests and nuns included, had no experience with change in their church and many weren't up to the challenge. To make matters worse, education about the teachings from Vatican II was spotty.

As Rome's reforms trickled down, priests began to say Mass in English, not Latin, although some parishes hadn't heard that the change was meant to make their prayer more meaningful. The substitution seemed arbitrary and the new

Anglo-Saxon sounds were much less melodious, especially when sung, than the familiar and mysterious Latin. When parishes stopped offering novenas and recitation of the rosary, took statues out of the sanctuary, moved the altar from its place on high to the middle of the room circling it with seats no longer accompanied by kneelers, the old timers threw up their hands and wondered what had happened.

People were angry and soon discovered some neighboring parishes had made no change at all because the pastor or even the bishop was dragging his feet in implementing Rome's directives. The migration from parish to parish started. Resistance was in the air. Some spoke of schism and groups did break away to keep the old practices, eventually being excommunicated by Rome.

The struggle to update was going on at St. Rose, too.

Father Missler, our chaplain, was the master of ceremonies for this unfolding drama. His daily homilies at Mass gave him his platform. One August day he approached the pulpit with a sheaf of papers in hand.

He began with a smile. "Sisters, your lives have always been dedicated to service. All Catholics recognize that about you as religious women." No doubt this priest's long tenure at the motherhouse was due, at least in part, to his elegant diplomacy. I tried to remember how long he'd been at St. Rose.

Fr. Missler's slightly raised voice interrupted my idle speculations.

"It's time for us to take seriously the new teachings from the Vatican Council." His special emphasis on the word "seriously" echoed in the large chapel. He shuffled a few pages, then wiped his brow with a large white handkerchief. I glanced at the row of nuns to my right. Sister Henrietta was in the first seat. He might need a white flag of truce with her. Last night in the dining room, Henrietta had had lots to say about the pastor of a nearby parish who had permitted "undignified English hymns at Mass, accompanied by some teenager's twangy guitar." I didn't envy Fr. Missler's task.

He began again. "The documents of Vatican II encourage not only the use of English instead of Latin in liturgy and music, which our choir directors and I have already begun, but also changes in our liturgical space itself."

Sister Henrietta straightened, as if a rod had suddenly been inserted into her backbone.

Fr. Missler saw her movement. His smile faded but he hesitated only a moment. "Sisters, it truly is better, when we pray the Mass, for the celebrant to be in the middle and face you all, not standing on high with his back to the group. You must remember, the priest is only one member of the community. You, the community members, your prayer is important, too."

He pushed his glasses up on the bridge of his nose. I wondered if I'd just imagined his jaw jutting forward in Sister Henrietta's direction. She was the only nun in the pew still wearing full garb. Of course, she wouldn't want other practices to change. My thoughts flashed to the penny loafers, cardigans, and slacks I'd left home when I joined the convent, trading them for the voluminous, floor-length habit and yards of veil supported by a mysterious contraption that had no relationship to the shape of the human head.

Then I remembered pictures I'd seen of the women who formed the earliest communities in medieval Europe. The founders of those orders kept the first nuns in the dress of their day so as not to be conspicuous. Styles changed, but habits didn't, and look at us now! The irony of it all made me smile. Rearranging the furniture and changing the music was a good start, but it was going to take more than that to change attitudes in the Catholic Church.

In the dining room that night, I made a point to sit far away from Sister Henrietta. As an added precaution, I came to table prepared to talk at length about the paper mills and cranberry bogs of Wisconsin Rapids, anything to deflect tense debates over dinner.

And I had my talk with Sister Maureen. Due to our earlier skirmishes, it wasn't easy, but I knew I'd be ill again if I returned to Wisconsin Rapids. Although my health had gradually improved, my spirits were low even here at St. Rose.

She listened to my story kindly enough, offering no comment. As summer passed, however, my classmates from Wisconsin Rapids and I were assigned to new schools for the coming year. Nevertheless, the Superior in Wisconsin Rapids remained in charge and no explanation was offered.

One glorious autumn afternoon, I walked the long blocks from my new school, Blessed Sacrament, to St. Rose, under elms turning gold. Sister Maureen had called, asking me to stop at her office. Dry leaves crunched under my feet sending their pungent aroma into the bright blue day. Fall was my favorite season, but I couldn't shake off a troubling heaviness. Why was I feeling so sad, so shriveled, like the leaves drifting in the breeze? I was glad to be here to finally finish the last class I needed to graduate, wasn't I? I shook myself and hurried along. No point in all this sadness.

Once at the motherhouse, I found Maureen's door open, shafts of autumn sunshine brightening the room.

As I came in, she stood to welcome me, stepping around

her desk. "Sister John Ann, how are you today?"

An embarrassing tear slid down my cheek. Before I could speak, she took my hands and drew me down beside her on the small sofa under the window. Maureen, one of only a half dozen nuns still in full garb, pulled her bulky skirt close to her, making room for me.

"I'm sorry, Sister. I don't know what's wrong with me."

"So, still having some hard days?" Her voice was soft.

I nodded. I didn't want to cry in front of Maureen. "I'm fine as long as I'm in the classroom." Blinking back tears, I took a deep breath and cleared my throat. "Being with the kids or at my own classes keeps my mind occupied, I guess."

She nodded. "It's just when you are alone and quiet that you feel sad? How are you sleeping?"

I'd been unusually restless lately, sad thoughts waking me in the early morning.

Sister Maureen nodded. "Your hands are like ice. And on such a sunny day." She squeezed them and laughed a little.

I didn't understand it either. I felt cold inside, too. "Maybe it's nerves."

The tall nun stood and went to her desk, rosary beads quietly clicking at her side. She turned to look at me appraisingly. After a pause, she spoke as if choosing her words. "Sister, you've been in a sad frame of mind for a while now. Would you like to talk with someone about it, perhaps a counselor?"

Feeling as if I'd just been thrown a rope, I quickly agreed, "Oh, yes, yes. I'm tired of all these tears."

Maureen smiled, and reached into her desk drawer. She handed me a business card that read, "Fr. James Bertrand, MC."

And so, in-between hours of teaching and taking classes, I began what was to be a three-year dialogue with a kindly listener. Sister Maureen scheduled my first visit within days. Once I arrived at the address, only a few blocks from the convent, Fr. Jim's receptionist seated me in his cozy office assuring me he'd be with me in a moment.

Glad for the chance to look around, I craned my neck to look at the shelves of books surrounding me, many written by authors I knew: Eugene Kennedy, Carl Rogers, Adrian Van Kaam, Hans Kung. Their familiar names reassured me.

Then, a lanky priest dressed in clerical black strode through the door, dropping a briefcase by the desk and reaching for my hand in one motion.

"Glad to meet you, Sister." His wide smile was warm.

I thanked him, smoothing my skirt over my knees. He settled himself in the chair across from me, not missing my nervous move.

"I heard that most of you Franciscans had changed your garb, but this is the first time I've seen it. How do you like your new look?"

I glanced down at my pleated black skirt, my short jacket.

"Grateful to be wearing less black serge." I carefully crossed my knees. "Still getting used to the shorter skirt, though."

He flashed his big toothy grin again, "I bet. And a new wardrobe for every nun must be expensive for the community."

I smiled back. He was doing a good job of putting me at ease. "Actually, our old black habits were altered into these suits."

Jim raised his eyebrows. "You must be quite a seamstress."

"Far from it. When we got permission to change out of the habit, I talked my mom into driving through the cranberry bogs to Wisconsin Rapids. She did the sewing, bless her heart. I think you know I was teaching there."

"Yes, Sister Maureen told me when she called." He offered me a cup of coffee from the carafe on his desk, glancing up as he poured some for himself. "Tough year, huh?"

His sympathetic tone was all it took to send a tear sliding down my cheek. I tried to laugh, hoping he hadn't noticed, but the look on Jim's face told me I hadn't fooled him. He leaned back, reaching for a yellow legal pad. "Well, tell me about it, Sister." He was obviously ready for my story.

And I was ready to plunge in. In the telling, to my surprise, the tale grew beyond the tough year in Wisconsin Rapids. I heard myself pouring out question after question about my life, even wondering how I had ever gotten into the convent.

After my long recital, Jim spoke. "So, you are really feeling very sad about all this and not sure of anything right now."

I looked down at the coffee cup warming my cold hands, mildly surprised that this stranger had so easily summarized what to me was such a tangle. "Yes, sad." I sipped the lukewarm coffee.

But it wasn't just sadness. What was it, exactly?

I reached to put the cup on the coffee table between us. "I think I'm swallowing anger here, maybe swallowing my individuality. I don't feel I can be myself in the convent, like it's not ok to just relax."

Jim nodded. He seemed to understand even though I felt I was only hinting about what troubled me. "Do you know why you feel this way?"

Suddenly, past episodes flooded into the room with all their pain. "Well, some of my classmates have been sent home for no reason I can see."

Jim nodded again, making a note on his pad.

I went on. "When things like that aren't explained, I feel

anxious. The decisions about who is accepted into the community seem so arbitrary. It bothers me that one Superior can either support or block my whole life."

Jim leaned back to listen more. I had lots to say, and as I said it, I heard my voice sharpen, felt my face flush.

Finally, after a spurt of note taking, he flipped to a new page on his yellow pad. "You're really angry."

Was I? The sudden change of focus from my complaints confused me. Anger wasn't part of my repertoire among the nuns. To ask a question was to take a risk. To express anger, impossible. I looked at Jim. His gentle smile said my anger was all right. Cold prickles on my arms reminded me of childhood, of how out of control and dangerous my father's anger had been.

Jim watched my face for a moment, then his eyes crinkled into a smile. "You are safe here, Sister. I know it can be unsettling to get at feelings." My eyes welled up at his gentleness.

He pushed a box of tissues toward me. "And, if you're up to it, here's some homework. Think about when you've felt sad or angry since you've been in the convent. Maybe some things about your earlier life will come to mind, too. We'll talk about all that next time."

The next evening, I sat quietly in chapel, hearing Jim's words again, wondering what would surge forward as I opened to my tumultuous feelings. Just what was it that had made me sad since I'd been at St. Rose?

Suddenly, I remembered sitting in nearly the same pew a couple of years earlier. The nuns were gathered for benediction after lunch, a daily routine. As echoes of the last hymn faded, Fr. Missler unexpectedly stepped to the pulpit. "Sisters, I have a very important announcement to make. Our President's been shot. No one knows just yet how badly he's hurt." An assassination? Fear grabbed my heart. What did it all mean? That afternoon, television sets were hurriedly rolled into the halls at college, something never seen before. Between classes, I lingered to watch, sharing the stunned anxiety of the country. Then the bad news came. President Kennedy was dead.

Across the street from Viterbo, the motherhouse's one television sat in the midst of gray metal folding chairs in the drafty, Music Hall auditorium. Silent pianos on stage awaited the student nuns who would practice there. Otherwise, the room was bare. No carpets absorbed the creaking of the old, wooden floor. No curtains muffled the rattling of the windows in the winter wind. We huddled like black birds, my sisters and I, watching the funeral of John F. Kennedy. From my place in the back row, I strained to hear the broadcaster's voice, caught a few words, and then lost it again. It didn't matter. The desolate scene spoke for itself. A drum roll harshly bounced off the walls around us as a rider-less horse and John-John's salute flashed on the screen. The assassination had assaulted the national psyche and mine. I shivered and wept. It was a cold, gray day.

I looked up at the gold and marble altar, candles flickering before the tabernacle and remembered how I'd wept there that night. I'd have to tell Fr. Jim about it.

Next time I sat in his office, his coffeepot steamed with a fresh brew. I gratefully wrapped my fingers around a warm mug, and began my cold, gray story.

He listened carefully, letting my words settle down around us like tame birds, and then confirmed, "So the atmosphere, the convent itself, and the funeral, were all very cold, very miserable for you."

Vision blurred with tears, I looked at him. The sadness of that historic tragedy was one tendril connected to a long root of other sadnesses. It led me from the political scene, to the disillusionment Mary Ann and I had shared on the way home from Wisconsin Rapids, to the general unease in the Church itself. Tendrils everywhere. Vatican Council II had closed less than a year earlier, mandating reforms that were strongly resisted in many quarters. Some of them mighty close quarters. Was I struggling with the loss of leaders? What was Jim's estimation?

"Am I too much of an idealist?" I asked. "Is that what's wrong? Do I just need to face up to the loss of everything I've wanted to admire?"

He leaned forward, picking up on one word. "Tell me what losses you mean, Sister."

The first thing I thought of was being ill in Wisconsin Rapids. He knew about that. Suddenly, my thoughts and feelings tangled together, refusing to go in a straight line.

"I guess that's the biggest one, but somehow that loss got bigger. The assassination and the council and my life all seem related somehow . . . so much disappointment, confusion, and turbulence." I paused, taking a deep breath, then spoke into the lengthening silence he'd allowed me.

"Well, we've talked before about the Vatican Council. I thought good would come from it, and it has. But, . . ." I hesitated. How would he, a diocesan priest, albeit a trained counselor, feel about my observations of the Church?

I glanced at Jim. He met my eyes. "Keep going. You're doing fine."

"It just bothers me that the rules have changed, and so quickly. Rome tells us it's a new era of freedom and that we are to make adult decisions. I was used to that before I came here, but the Church isn't egalitarian. The way we practice obedience feels like I've lost my rights over my own life. I have no voice in this community. How long will it take religious orders to let all their members, new ones included, have a vote in who their Superiors are, for example? That would be a big improvement, but the nuns who don't want change seem to judge those of us who do. On one hand, I feel restless that change is so slow, and on the other, I feel boggled by the uncertainties. When I came to the convent, the way of life was clearly defined. Now it's not. With the new emphasis on lay leaders, maybe our roles will be lost—"

His voice was soft, "That is a big loss."

I sat silently, overcome by sadness.

Jim edged a box of tissues within my reach on the coffee table between us.

"I don't know if I can get through it all. I used to think I was pretty strong and able to cope with things, but now I'm not sure I can survive in religious life, or if I want to."

His reply was immediate but gentle. "I think you can, Sister, but maybe not the same way you have survived until now."

Walking back to St. Rose on sidewalks shaded with budding elm trees, I turned his words over in my mind . . . "Not the same way." What did that mean? Would I survive, somehow?

Once back at the convent complex, I stopped at the college library to return an anthology I'd borrowed for a term paper on Shakespeare.

As I came in the door, Sister Celestine caught me by the elbow. "I've been looking for you all over campus, Sister. Please come into my office." In a swirl of energy, she trotted down the hall, fully expecting me to follow her, which, of course, I did.

Sister Celestine, the talented and sharp-witted chair of the English department, had the distinctive honor of being the first nun I'd ever heard say "damn" in front of a classroom. Needless to say, I loved her. I followed her into her sunny office, windowsill lined with African violets. My Shakespeare term paper was on top of a pile of assignments on her credenza. Was she going to review it with me?

Before I could ask, she gestured me to a chair in front of her desk, and stood beaming at me from the other side.

"Sister John Ann, I've got some good news for you." She waved an envelope embossed with an official-looking seal. "You have been accepted to Ohio State's graduate English program. As soon as you finish, we need you to teach here at the college."

I gasped, nonplussed. Was this how the nuns were sent to grad school, just signed up by the professors?

"Sister, I just . . . I just . . ." The questions racing through me created a traffic jam in my vocal chords. "That's great." My voice sounded squeaky. "I'm really excited. I'm so surprised." Celestine's grin told me she was thoroughly enjoying this exchange. Stuttering wasn't like me.

"You can save your brilliant gems for your next term paper," she joked, tapping my recent assignment. "You'll need those pearls in grad school."

My face felt hot. Would I ever outgrow my blushes? Hoping she didn't notice, hoping to gather my scattered dignity around me, I turned to practical matters. "Ohio State? Is that in Columbus?"

Sister Celestine sat down placing my acceptance letter

squarely in the middle of her desk. "Yes, Columbus. I studied there last summer. The graduate English program is excellent. Your credits for the master's degree will apply toward doctoral studies. You'll begin this summer and go straight through." Her voice was all business.

"Summer school?" My voice squeaked again. It was already late April. I thought I was to teach English at Aquinas High School here in LaCrosse in fall. Maybe I'd heard her wrong. I asked again. "This year?"

Celestine laughed a hearty laugh. I squirmed under her amusement. "This year, Sister John Ann. Pack your toothbrush!"

Within weeks, I found myself at the "big farm" on the banks of the Olentangy River with its forty thousand students. If I had been dazed in Sister Celestine's office, it was nothing compared to the effect of Ohio State. The Big Ten University's immense campus couldn't have been more different from friendly little Viterbo College in LaCrosse, Wisconsin, enrollment 550.

It was summer of 1967, as I stood at the housemother's desk checking into the graduate women's dorm in my black serge suit. Eyed by friendly but curious peers in blue jeans, I was glad at least to not be in full medieval regalia. As Bob Dylan reminded us, "The times they are a' changin',"[6] I knew, clearly, mine hadn't changed enough yet. My own personal Age of Aquarius had yet to dawn.

As summer school metamorphosed into fall quarter, I found my way around campus, from dorm to classroom, to the memorial union, to greasy spoons surrounding the complex, and even gradually overcame my phobia of the immense university library.

By late fall, I was confident enough most days to huddle in the tiny library carrel that had become my home away from home. There, I inhabited a fortress of silent books, moving among folktales, novels, and poetry, as if from room to silent room.

"Psst. Hey, Shirley, wanna go out for pizza?"

A freckled face peered over the protective wall of books and into my cubicle. It was Sister Anne Kerrigan, a Mercy nun from Michigan, and a grad student in music.

I couldn't help but grin at her. "You're the only person on this whole campus to find my carrel, Annie. I shoulda known!"

Her eyes sparkled behind thick glasses. "Come on, you big brain. You can't work all the time. It's Friday night. I've got wheels. Let's go."

I stretched. My watch read 5:30P.M. I'd been there since 8:30A.M. I must've hypnotized myself. "You're right, and I'm starved."

Annie's ten-year-old chevy was a real luxury for the handful of student nuns in our dorm who bummed occasional rides with her. None of us had transportation. The car wheezed as she backed into the only parking space in front of the already crowded pizza parlor. "Sure hope this jalopy can get me home for Christmas." Worry creased her smooth forehead.

Already? I hadn't thought about the upcoming break. "When will you go?"

"Term ends the 15th."

I tugged on my door handle. It reluctantly turned, releasing me. "You driving alone?"

Annie held the restaurant door open for me. "I think so. No other Mercy nuns on campus right now." A busy waitress waved us to the only empty booth.

Annie's nostrils flared. "Smells so good in here."

"Yeah, pizza and pine trees." I slid into the booth, pulling off my jacket.

In the corner next to us stood a festooned Christmas tree, twinkling with tiny, white lights. Its woodsy fragrance filled me with homesickness. A lonely little voice in my head started making pronouncements: *Annie shouldn't be alone. I shouldn't be alone. Nobody should be alone at Christmas.*

"I wish I could ride with you, Annie."

She scrutinized me over the tattered menu. "Did your Superior already send your plane ticket?"

I carefully studied my menu. "Yeah, the ticket came last week." I knew she thought our community was far too protective of its young members. Anne turned a page of the menu, willing to let the subject drop. I was glad. My hunger pangs put me in too foul a mood to debate the merits of the FSPA's parenting style versus the Mercies. A burst of laughter from a girl in the next booth made me suddenly lonely for my classmates in Wisconsin.

Annie read my face. "What's the matter, Shirl?"

"I guess I'm dreading the trip home, all alone." She reached across the table, giving my hand a quick pat. I smiled at her. "But I am looking forward to seeing everybody when I get there. Bet you are, too."

Anne shifted in the booth, stretching her legs. "Actually, not so much. I've been here so long, I guess I'm closer to my friends from class now than I am to most of the Mercies." The crowded restaurant was warm. I watched as Annie tugged an oversized Ohio State sweatshirt off over her head revealing a white T-shirt drooping down over her jeans.

The harried waitress padded up to our booth. I glanced

at Annie, "Mushroom and sausage?" She nodded and the waitress, grateful for our decisiveness, left as quickly as she had come.

Annie closed her eyes and made a little slurping sound in anticipation. "Pizza is such a treat. We almost never had it at the motherhouse, and when we did, the homemade version was nothing like the real thing."

I pushed the napkin dispenser across the table. "Here. You're going to need these. This is the juiciest pizza in town."

She obligingly pulled out several napkins. "And meat on Friday night, too. Ain't it great?" Her voice was a happy lilt. We both liked this outcome of Vatican II.

"I remember waiting for midnight on Friday night so that my boyfriend and I could go out for pizza."

She grinned. "A boyfriend in your shady past? I'd better watch you at the Newman Club with all those cute guys."

"Ok, Annie. You're the one who looks like all the other coeds. In this black suit, nobody is going to make that mistake about me."

"I know. I know." She shoved the sleeves of her T-shirt up to her elbows. "When is your community letting you out of the uniform?"

"I'll probably come back here after Christmas in civvies. Everybody who wants to change now can do it. I don't know what I'll find when I get back to St. Rose. Maybe I'll be the only one still wearing a black suit."

Conversation halted with the arrival of an immense pizza wafting aromas of Parmesan, oregano, and sausage to our delighted noses. After the first bite, wiping a string of mozzarella from my chin, I brought up a question I had for Anne, a music question about Vatican II.

"You've been playing guitar Masses at the Newman Center for quite a while, right?"

She slid a piece of pizza onto her plate. "Well, when I came here five years ago to start my doctoral program, the Center was like all the parishes, still singing Gregorian chant to a small organ. It's only been about a year since we started singing in English. It took a while after that for the chaplain to get brave enough to give the organ a rest and try guitar. I guess the bishop didn't like the idea."

I tried to piece together the history. "So, then, guitar Masses in English started here not long before I arrived?" No doubt it had been a less tense transition than in LaCrosse.

Annie took another bite of pizza. "Yeah, I'd say so. The music changed about the same time our community gave us the ok to go back to our baptismal names, if we wanted."

Her community was ahead of mine in making name changes. I had permission to use my family name here on the secular university campus, but the nuns at home were still waiting for that option.

I studied Anne's freckled face trying to imagine her with another name. I drew a blank. "So, what was your name before?"

She pointed a bony index finger speckled with tomato sauce at me. "Promise you won't laugh."

I could see Annie was half-serious. I handed her a napkin. "Not if you clean up your act."

She wiped the pizza sauce from her finger. "Well, promise you won't tell?"

I nodded assent.

"It was Sister Dennis Areopagite."

A large snort escaped me. What a name!

Annie leaned across the table, nearly overturning her coke. "You promised!"

"Ok, ok." I helplessly guffawed again. Poor Annie's face was red as she noticed the girl in the next booth looking at her.

I took a deep breath, trying to smooth out the spasms of laughter. "It was just a shock. How did you ever get such a name?"

"God, I don't know." Anne wilted against the back of the booth. "I think the Superiors hated me. In those days, they picked our names. When I heard my name in the investiture ceremony for the first time, I was totally shocked!" Still blushing, she took a big swig of coke. "Then, when I got here, I really wondered how my classmates would react."

I could imagine Anne's embarrassment, wearing full habit and using such a name among all the blue-jeaned coeds named Debbie and Lisa.

"Was it pretty awful?"

Annie grinned. "I got an unexpected break. My professors called me Sister Kerrigan. They picked up my family name from transcripts. I was in college before I joined the Mercies."

"You must have been so relieved."

"Absolutely! Yes!" She giggled, then went silent. "But, you know what? I've made friends with those Debbies and Lisas." Her eyes looked misty behind her thick glasses. "It seems so much easier without the frippery of weird names and long black veils."

I was still thinking about my conversation with Anne when I arrived home a few days later. I couldn't imagine not missing my Franciscan sisters. A light dusting of snow swirled around my ankles as I quickly pulled the convent's heavy, brass-studded door closed behind me in the dark entryway.

Nobody was in sight as I hurried down the shadowy corridor toward the refectory. I hoped I wasn't late for the evening meal.

Just outside the dining room, I shoved my small suitcase under the coat rack, hung my damp winter jacket, and slowly pushed the door open.

The usually bustling dining room was eerily silent. To my surprise, the room was nearly empty. Gone were the diagonal rows of wooden tables and stools. In their place were large round tables covered with white tablecloths. At the far end of the room, under a large oil painting of the Last Supper, a buffet counter was set up where Reverend Mother's table used to be. I hardly recognized the place.

An elderly nun in full habit was serving herself at the buffet. Taking a tray, I stepped next to her. She turned, startled. "Oh, who are you?"

"I'm sorry I startled you. I'm Sister Shirley Cunningham. I've been away at school."

She turned back to ladling green beans onto her plate. "Can't keep you young'uns straight with all the comings and goings around here."

I served myself a piece of lukewarm chicken. "Maybe you knew me by my old name, Sister John Ann."

"I never heard that name around here before." She slowly made her way to an empty table near a small Christmas tree and seated herself with a jerk, as though favoring a sore knee.

I followed her wondering what had happened since I left the motherhouse in June. "Don't the sisters eat together any more?"

My companion made a huffing noise. "The kitchen puts

the food out and everybody comes and goes. We hardly ever sit down together or have reading. It's just not like the old days."

Two other sisters in full habit were seated at a table nearby, not speaking. Their faces were unfamiliar to me. The clinking of glassware echoed against the dining room walls. I looked at the empty tables wondering if this was better or worse than the conflicts of the previous summer. Where was everybody?

"Very few are here for Christmas. Several from the first year class have left." She looked at me appraisingly. "That your class?"

"Yes, my class."

Her eyes dropped to my black suit as if it offended her. The thought irritated me, but I kept my voice even. "I heard Sister Aaron left."

My companion looked at me over her bifocals. "Yes, along with the rest of the bunch, all at one time. Even Sister Maureen."

A cold draft sent a shiver down my back. "Sister Maureen has left the community?"

"Oh, yes, with those Ph.D. nuns at the college. Just at Christmas, too." She slid her chair away from the table, supporting her weight on the arms as she rose. "Don't know what they were thinking."

She walked away without a goodbye, veil swaying crookedly with each jerky step, leaving me alone with my stunned thoughts.

Some of the departing nuns had probably decided the community's adjustment to a less autocratic way of life would never come, and they could accomplish more good as laywomen. Others may have felt change had gone too far, tearing the heart out of the old-time practices. Either way, the worrisome news scared me. Was all the leadership splitting from the order, like driftwood breaking up in a storm? I'd never dreamed such a thing could happen, and in such a short time.

A sudden wave of fatigue swept over me, like the old weakness from mono. I leaned back in the chair and closed my eyes, hoping the heaviness would pass. In a few moments, I knew I needed to sleep.

Exhausted, I made my way through dim corridors to the dorm. Most of the beds were empty, untouched. I sat down wearily on the first one I came to, mildly consoled that at least the dorm looked the same but wishing Sharon would appear, or Marlene, or Mary Ann, or Aaron.

In the dim light at the far end of the room, two junior sisters quietly padded around. One had permed and dyed her hair an unflattering shade of red. The other was rubbing make-up off with a tissue.

Before any further revelations, someone snapped off the light switch. It didn't matter. I undressed in darkness and slid between cold sheets, a tear trickling down my cheek. My long-awaited homecoming was a disappointment. I had yet to see one person I knew.

Because it was Christmas holiday, Fr. Jim's schedule was open. His voice was warm on the phone: "By all means, Sister. Come on down. I'll meet you at the office in an hour."

The thin tread on my rubber boots couldn't keep me from slipping on the icy sidewalks as I walked the few blocks to my appointment. Hoping not to lose footing, I hurried along between high banks of recently shoveled snow, shivering despite the black wool scarf over my chin and mouth. Once in the warm vestibule of Jim's office, I unwound the scarf. My nose felt numb.

His hearty voice boomed through the half-open door. "That you, Sister? You must be frozen. Come on in."

Jim, still in clerical blacks, hadn't changed. "Coffee's hot." Pot in hand, he flashed me a grin. It was truly good to see him.

I handed him a small box. "Merry Christmas."

His grin widened even further. "Well, thank you, Sister." I had tied the brightly wrapped holiday package with a silver ribbon proclaiming, "A gift from Ohio State University."

He chuckled, pulling the ribbon from the package. "I can use this as a necktie when I go out in my civvies." We laughed an easy laugh together as he opened the box. "Candy. Goodbye waistline! Have some."

I sampled a maple cream while Jim made his choice.

"Carmel! My favorite." He leaned back in his chair, chewing contentedly, then took a quick swipe at his mouth with a napkin. "So how're things going for you out there in the halls of academe?"

I smiled, relaxing. It was so good to talk with him. "I'm half finished with my program now. Next quarter, my classes will be done. Then I'll write my thesis."

He raised his eyebrows. "You're really moving right along." He reached for his ever-present legal pad and poised his pen over the page. "Does that mean you'll graduate in June?"

When I nodded, he wrote a date on the page, then looked at me inquiringly. "So, what's next?"

I hated to tell him that no matter how hard I tried to decide, I still didn't know.

He leaned forward to drop a crumpled napkin on the table. "I heard some nuns just left the FSPAs, including Sister Maureen." He shot a quick glance at me to see if I was ready for this topic of conversation.

I guessed I was as ready as I'd ever be. "Someone told me last night, right after I got in. I just can't believe Maureen would leave. She was my Superior. I don't even know who to report to right now."

"You look scared."

"I *am* scared. The nuns who left were leaders. I didn't know there was so much polarization going on. Is the community splitting in two, like a family breaking up?"

"It could happen." Jim's voice was smooth.

How could he be so matter-of-fact when the earth was crumbling under my feet? I looked up to see his eyes measuring me carefully. "What frightens you the most, Sister?"

The most frightening part? The possibilities milled around in my mind like anxious cats. Was it the fallout from the turmoil of the Vatican Council? With the new value placed on lay leadership, maybe we weren't needed any more. Even if we were, how could I live with these women who differed so sharply on how we should make changes? It was very unnerving to imagine myself alone in a house full of conflict, with no close friends, without the sisters I'd come to think of as family.

Suddenly cold, I pulled my jacket closer around me. "I fear what I can't see in the community. These women who left, what did they know that I don't know? Sister Maureen and I may have had our differences, but I respected her. Nobody was more dedicated."

Jim's voice was a soft murmur. "So, here you are, a newly

professed sister and your future looks very shaky."

I wondered if he could see just how shaky I really felt.

"The motherhouse doesn't feel like home any more."

"Are all the nuns you knew gone?"

"It looks like it. The ones still here are either in full habit with no plans to change or else they're wearing makeup and dying their hair." I felt foolish remembering the months I'd worn my prescribed suit at Ohio State, never considering even a dab of lipstick.

Jim sat silently, waiting, watching my face. "What else?"

Tears welled up in my eyes. "I never expected to feel so alone in the convent. I've been gone for months, and couldn't wait to come home, but no one noticed I was gone."

"Are you asking yourself, then, what community life really means? Is that it?"

He had framed my question exactly. I knew I didn't want a life without love. I doubted I could survive. Then I thought of the hours I'd spent in silent prayer. I knew in my heart that I was called to be close to God. How could I leave? But I was so lonely! I hardly dared let myself think of it, but maybe I had underestimated how much I needed the intimacy marriage could bring. It was another issue I had to face. My mind raced between the alternatives I'd agonized over for so many months.

"I've made vows, Fr. Jim. I meant them with all my heart. But now I'm afraid I really need to leave, get married, have kids."

He smiled. "I've wondered about that."

"It's funny. The Council told us the lay state is as important as the religious state or the priesthood. I guess I always thought I couldn't be close to God unless I was a nun. But now, this awful loneliness seems to even be getting in the way of my prayer."

"That's serious. You don't want to lose communication upstairs." Jim smiled, jerking a thumb toward the ceiling. "Well, there is such a thing as existential loneliness that all of us feel. But you seem to be talking about something else here. What about before you came to St. Rose? Lots of lonely times then, too?"

"I never felt lonely when I was dating Peter."

"But your boyfriend wasn't Catholic, right?" Jim had a good memory for the stories I'd told him about Peter.

"That's right, he was a skeptic."

"So maybe you could feel close to God with a husband who shared your deep faith."

I thought about it awhile in silence, remembering what Anne Kerrigan had said about her closeness to the friends she had so much in common with at the university. Maybe Peter just wasn't the right guy for me.

As for having kids, I'd long since recovered from my irritation with the stints of babysitting I'd endured as assistant Mom. I knew I'd love having my own children. As always, Jim had given me much to ponder.

"I'll think about all that, Fr. Jim." I took a deep breath and changed the subject. "There's another matter, too. I feel guilty even wrestling with these questions about leaving. The nuns are investing in my education. They expect me to use it for their work."

"Of course," his voice was smooth. "Well, you can't force a big decision before its time, but we can explore your other concerns about school. What do you feel would be the fair thing to do?"

"I don't know."

The silver Ohio State ribbon from Jim's package sparkled at me from the floor. The expenses I was tallying up at Ohio State were becoming a pain in the neck. "How can I leave the community right after finishing this degree when so many other nuns have just left? The timing is terrible and I feel obligated. The others have given years to the community, but I'm not sure I can last long enough for that." Even the thought made me restless. I shifted, stretching. "I feel stuck."

Jim's reading glasses couldn't hide the smile wrinkles gathering around his eyes. "May I make a suggestion?"

Why was he grinning? Was there some obvious solution I'd missed? I nodded dumbly.

"Have you considered talking to your new Provincial?"

How simple. Of course. My angst needed to be talked about with someone directly involved, a Superior, not just with Fr. Jim. I sheepishly smiled back at him. I'd assumed I had to sort myself out first, but Mother Rosanne was approachable. I hadn't officially been introduced to her since she had been called home from San Salvador by her election to office. Nevertheless, she'd greeted me warmly on the way to chapel that morning. I was relieved to have a course of action.

Next day found me at the provincial house, a modest, two-bedroom bungalow across the street from the college. Mother Rosanne was on her knees in the kitchen scrubbing the faded linoleum floor. She smiled but refused help as she stiffly raised herself, leaning on the scrub bucket. The elderly nun hugged me with surprisingly strong arms then pointed to a coat rack in the hall. "You can leave your things there. Let's sit in the parlor where we can chat." Something about Mother Roseanne reminded me of my grandmother. I followed her, telling my anxious stomach I was safe on this errand.

The small front room's dim light revealed two worn wingback chairs, a well-used sofa, and a lovingly polished but far from new coffee table with a wooden statue of the brown-robed St. Francis. A small Christmas tree twinkled in the front window. Mother Roseanne gestured for me to sit in the chair facing her.

"Well, as you can imagine, it's taken a while for me to get to know all the new sisters who've come to St. Rose since I left years ago." She smiled broadly. "It's good to meet you, Shirley."

I'd been Shirley much longer than I had ever been Sister John Ann. Hearing my name and her kind voice was all I needed. I burst into tears.

"What's the matter, dear?" She reached for my hand, taking it in both of her own still damp hands.

This was no way to get acquainted with my new Superior. "Oh, Mother, I'm sorry." I struggled for composure. "I've been worrying—"

With a gentle laugh, she stopped me mid-sentence. "Well, that's not such a good idea."

I looked at her, surprised.

"The worry, I mean." Her voice and eyes were soft. "You've been away at school, I think? Some problems there?"

I took a deep breath. Mother Roseanne, close to seventy, was more than ready for the likes of me. I might as well plunge in. "School is no problem, Mother. It's all those sisters who left the college." I groped for my handkerchief. She'd probably entered the convent at age thirteen and been a nun for fifty years with never a doubt. I glanced down at our interlocking fingers hoping she could understand. "I'm not sure if I should stay, Mother."

Roseanne slid her chair closer to mine. "Ahh, yes. That's not easy. We all have our times of doubt." Her words surprised me.

She paused a moment, studying me. The achy tightness in the back of my head eased a bit. "How long have you been in the community?"

"Nearly seven years."

"That's a long time, a very long time." The nun's eyes seemed to look right into my heart. "It tells me you take your religious life seriously." She sat back, released my hand and, as if from long habit, began fingering the rosary hanging at her side.

"Have you asked God to show you how He is leading you?"

I could see she knew this was the most important decision of my life. "I pray about it every day, but I can't get clear. I just haven't been able to decide."

"So often it's like that." Mother Roseanne smiled and sighed. "Well, Shirley, one thing is for sure. To resolve this you need to be at peace. Go back to the university and continue to pray."

"Mother, that's the problem. I don't feel right about the community paying for my education when I'm not sure I'll stay and teach."

"Oh, I see. You're worried about your responsibility. That's why the others leaving has troubled you."

I nodded.

She brushed away my concern. "You mustn't worry. Worry will cloud your prayer, your ability to hear God's voice in your heart."

Her words rang true. Before, I could often sit in silence

and know what God was asking, but lately, my quiet time was filled with struggles and confusion.

She went on. "Should you decide to leave the community, you can repay us for your education. I will pray for your peace, Shirley."

Before I could respond, Mother Roseanne stood, picked up the bucket near her chair, and smiled at me. "Will you promise to write and let me know how you are?" As she spoke, she reached for me.

Grateful, I stepped into her motherly hug. She even smelled like Grandma, like clean linen that had been folded in a drawer with sachet. I promised. As I crossed the street to the convent, a soft snow was falling. Brushing it from my jacket, I swung the heavy brass door of the chapel open and walked in. In the darkness, the sanctuary lamp threw shadows on the comforting marble angels hovering over me from every corner. I settled in the last pew, grateful to be alone, grateful to release the worry that had plagued me for months. I closed my eyes. The perfume of fragrant pine trees clustered around the crèche reminded me of St. Gabriel's and that last Christmas before I came to St. Rose. What I'd give to hold my mother's hand at midnight Mass once more. I was so lonely.

After the holidays, I left LaCrosse for school again with Mother Roseanne's reassuring words still echoing inside me. As it turned out, I needed them for more reasons than I knew.

Once in Columbus, the cabbie took a long, circuitous route from the airport to the campus. I sat in the back seat wondering if I was the target of a ruse.

"Can't get through those streets to your dorm, Miss. There are riots on campus." A chill went through me. Last term, angry protests, sit-ins, and takeovers had been all around me. I clutched my book bag, silently wondering how dangerous it would be on campus, as the driver wound through unfamiliar neighborhoods to the university.

As soon as I arrived at the residence hall, the house-mother summoned me to the phone. Mom had seen network news in Iowa about the violence and shooting at Ohio State. As it turned out, no one had been hurt and little damage had been done that night, but fear was in the air. For months, feelings about Vietnam ran high on campuses, a prelude to the student killings by Ohio National Guardsmen at Kent State. Before the term was over, national events horrified us again.

Martin Luther King, the great warrior of civil rights, was shot to death on his balcony. At the Newman Center, a special memorial service was hastily planned for the leader so much admired by our generation. Sister Anne and I squeezed inside to find a place in the standing-room only crowd of students and professors.

Tears streamed down my cheeks as I looked at the anguished faces around me. This suffering world was a far cry from the quiet of the cloister. It was a world in need, not a world to be escaped and avoided. When the service began, we joined hands and raised our voices. As we sang, "We shall overcome someday,"[7] the words of a priest I'd met before I joined the convent floated through my mind: *If you want to change the world, go into politics.* I prayed that some great-hearted leader would one day fill Martin Luther King's shoes.

By spring break, it was a relief to escape the turbulence at Ohio State for LaCrosse. I needed to talk to Fr. Jim.

Green buds graced the elms arching over me as I retraced

my familiar walk to his office. The trees, now full of promise, had looked so dead, so bare, on my last visit home.

Once at Jim's office, Joanne, his secretary, waved me through his open door. My eyes were immediately drawn to one yellow rose standing tall on the coffee table. Jim was bent over it, breathing in its perfume.

He turned with a smile. "Joanne said we couldn't wait for spring. We needed some color in here now."

"Thank God for flowers in winter! And roses are my favorite." I leaned, too, to inhale the flower's sweetness, then sat down. My knees were shaking. Why was I so jittery today? "Would you mind if I have some coffee? The stress is getting to me."

Jim nodded. "How about cocoa? Less caffeine?"

"That'd be great."

He stirred chocolate into the cup of water, hot from the warmer on the table between us, and handed it to me. The first sip calmed me.

"It's been some months since I followed your suggestion to talk with Mother Roseanne, and it did relieve me."

He met my eyes. "Glad to hear that, Sister. And have you been able to get clearer about what you want to do?"

I smoothed my skirt over my knees, wishing I could say yes. "I'm still wrestling. I vacillate and vacillate. I know I've grown these years in the convent. I've felt God's closeness many times. Mother Roseanne was so understanding, and when I was ill, Sister Agnes was very kind. Over the years, I've felt close to my friends and classmates. I know I'm stronger, in spite of everything."

Jim nodded again, reaching for his own cup. "Yes, your life with the nuns has been a good thing in many ways, but that's not the end of the story, is it?"

I could always count on him to understand. I shook my head.

"It must be pretty uncomfortable to be unsettled for so long. You must feel like you're running back and forth on some kind of edge."

How did he find the words to describe my turmoil so clearly? "Yes, yes. It's so ironic. In this celibate life, I've been nurtured somehow. I'm stronger as a woman now. The nuns made up for something I missed as I grew up, I guess. It's odd. I never seriously wanted to marry or have kids before, but now . . ." Words stuck in my throat, stopped by sadness.

He allowed me a moment of silence, then spoke softly. "So you've learned some new things about love."

I blew my nose and nodded. "Yes, many of the nuns have been like real sisters to me. They've been so kind and generous."

"And you've also been hurt and disillusioned about community life."

"Yes, and lonely. But I know God called me here. I'm not sure of much, but I am sure of that, and I can't say no to God and walk away. Otherwise, I'd just leave and get married."

Outside Jim's window, two loudly chirping robins landed on a bare branch. Even the robins had each other. Desperation washed over me.

"I've prayed. I've struggled." I could hear my own voice rising. If only someone could tell me God's will. . . ." Finally, I burst out, "Fr. Jim, what does God want me to do?"

The priest looked at me with a clear gaze, smiled slightly and replied without skipping a beat. "God doesn't care, Shirley."

I looked at him, thunderstruck. How could God not care what I did?

He went on. "God loves you, right?"

I nodded.

"You have free will, right?"

I nodded again.

"You love God?"

Another mute nod.

"Then, you can do what you want about this. You're yearning for a husband and children, the closeness of your own family. And, it's all right. All desire for love comes from God, after all. Believe me, God really doesn't care if you go or stay."

I didn't know what to say. Could he be right? I sat there a long time, wordlessly trying to take it in.

As I walked home, a robin hopped across my path. The chubby, red-breasted bird, hardly more than a nestling, stopped and looked up at me, singing one note. As if on cue, a second robin landed nearby, at the edge of the sidewalk. Was this the couple I saw from Jim's office? I stood looking at them, never a more sociable pair of robins. I wondered if they were following me.

As if to answer my unspoken question, the first robin hopped sideways and sang again, still looking at me, then flew to a low branch just above my head and trilled. His little companion twittered, then flurried up, settling beside him and the concert began. It was as if the two birds had been waiting to pour out their music for me.

Somehow the song flowed into my heart and with it, the simple, clear message: *You can still serve Me. I know your love and I want it, always. You gave Me your life. It belongs to Me. You aren't taking anything back.*

The robins warbled one last trill and the music stopped. After a moment of silence, they lifted off the branch, flew a loop around my head, and disappeared from view as if their mission had been accomplished. I looked after them, then laughed out loud, too delighted to care if passersby noticed.

My heavy heart had lightened. I could fly, too. I finally knew my life belonged to God. That would never change. It didn't matter where I lived it.

When the day came to take off my gold ring and walk out the convent door, it didn't matter. God and I had it straight. We would be close wherever I was.

Many difficult conversations with family and friends were still ahead, along with anxious moments, returning to a world that I'd left seven years earlier. But I had what I needed to go on, a peaceful heart. God had called me into the convent and now was calling me out.

I packed the small black suitcase I'd brought to St. Rose. God and I were going on the road.

3

Love is the Answer

TOO LATE

It's too late — it's too late.
I have breathed your breath.
I have melted in the heat and pounding of your blood.
I have been swept away on tempestuous rivers,
Submerged in the depths, the flood.

It's too late — it's too late.

I can never again walk quietly where I used to walk alone.
My innermost places are now filled with you.
You are under my eyelids,
In the air I breathe,
In my heart pulse
Roaring there.
It's too late — it's too late.
I am lost
In you.

The windowpanes on the old Victorian house at 2611 N. Maryland rattled in the winter wind. I put down my novel, turning to peer out the window by my chair. The light of the street lamp glistened on the snowy scene below. Patches of frost blocked my view, etching the glass with whorls and scrolls like some unknown language, as if they could tell me how I might meet the love of my life.

Milwaukee could be freezing cold in January. Cookie, Sue, and Theresa had all decided to get out of town for the weekend. I didn't mind, preferring to curl up and stay warm in our upstairs apartment rather than brave the elements. I needed peace and quiet to grade the week's accumulation of student papers and to sort myself out a bit.

Shirley

I smiled, remembering the happenstance's that had brought me, step by step, to this slightly shabby but cozy apartment and my new identity as "Miss Cunningham, English teacher." Life had carried me from the convent gate in August to a job at Nathan Hale High in suburban West Allis.

I could smile now, but the summer had not been without headaches. Sue, Theresa, and I all had left St. Rose within weeks of each other. We were teachers and school was about to start. The adjustments to civilian life and work had to be made simultaneously, and quickly.

Sue was confident: "Don't worry. Cookie says there are plenty last-minute teaching jobs in Milwaukee." Sue's cousin, Cookie, should know. She'd taught high school chemistry in the city through the years that Sue, Theresa, and I had spent in the convent. As it turned out, she was right. We each signed teaching contracts in the few weeks between our exit from the Franciscans and the beginning of the school year.

Then, the next problem arose. Where would we live? We trekked the hot streets of the city, newspaper ads in hand, finally settling on the somewhat dingy but completely furnished upstairs apartment of an old house near Lake Michigan and the University of Wisconsin campus.

I was broke except for the small dowry the nuns had returned to me, but I managed to buy some clothes. Even at age 28, I didn't mind my insolvency, until time came to buy a car. Because I had no collateral, Mom had to cosign for a $2,600 loan, the sticker price on my new 1968 Chevy Nova.

I quickly learned that the seven years I'd spent in the convent wouldn't convince a banker that I was honest. With some chagrin, I realized the dollar said, "In God we trust" for a reason. It meant, bankers, among others, trust only God.

Somehow, the first months of adjustment had passed. I'd upended my existence as a nun with the sureness there'd be a man in my life. Several showed up. The first was an attorney with a red sports car, the next, a science teacher at my school. Although I was ready and they were willing, strangely enough, no emotional connections developed. So here I was, six months later.

I turned away from the window and picked up the newspaper. The Calendar of Events listed a singles dance at a downtown hotel starting just about now. It sure would be fun to get out of the house and maybe meet an interesting guy, but I doubted the wisdom of going alone. Even my roomies wouldn't know where I was.

My ruminations came to a halt as Cookie breezed in the door, her miniature Chihuahua snuggled in the crook of one arm. She dropped her suitcase with a thunk. "Hey, Shirl, it's a cold one out there! I was afraid the dog'd freeze before we got home."

I laughed at the thought, getting up from my easy chair to shove her suitcase across the hardwood floor, out of the entryway, into her bedroom. "Well, we don't want any frozen Chihuahua around here."

Cookie lit one of her king-size menthol cigarettes, squinting the smoke away from her eyes. "So what've you been up to?"

"Not much. Got my schoolwork done. I've been bored crazy tonight. I guess I've had too much solitude. I'm really glad you're home early!"

Cookie's round face beamed. "My weekend wasn't exactly exciting either. My family can be . . . well, . . . tranquilizing." I could believe it. Cookie was easy going, unflappable. Likely it was a family trait. And, she was a night owl. Here in our little, bachelor-girl pad, she was the only one who faithfully watched Johnny Carson every night at bedtime. She seemed full of energy now. I decided to try my chances.

"How would you feel about checking out this singles dance at the hotel tonight? Are you tired? Do you think it's too cold?" I wasn't sure she liked to dance. She didn't have a boyfriend. Maybe she wasn't interested in meeting one.

My doubts were soon put to rest. Cookie flashed me the biggest smile I'd ever seen on her face. "I'm game. What's a little frostbite when you're having fun? Besides, the two of us have never gone out howling together."

I grinned at the thought. While Cookie bedded down her dog, I circled the address of the hotel in the newspaper, stuffed it into my purse, and then dabbed some cologne behind my ears. I was ready for adventure.

By the time we walked into the crowded hotel ballroom from the frosty night, the party was in full swing. Music pounded as a Jim Morrison wannabe pleaded, "Come on, Baby, light my fire."[8] A sea of dancers flung arms, shook hips, and stomped with abandon. This definitely was not the convent recreation room!

As the song ended, Cookie and I found the bar. Before we could sit down, the band started again. A large, red-faced, slightly winded man was at my side. "Would you like to polka?"

Why not? I'd braved the cold night air to dance, to have some fun, to survey the scene. My partner's hand was hot, hard, and damp as he led me onto the floor.

"Roll out the barrel. We'll have a barrel of fun . . . omm-pa-pa . . . we've got the blues on the run. It's time to roll the barrel. The gang's all here." My burly partner took me firmly in his grasp and hurled us both across the dance floor, completely disregarding the elbows and shins of any unfortunate victim in our path. Were my feet touching the floor at all? Breathless, panting, I clung to him with a death grip, fearing imminent collision, broken bones, and untimely death. My heart pounded from the exertion. As we galloped around the floor, other dancers left to give us room. Sweat trickled between my shoulder blades, and down the back of my legs. When I dressed in a turtleneck sweater, woolen vest, and mini-skirt, I wasn't expecting the aerobic workout that polka turned out to be.

Cookie sat at a nearby table watching the spectacle. As the last strain of the accordion faded, I mopped my wet brow and headed for her, eager to escape.

But I was intercepted. A smiling, sandy-haired man touched my elbow as the band eased into a slow ballad. "Would you like to dance?"

Calmness emanated from him and the music was quiet. I took his hand, grateful to see my death-defying former partner turn and walk away.

"So, you survived the polka." Little wrinkles of mischief spread at the corners of his eyes belying the innocence of his toothpaste-ad-perfect smile.

"Just barely!"

His name was Bob McCauley, a pronounceable Irish name among the many tongue-tangling names I'd heard in Milwaukee.

As he led me across the floor, I noticed the large, firm shoulders under the slightly nubby fabric of his well-tailored, green sport jacket. Thankfully, he was less vigorous than my first partner but seemed athletic. As we swayed to the soft music, his arms were strong and secure around me.

"I'm from Lake Delavan," he offered, "but I've been here teaching high school for a few years."

So, he was a teacher and Irish! Grandma always warned me to watch out for those Irish boys. I wondered what she'd say about this one.

He wanted to know all about me. I started off with a few of the basics.

"I'm an English teacher, but this year I have a journalism class, too. The kids want to make movies. Maybe we will, once I figure out how to get them started."

Bob grinned broadly. "My classes have made movies. It's great fun. A couple years ago, I found some films that show kids how to do it. If you like, I could call you with the information about them."

This guy had a smooth way to get a phone number. I looked him over. He seemed sincere, a white-picket-fence kind of fellow, probably in his late thirties. I could imagine buying a used car from him. I wondered why he was single. He didn't seem wounded or cynical, like a divorce survivor. He had mentioned Loyola, a Jesuit school. Maybe he'd been in the seminary.

As the music stopped, Bob bought fresh drinks for Cookie and me but soda for himself. We had lots to talk about, trading gossip about our schools and kibitzing about the dancers on the floor. When the conversation slowed and I fumbled for a cigarette, he bent to offer me a light.

The match in his strong hands flared, casting a glint on the tinge of red in his sideburns. I wondered if the hair on his chest would be that color or light brown like the rest of his thick head of hair.

Straightening up, he twisted slightly. "Ouch! I fell on my shoulder skiing yesterday." So, he was outdoorsy and a non-smoker. As he flexed his arm and stretched, I caught a whiff of after-shave. It was like a breath of fresh air in the smoky ballroom.

Later in the sub-zero parking lot, it was far too cold to linger. We hurriedly exchanged phone numbers and waved our good-byes. Bob, in his black overcoat, quickly faded into the darkness. I wondered if I'd hear from him again.

Next day, when my prep period arrived, I was already caught up on lesson plans. After my weekend of schoolwork, I actually had some rare free time. I decided to write to my sister, Jane.

"I met an interesting guy last night. He's not handsome exactly, but he seems kind and interested in helping people. I'd guess he's about ten years older than I am. I can only think of one reason why he's still single: he's probably been in the seminary. He mentioned Loyola and we've read all the same books. I wouldn't doubt he's figured me for an ex-nun, too, even though I was wearing a mini-skirt. Well, we might not be such a bad combination. You have to meet him."

Both prep period and my letter quickly ended. The rest of the day was full of deadlines and frustration as the newspaper staff struggled to finish the last few articles for the February issue.

It was later than usual when I dragged home into the dark kitchen of my apartment. Pushing the door open with one hip, I precariously balanced an armload of file folders while fumbling for the light switch. Silence told me my roommates were out somewhere. As I snapped on the light, a sudden jangle of the phone startled me. I grabbed for it, only to see my students' newspaper galleys slide out of their folders creating eddies of paper under the table on the linoleum floor.

"Is this Shirley?" My mood shifted immediately as I recognized the pleasant, masculine voice of the night before. "I know where we can find a good pizza in about an hour, unless you have other plans. . . ."

The newspaper galleys could wait. He had called and right away! I hurried into my bedroom to check my makeup, slip on high heels, and make one last inspection in the mirror. As the doorbell rang, I winked at myself and turned out the light.

Bob bundled me solicitously into the bucket seat of his already warm car.

His smile was warm, too. On the short drive to the pizza parlor, wheels crunching in the cold snow, we chatted about the day's events in our classrooms. Once in the crowded parking lot, he turned off the headlights but kept the heater running, making no move to go in.

I had a million questions left over from the night before. Maybe he did, too. But before I could launch in, Bob spoke. "Shirley, there's something I should tell you."

I turned to face him across the gearshift and laughed, pleased. "Oh, I know."

"What do you know?" He sounded startled.

"That you are either a priest or were a seminarian for a very long time."

His eyes widened as he twisted in the seat to look at me.

I'd noticed his black overcoat, black slacks, and shoes. Besides, how many other single thirty-five-year-old men read Eric Fromm, Hans Kung, and talked on the dance floor about Pflaum Publishers, a Catholic catechetical text-book source?

He found his voice. "How did you know that?"

"Well, it takes one to know one. I was a nun for seven years."

Dumbfounded, he let out a lung full of air. "Well, I'll be! And I always vowed I'd never get involved with a nun or an ex-nun." He squinted at me in the half-light filtering through the frosty windshield. "You sure don't look like one."

"I did let my hair grow, that's true."

I followed his glance from my face to my bare knees and high heels, enjoying his consternation.

Over dinner, the story unfolded. Bob wasn't merely a long-term seminarian. He had been ordained in the Milwaukee diocese some years earlier.

"I've come to the conclusion I need to leave the priesthood and marry. I don't want to. I love the ministry." His eyes asked my understanding. "It's the celibacy. If I could remain in the priesthood and marry, that would suit me perfectly."

I shivered and looked away to pour myself a cup of coffee. This man's sentiments echoed mine in an uncanny way. I remembered my many conversations with Fr. Jim. If I could have continued my life as a religious with a husband and family, I'd probably still be there.

He went on. "I had to tell you all this now, Shirley, because I want to be honest with you."

I placed my coffee cup on the table and reached to touch his hand. "I can understand that, but why did you go to the dance?"

He looked uncomfortable. "Truth is, it was a whole new experience for me, and not an especially easy one." His blue-gray eyes were serious. "I confided to some close friends, a couple, that I'd like to get married. They told me they'd met at a singles dance."

I had to respect that this was the first time he'd been alone with me, the first chance he'd had to tell me his story. Maybe he was struggling with the same loneliness I'd known. Maybe he was ready to go on leave.

He dropped a napkin in his lap. "I'd never been to that hotel before. By ten o'clock, I'd danced a few times, but there wasn't anyone I wanted to meet. I was ready to leave. Then, you walked in."

I caught my breath wondering how my path had crossed Bob's like this. I'd never attended a singles dance or been at the hotel before either, and if Cookie hadn't come home unexpectedly, I wouldn't have shown up last night, given the cold, unwelcoming night that it had been.

Bob sprinkled Parmesan on the juicy wedge of pizza before him. "I've applied for my dispensation, but it takes a long time for Rome to process these laicization cases, and I'm ready to change my life now. It's up to the bishop how soon I go on leave."

He handed me the cheese shaker. I surveyed my pizza, glad for a moment to gather my thoughts. Though I felt I'd known the man across the table from me a long time, my better judgement reminded me that we had just met. I now saw that many unknowns were concealed under his laughter and banter on last night's spin around the dance floor. I looked up to find him studying me, waiting.

"I think I understand."

He nodded silently, winding a strand of mozzarella round his fork, then came back with a question of his own.

"Why did you leave the convent?"

I hadn't talked about this with any of the other men I'd dated and wasn't crazy about doing it now. Was it really necessary? I speared a mushroom, hesitating. I guessed it was. Bob's background was like my own, after all.

"I left the convent because I wanted to get married and have kids. I was very lonely, so I can understand that you're going through something tough. Your situation may even be harder than mine because of the way the Church treats priests who leave." I knew well my vows had been easily dispensed, but every Catholic grade-school kid learns that ordination can't be undone or allowed to simply expire. Once a priest, always a priest.

Over the next weeks, I thought long and hard about Bob McCauley and kept him at arm's length. I liked the guy, but we didn't meet often. We'd have long phone chats, each of us eager to hear the other's stories, opinions, and feelings. Bob was a good listener and seemed open about himself.

Meanwhile, I made solo plans each weekend, heading off to visit a classmate in Omaha, back to see another in Illinois, anything to avoid those long hours I knew I'd love to spend with him. He offered to take me to the airport, or to pick me up, but I wouldn't accept any favors, wouldn't encourage him. On one hand, I was drawn to him, but on the other, I wasn't sure that it would be safe to fall in love, that he really was available. He loved the priesthood.

Finally, the confusion was too much for me. I flew to LaCrosse to consult Fr. Jim.

Once at his office, I quickly settled myself to talk as he poured the cup of coffee I never refused. "I really need the chance to talk."

He folded back a sheet from the always-present, yellow pad and smiled. "So, shoot."

"Well, I've met somebody I like. He's a really fine guy, and I think he's been honest with me, but he's a priest."

Jim shot me a glance over his reading glasses. "So, how did you meet?"

I told him the story of the dance and the next night's date for pizza.

"He's been ordained quite awhile. You can imagine how much we have in common. I really love to be with him, but I've been holding him off. I can believe his life is lonely, but I don't want to be the cause of his leaving his ministry. Yet, it seems he's already made the decision."

Jim, a celibate himself, nodded, still listening.

I hesitated, wondering exactly what reassurance I needed from this counselor.

He asked, "Do you trust Bob?"

"I want to trust him . . ." My voice dwindled.

Jim coached me, . . . "And?"

I smoothed my skirt with both hands and took a deep breath. "Yes, I do trust Bob and I'd like him for a friend. Do you think it would be ok?"

The answer was quick and clear. "Sure. Think back to when you were lonely as hell at Ohio State and struggling to decide what to do."

I remembered those solitary days well, relieved only by the chats here, cuddled in this same deep chair where it was finally safe to talk. "Yes, I really could've used a friend." My tense stomach relaxed at the truth of it.

Jim flashed me a smile. "And, if this turns into a courting situation, let it be."

I fell silent. Bob had made promises, freely, just as I had made religious vows. Celibacy was one of them. This observation from Fr. Jim set me back on my heels, calling up a host of questions. What was holding me back from Bob? My own legalism? Or was I afraid to fall in love, afraid of being hurt?

He was watching my face. "Shirley, you may be worrying unnecessarily. It's possible Bob is dealing with the same kind of free choice you made. With prayer, you came to the decision that was right for you. He will, too. It may not be his calling to stay in the priesthood."

Jim eyed me thoughtfully. "It takes courage to love, Shirley. This budding friendship may be a call to love for both of you. Remember, celibacy in the priesthood was introduced centuries after the Church began. If that's Bob's issue, he may find his ministry outside the ranks as a married man with a family."

Once again, he had given me something to think about. "So, my not feeling right could be scruples?"

Jim smiled. "I know you're praying about all this. What God wants, above all, is your free choice to love."

As I sat silently taking in his words, my glance drifted to a plaque behind his desk. I'd never noticed it before. The scrolling calligraphy read: "You are free with the freedom of the children of God."

I returned Jim's smile, squeezing back a tear. "God doesn't care what I do, right?"

A few days later, Bob and I sat together in my kitchen. He'd delivered the Loyola film on how to make movies. "I picked it up while you were gone last weekend. How was your visit to LaCrosse?"

When I recounted my conversation with Fr. Jim, he laughed. "I'm with him. Love is the answer, for sure. Just think. If we were Lutheran, we wouldn't even have a problem."

It was true enough.

Though it was early April, the late afternoon sun slanting through the window made the room stuffy. "Want some ice-cold lemonade?" I emptied ice cubes into our glasses.

Bob swung his legs out from under the table, took the empty ice cube tray from me, and walked to the sink. "I've got some news for you."

A splash of water punctuated his words as he passed the tray under a faucet. "My folks are coming to visit. I want you to meet them."

"They're coming from Arizona?" Bob had told me of his mother's death a few years earlier. His dad, devastated at the sudden loss, had remarried soon and moved from their Delavan Lake home to Sun City with Millie, his new wife.

"I wrote Dad that I plan to resign from the priesthood. I guess he just wants to see for himself that everything is all right." Bob walked slowly to the refrigerator, careful not to spill the tray. He slid it into the freezer, then sat down again, smiling at me.

He seemed so even in this major life transition. I wondered how he managed, and how his dad was managing.

"Well, Shirl, Dad's seventy now and an old-time Catholic. It's not easy for him, but he's getting used to the idea."

I thought of my mom's support when I left the convent. Parents like ours could be counted on to understand. No doubt Ben dearly loved this only son of his. But what about Millie?

"Well, that's another story. Dad tells me she doesn't like

my plans at all. She was a widow when Dad met her, but apparently was married the first time while in her fifties, so she's never had any kids."

I could well imagine her viewpoint. Bad enough for Bob to leave the priesthood, but to get married, too? And to an ex-nun? The role of scarlet woman was new to me, and I wasn't anxious to meet the woman who'd cast me in it.

It wasn't long before Ben and Millie arrived, specifically to meet me. That Saturday when the doorbell rang, I anxiously peeked out the upstairs window through budding trees to see them waiting in the car parked across the street. I guessed they were hoping to stave off disaster.

Ben

Bob bounded up the stairs to get me, his usual enthusiasm written all over his face. Keeping my trepidation to myself, I smiled and let him lead me down the steep stairwell and to the car. As I folded my legs into the front seat of the sedan, Ben reached from the back to grip my hand in hearty greeting.

"So, this is Shirley. We've been waiting to meet you, young lady!"

The ruddy, energetic face in the back seat was an older version of Bob. I was charmed. Ben, at seventy, exuded megavolts of warm, extroverted energy.

"Do you like German food, Shirley? We think the sauerbraten at Carl Ratch's is the best in Milwaukee."

Over dinner, Ben's affable joking never stopped. He was reaching out to me for Bob's sake, to show his son a fatherly acceptance, but Millie was politely subdued. As we left the restaurant, Bob and Millie went to the valet station for the car while Ben and I waited in the foyer. As soon as they were out of earshot, Ben took my elbow and whispered, "Do you have an aspirin in that big purse you're carrying there, young lady? I've got a bad headache."

I could see the strain on his face. I'd felt the tension of Millie's reserve, too. He winked at me as we took turns at the water fountain, co-conspirators, dosing ourselves with aspirin.

That same afternoon, they left to fly back to Arizona, and I knew Bob was exactly what he appeared to be. He was just like his father.

On the last Friday night of the school year, Bob and I sat knee to knee in our favorite booth at Kalt's, a deli near my apartment, waiting for an order of their great pastrami sandwiches.

I'd known when I opened the apartment door that he was

eager to talk, but not in front of my curious roommates. "The girls aren't hiding under this booth, Bob, so tell me what's up!"

His voice was pitched a few notes higher than usual. "I had a meeting with the bishop today. My papers are on the way to Rome. In three months, they should be approved. Meantime, I'm to go to Loyola for the classes I need to finish my master's next year. When summer school's over, instead of coming back here to the diocese to work, I'll go on leave 'til the dispensation comes."

I was nervous. Just how priests shed their roles as clerics was hazy to me. What I didn't know made me anxious.

"Rome has to give the formal approval, of course," Bob explained.

He seemed to have more patience than I had with what was turning out to be a complicated ecclesiastical process.

"My leave from assignment here is like an informal approval from the bishop, honey. With that, I remain in good standing to work in any diocese. That's all I need to get a parish job in education somewhere away from here."

This was good news. I knew he wanted to work for the Church, to use his graduate degree from Loyola.

The waitress placed two frosted mugs on the table. Mine, a Heilemann's Old Style Lager; his, a root beer. I hoisted my heavy stein to a toast. "Here's to your new life, Bob."

He raised his. "To *our* new life, Shirley! I want you to come with me in August. The dispensation will be here, and we can be married."

My heart skipped a happy beat. I reached across the red-checkered tablecloth for his hand.

"Oh, Bob. I hope so. Just promise me, now that I've fallen in love with you, that some process in Rome won't go haywire and keep us from marrying in the Church."

"It'll all be fine, honey. You'll see."

He hadn't admitted it, but I knew he was worried about finding work. It was a long shot. Though the Vatican Council had closed four years earlier, it was still rare to find a laicized priest employed by a parish, even as a religious education director.

I took both his hands in mine, squeezing them tightly. "Don't you worry, either, no matter what happens. I'll sit in the gutter with you, if necessary." I loved this guy, and I wanted him to know it.

He leaned across the table, eyes misty, for one sweet kiss. He knew.

The summer passed quickly. I was busy teaching at Coe College, a small liberal arts school in Iowa, near my family. Bob came to visit some weekends; I flew to Chicago on others. We were in love and celebrated all over the city that summer of our courtship. Bob spent his small paycheck squiring me to plays at the Schubert Theatre, concerts at Ravinia, jazz on Rush Street, and steak dinner at the Stockyard Inn. Life was good.

One breezy night, we sat on a blanket in Grant Park, watching the lights of the city reflect in Lake Michigan. Bob wrapped his sweater around my shoulders.

"I've got a surprise for you," he said.

He took a ring box from his pocket and snapped it open. It was the beautiful solitaire we'd chosen from a black velvet tray at Carson Pirie Scott. I shed a happy tear as he slid it on my finger, then threw my arms around his neck. He laughed and hugged me back before gently disengaging himself.

"I knew you'd be happy, honey, that we're formally engaged. But, the ring isn't the surprise. I was hired today as religious education director at Immaculate Conception Parish in Northville, Michigan."

The long shot had worked. Immaculate Conception was one of the first parishes in the Midwest with an advisory lay council.

"I knew the president of the council liked my background when he interviewed me. I guess he convinced the panel and the pastor I was the best candidate to run their programs."

Bob's eyes sparkled. He was obviously delighted, and so was I. Our life together was about to begin. I laughed and hugged him again, nestling my head happily on his shoulder to watch the city lights twinkling on the lake.

Then I sat up. Michigan? I'd already signed a teaching contract in West Allis for another year.

My new fiancé was unperturbed. "Shirl, administrators are used to last minute resignations, and Northville is near Detroit. In the city, there'll be plenty of teaching jobs." I looked into his smiling face.

Of course there would be. Cookie had been right about that last year in Milwaukee. There were many teaching jobs open in August. I'd find one in Detroit, and this year, another teacher would walk into mine at Nathan Hale.

Bob went on. "And, honey, it'll only be a few weeks until my dispensation comes, so start shopping for your wedding dress!"

I called Mom excited about our plans. When I told her about the move to Michigan, there was silence on the other end of the line. 1969 might have been the middle of the sexual revolution, but that didn't cut any ice with her.

"Shirley, why don't you wait until you get married before you move away with him?" She'd weathered my exit from the convent and my love for an undispensed priest, but this latest turn of events taxed her.

At age twenty-nine, I still enjoyed my status as her fair-haired girl, but whether she understood or not, I was going to Michigan with Bob.

"If I wait, Mom, I'll have trouble changing jobs in the middle of the school year."

She still didn't like it. "When does Bob think his papers will come from Rome?"

"Any time now. The bishop told him it'd be three months when he applied, so I'm shopping for my wedding dress now."

She sighed. "Well, Bob is a good man and I know you're in love. I would never interfere."

I knew that was true. Her young heart had been broken when her father had forced her to break an engagement.

"I just worry about you so far away. You let me know as soon as you have a new address."

"Of course, Mom. I'll call. And don't worry."

Days later, we found an unfurnished apartment between Northville and the next village, Novi, where I'd signed a contract to teach. We bought a few pieces of furniture and Bob moved me in.

I called Mom with the new address.

She was pleased. "So where will Bob stay?"

I laughed. "You won't believe this story! After we had the last end table in place, Bob dusted off his hands and walked out the front door. He looked across the parking lot to the nearest house and decided to see if they had an extra room."

Mom laughed, too. "He asked a total stranger?"

"Yeah, and wait 'til you hear the rest! When the door opened, it was the president of the parish council, a guy named Wortski. He was the one who had hired Bob."

"Oh, for heaven's sake!"

"I know! Well, When they finally got past just standing there, Bob asked if he had a room to rent. The guy couldn't have been more profusive, said he was so honored to have him, and on and on. So Bob moved his toothbrush and pajamas into the Wortski's extra room!" Mom was relieved, and Bob and I soon settled into a routine even she could approve.

We watched for word from Rome, making a ritual of opening all the mail together at the dinner table each night, hoping, day by day, to find an official-looking envelope from the Diocese of Milwaukee. It didn't come and didn't come. Weeks became months. By December, the Michigan nights grew frigid, but Bob and I continued to wistfully part after a goodnight kiss, often to the strains of "The Marines' Hymn," one of the few records in our small collection. He'd sprint across the cold parking lot to his room next door. Chagrined to still be playing the role of good soldiers night after night, we re-named our theme song, "The March to Wortski's."

It wasn't long until Christmas cards started to arrive in the mail. One evening, an especially tall pile waited on the kitchen table. The card on top of the heap was from Father Tim McIntyre, but was signed "Tim and Janet." I suddenly lost interest in the tuna casserole steaming on the dinner table between us.

"Bob, what do you make of this?" I shoved the card over to him. I'd known Tim from LaCrosse. He was the chancellor who handled dispensations in a nearby diocese. When

Bob's paperwork hadn't come as expected in autumn, we called Tim for advice. He'd reiterated what we'd been told, that it should arrive any day.

Bob folded his napkin, and reached for the card. "Tim and *Janet?*" A frown line formed between his eyebrows. "Tim's married? What does he know about dispensations that we don't know?"

We both wondered. That Rome moved slowly was no mere platitude to us. Despite the optimistic estimate of a three-month turn-around time, here we were six months later with no marriage plans, faithfully re-enacting the nightly March to Wortski's. It was getting old.

"Let's call Tim." The words were hardly out of Bob's mouth when I had located the McIntire's new number scrawled under Tim's signature.

He answered on the first ring.

"Bob! Hello, Merry Christmas, Merry Christmas. Glad you got the card. How are you?"

"Tim, happy to hear from you. It's been a long time since September. Looks like you've had as many changes as we have the last few months."

Bob was much more diplomatic than I would have been. Leaning close to the receiver, I could faintly hear Tim's voice.

"Yes, yes, you got it right. We were married a couple months ago. Lots of guys out of this diocese are getting those papers through Rome fast. How about you?"

Bob explained our long wait. When he stopped speaking, I held my breath, straining to hear a few words. No luck. I sat back and poked a fork into the now-cold casserole on my plate, watching.

He nodded, listening to Tim's voice on the other end,

then scribbled a name and address on the greeting card in front of him, glancing at me.

"Yes, Merry Christmas to you and Janet, too." Bob set the receiver in its cradle.

I couldn't stand the suspense. "What did he say?"

Bob looked at me, hesitating before he spoke, "Tim asked if we'd sent money with our papers."

"Money?"

"Yes, he says it helps. About $300. He gave me a name and address."

My voice came out in a whisper, "You mean, a bribe?"

He looked crestfallen. "Well, if we'd needed a fee, I'm sure the bishop's office would've asked for it when I submitted my papers."

The heaviness in my chest didn't lighten with the long sigh that escaped me. "Oh, Bob, do we have to bribe somebody so we can get married? I don't like this."

He saw the tears in my eyes and quickly slid his chair across the kitchen's shiny, tile floor until he was beside me, wrapping me snuggly in his arms. "It's ok, Shirl. We aren't going to bribe anybody. We'll be married in the Church somehow, even if it takes a little longer." He handed me a rumpled handkerchief.

"I'm just shocked. Delays or even deliberate foot-dragging are one thing, but this—"

Sobs choked me. Tim's suggestion about money had triggered the old pain of convent days. "I know you want to work for the Church, but this is hard, especially after all these months of waiting."

He sat silently, studying the words he'd written on the Christmas card. "Well, one good thing has come out of this.

We have a contact in Rome. That's more than we had before. At least now we know how to check on the progress of my papers."

He was right. I felt a little better knowing we'd broken through the nameless, faceless wall of Vatican bureaucracy.

I leaned over to read the unfamiliar Italian name. "So, will you write to this Monsignor?"

Bob kissed my nose and smiled. "I sure will, honey. Hang on. It'll all work out, you'll see. We'll just give it a few weeks until the holidays are over."

That became my Christmas prayer: *Dear God, help me to hang on and to believe that our efforts to be married in the Church will be blessed.*

In early spring, more important mail arrived, this time from Loyola. It was time for Bob to register for summer school and the last few classes needed to finish his master's. I snuggled close to him on the flowered sofa, looking at the form in his hand. Bold, black print leaped off the page at me: Housing Reservations. Married?___ Single?___

A cold finger of anxiety ran down my back. "Yikes! What are we going to do about this housing? We don't know when we'll be married."

He frowned, crinkling the form as he turned it over. "Let's see. The deadline is April 1st. I guess they really need to plan early."

The cold spot spread to my stomach. I shifted to look straight at him. "Will we be married by June when summer school starts?" My voice trembled. "I'm sorry, Bob, but I just hate this uncertainty. I mean, I'll definitely go to Chicago with you this summer, but this has been going on since last summer. I thought when we came to Michigan that we'd be married in a few weeks."

My mother's voice echoed in my head: *Wait 'til you're married before you move away with him.*

Mom hadn't liked my plans then. I didn't want to speculate on how the family would react to more delay.

Bob reached for my hand, kissed it, and looked long at my solitaire. Then, his eyes met mine. "I'm going to call that Monsignor in Rome and get some action. He needs to do his job and process my papers. It's high time, and money is not what this is all about."

I brightened up. It *was* high time for that phone call from Michigan to Rome.

Within a couple of weeks, plans firmed up.

Many new friends at Immaculate Conception had warmly welcomed Bob. Ann Moran was one of them. She sat on the affluent parish council that had hired him, and was a little embarrassed at the modest salary he'd been offered. "Why don't you two come over to my place to make that call? Could be fun, middle of the night and all? And we can save you a couple bucks. Besides, I'd like to hear what this Italian bureaucrat has to say for himself, if he's lost your file or what!"

Not since I was a little girl had I been bundled into the cold car at night for a social excursion, pajamas and robe under my long winter coat, but the intricacies of my fiancé's complicated legal dealings with the Church had produced one adventure after another.

The Moran family, beneficiaries of Detroit's thriving automotive industry, lived in a beautifully appointed home in the woods at the end of a winding drive. Ann greeted us at the door in her quilted bathrobe.

"Do you think the McCauley file is covered with dust?" Her eyes twinkled as she led us to her family room, bedroom slippers whispering across the tile floor of the entryway.

As the long awaited communication began, our hostess moved quietly around the coffee table serving hot toddies. The transatlantic call went through easily. In heavily accented English, the Monsignor muttered, "MaCowley? MaCowley? Where's a MaCowley?" as he ruffled through the neglected papers on his desk. Obviously, the McCauley dossier was not on top of the pile of requests for dispensation flooding Rome in 1970.

Bob frowned, concentrating on the voice from across the world that held the power over our future.

I murmured to Ann, "This is clearly not a first first-come, first-serve operation." She rolled her eyes.

Mid-conversation, Bob quickly glanced at me, smiled broadly, then continued writing.

Ann whispered excitedly in my ear, "Must be good news."

I grinned at her, silently nodding.

Before we could speculate further, he hung up and turned to us, still smiling broadly. "The Monsignor said I should call the bishop's office in about eight weeks, but not ask any questions or volunteer any information. He said I should just inquire if the dispensation has arrived. And," Bob reached over to hug me, "he said it would be there."

I let out an excited yip and jumped into his arms, kissing his cheek.

Ann bounced up from her chair, warbling a funny off-key song, "You're getting married in the morning," as the three of us did a little jig across her elegant, family-room floor.

By the time eight weeks had passed, we were in Chicago

for summer school. I rode the bus every day from married housing to my day job in the loop. Bob cut across campus to class from his single room. We were rent poor. Besides two places at Loyola, we were supporting my apartment in Northville and Bob's room at Wortski's. If our Italian connection slipped up, we'd still need two roofs over our heads when summer school was over. As I balanced my depleted checkbook, I was grateful I'd bought my wedding dress months ago. Today, I wouldn't have been able to scrape up the money.

Finally, the long-awaited day arrived. Bob called the bishop's office. It was just as the Monsignor had said. The McCauley dispensation was already on its way to our mailbox. In the weeks since our call to Rome, wheels had turned.

However, my lacy, white wedding gown was not to be worn—not yet.

The dispensation did indeed arrive, but with it came an unexpected disappointment. I read the document in disbelief:

"A condition of this dispensation for return to the lay state for Robert Benedict McCauley of the Diocese of Milwaukee is that any future marriage in accord with the discipline of the Roman Catholic Church shall be done in private with no witnesses other than those officials formally recognized by the diocese to function in the capacity of witnessing this sacrament. Further, to avoid scandal, the marriage of a laicized priest of this diocese shall be kept private and not revealed by either husband or wife to other parties prior to its occurrence. It is also required that the laicized priest not attempt to assume employment in any capacity, in any parish of this diocese."

My Irish was up. I hadn't left the convent dreaming of a beautiful wedding for this. I suddenly wished I were Episcopalian, Methodist, or Presbyterian—anything but a Catholic caught in an unending maze of crazy rules.

"Bob, this is ridiculous. We've been jumping through hoops for more than a year to get this dispensation. What does this mean? We can't have a wedding? Besides that, what's all this secrecy stuff? Who's scandalized? Good grief, there are thousands of priests and religious these last years who have left the Church to marry, and lots of them didn't bother with the dispensation process either. Are we being punished?"

He hadn't expected the strings on the dispensation either. I suddenly realized that leaving the priesthood, though more complicated than leaving the convent, had one big similarity to my experience. The men who left the priesthood, with dispensation or without, were as shrouded in mystery as the nuns had been. The Church's style was to take unilateral action silently, without discussion or explanation.

I fumed, but I intended to marry this man. The legalism didn't matter. I would tolerate it to hold the door open for his ministry. He was a priest in his heart and wanted to continue his work as a religious educator. I was determined to be at his side. Despite what the Church might say, I knew that I was ok with God and so was Bob. That was all that counted. I was ready for whatever was next.

It turned out to be a hurried trip to the bishop's dark mansion in downtown Milwaukee, after business hours on a Friday afternoon in July. It was late, but we were expected. As we stood on the doorstep, black clouds rolled overhead. A thunderstorm was brewing. A tall, thin priest in dusty clericals answered the bell. We hurried inside.

Without introducing himself, he led us through a narrow, darkly paneled, over-furnished hall to the bishop's small office under a large, spiral staircase that dominated the entryway. We all ducked our heads to avoid hitting the low angle of the ceiling in the dimly lit space. An altar to the side of a large desk identified the room as a sometimes chapel.

"Please be seated." The priest's greeting was stiffly formal. His gray, tired face was covered with black stubble. Wasting no words on pleasantries, he got right to business. "Miss Cunningham, you have the original of your dispensation?"

I produced it from my purse, wondering if he meant to intimidate me with his manner. He glanced at me, eyes as cold as his voice, then scanned the document, copying a few words into a ledger open before him on the desk.

He turned to Bob. "Your dispensation is already here, Mr. McCauley."

Anxiety and anger both arose in me at the same moment. I felt my cheeks flush hot. What attitude toward women, toward sex, toward marriage was this? My inner voice began a pep talk. *Hold on! Never mind this man's judgment. You are only going through a formality here.* I bit my tongue.

The priest thrust a form in front of me on the desk. "Please sign here." It took effort to hold down my anger. My hands trembled as I signed in jerky handwriting the papers validating who I was, and that I intended to marry Robert Benedict McCauley on this day of July, 1970.

That done, the priest handed Bob the pen to sign on the line just below my signature, then stood and walked to the altar where he lit two candles with a cigarette lighter.

He gestured to us, "Please stand here."

Bob took my hand as we walked to the altar. Somehow, I mouthed the repetitive formula of words entitling Bob and me to be viewed legitimately married by the Roman Catholic Church. It was sad, spiritless, and perfunctory, a travesty of the celebration appropriate for the loving commitment of a man and woman.

Once the ritual was done, our unfriendly host quickly ushered us out of the front door and closed it firmly behind us.

While we'd been about our business, the storm had rolled in. Rain fell in sheets around as we huddled on the steps of the mansion's entryway. Despite the weather, we were relieved to have the brief encounter with the bishop's functionary finished.

As lightening flashed, Bob put his arms around me. I leaned into him looking up into the dark sky. Standing there on the shadowy, wet steps of the bishop's mansion, I had a sudden thought.

"You know, we promised to keep our marriage secret beforehand, but that paper didn't say we had to keep it secret later."

He hugged me closer. "Right. Wanna put an announcement in the paper, ducky?"

I laughed. "I don't care about that, but let's have a real wedding now, as soon as we can, and let's make it a party, a big celebration!"

He laughed out loud. "Whatever you say, Mrs. McCauley!"

I blinked back happy tears. The party was on.

On the night of our second wedding, Lake Delavan was unrippled, blue smoothness, reflecting a full moon. Seventy guests, family and friends, were gathered at the home where Bob had spent his boyhood summers, now owned by his Aunt Irene.

She'd been so excited when we asked if we could be married at her house. "Of course! Uncle Scottie will rent the chairs and help me set up and decorate. We'll put the champagne table on the porch."

Irene created a beautiful setting for a simple altar banked with candles and flowers. Bob's chalice was the proud centerpiece, glistening in candlelight.

Crowned with roses, I finally wore my white-lace wedding gown. As our ceremony began, strains of "Dream the Impossible Dream"[9] floated out over the lake from the crowded living room. Our love had been an impossible dream over the long, lonely years of our lives in religion, but we had followed our star.

I forgot my earlier bridesmaid with five o'clock shadow as I focused on Bob. His face was glowing as he waited for me at the altar. Moving down the aisle, I saw my mother's smile among the many radiant faces gathered there, reflecting our happiness.

When I took Bob's hand at the altar, love rose in beautiful waves around us. His vows went like arrows to my heart. His eyes as he heard my promises were never before so tender. I couldn't look into them or my throat would burst. The red roses of my wedding bouquet rippled in my watery vision. No matter. My heart clearly saw that my prayer for love had been answered.

4

A Precious Child

It all began when Dr. Hanss said, "Yup, you're pregnant!" I was ecstatic. Bob and I had been trying to conceive for about a year. At the ripe old age of thirty-three, I'd been on medication, trying to rev up my ovulation. Today I'd hurried to my appointment with Dr. Hanss, hopeful, but almost afraid to hope. Now, behind the wheel of my little Nova, speeding home with my news, I smiled to myself. This explained why my daily commute to Dysart High through the onion fields of west-side farms had begun to nauseate me. I should have guessed.

Bob's car was in the driveway when I drove in. I couldn't wait to tell him!

I jumped out of the car, and ran into the house, dropping schoolbooks, purse, lunch bag, and sweater in my trail. Hearing the commotion, he poked his head around the doorway from the kitchen where dinner preparations were underway.

"I'm pregnant this time! We're going to have a baby!"

I rushed right into his arms, not noticing the casserole dish and hotpad in his hand. He let out a little yip, hugging me hard with his free arm.

"Oh, honey!" He stretched to give the hotdish a safe landing on the cupboard behind us, but not before I saw his eyes well up. "You knew it, didn't you?"

I wiped away a quick tear and hugged him. "You mean in church Sunday? Yes, I did!"

"You had a definite inkling, Shirl." Bob squeezed me, then pushed back a few inches to look into my eyes. "You knew before the doc had a chance to check you out."

I'd told Bob about it in the parking lot after Mass. So often had I recited the words of the Creed at the million Masses of my life, I hardly heard them. But last Sunday, the words "Giver of Life" had made the small hairs on the back of my neck prickle.

I laughed and hugged him back. "I doubt my inklings'll ever replace the rabbit test."

He pulled me to a chair at the table already set for dinner and slid up next to me. My husband sat looking at me with wonder. I leaned into his embrace in our little kitchen, my heart melting. Years of loneliness seemed to melt with it. I had wanted this man and this child for so long! I must be lighting up the entire neighborhood right now, causing blips on radar screens.

We were full of anticipation as the weeks of pregnancy passed. Gagging over toothpaste and cologne slowed down my morning rush to get myself off to school. Next, I outgrew my bra, and then my tummy started to bulge. I wondered what the rest of pregnancy would be like.

In bed one night, Bob put his hand on my abdomen. "Can you feel the baby move?" It was a fair question. My waistline had long since been gone.

"No, not yet." Nothing was wrong. It was just too soon,

too early to feel the movement of the new life inside, but it was coming.

By November, nights were chilly in the desert. Bob and I were at the Casa, a retreat house we'd heard about while still at Loyola in Chicago. In the early 1970s, the Franciscan Renewal Center in Scottsdale was known for its enthusiastic implementation of the aggiornamento of the Vatican Council. Liturgy was lively, priestly vestments were festooned with rainbows, lay leadership was actively recruited, and the chapel overflowed with a standing-room-only crowd every Sunday.

We were eager for the renewal. Bob had met with disappointment in his attempts to work for the Church in the Midwest. After the death of Pope John XXIII, the Vatican decreed that laicized priests were not to be hired by parishes in what looked like an effort to stem an exodus from clerical ranks. The first year after we were married, an Illinois bishop told Bob his contract as religious educator in Chicago would not be renewed. In a last ditch attempt to do the work he loved, he flew to Phoenix to check on prospects.

Bishop McCarthy was welcoming. "We see things a little differently here in the West. The diocese is growing and we need help. We'd be glad to have you." The bishop was willing to disregard Rome's ruling. With that encouragement, we packed up and moved.

It didn't take us long to get involved at the Casa.

And now, we'd been invited to help present the first Marriage Encounter weekend ever offered at the center. We were delighted. We spent Saturday talking with couples.

What I hadn't counted on was the fatigue of pregnancy. The retreat, hard on the heels of my week at school, drained my energy. At the end of the day, I collapsed into bed and was just on the verge of sleep, cuddled under all the covers we could find, when I felt it. Down deep in me, something moved slowly like butterfly wings fluttering in water.

I caught my breath, then sat straight up in bed, jostling my sleepy husband. "Bob! I felt the baby move." I grabbed his hand under the pile of blankets and put it on my tummy. The baby moved again. Now wide-awake, Bob was excited, too.

He quickly dived down to put his ear on my stomach, mumbling something, his words muffled by the bedclothes.

His ear was cold. I giggled, pulling the covers back. "What did you say?" I couldn't help but grin at his awkward position, bare rear end in the air.

"I said, I can't hear anything."

I pulled him up next to me and poked him in the ribs. "What did you expect, an Irish tenor?"

After that gentle beginning, the next months brought plenty of rock 'n roll to my solar plexus. As the hot weather of Arizona set in, the extra thirty pounds around my middle weren't easy to arrange in the sweaty sheets at night. I couldn't sleep, and the increasingly energetic frolic in my innards made me ready to get on with things.

On Mother's Day, I wondered aloud to Bob if the new pressure in my pelvis and lower back meant the beginning of labor. The look of alarm that flashed across his face was almost laughable.

We both would have felt safer if the hospital were nearby, but the only obstetrician who invited husbands into the delivery room practiced across town at Phoenix Memorial. "We're not going to hang around here to find out." My nervous husband hustled me to the car and sped through yellow lights to get me there.

Mother's Day would be a neat day to have a baby I told myself as the hospital doctor on call gentled me back onto the examination table. He probed silently for a minute, then took my hand, helping me sit up.

"No, not yet, Mrs. McCauley. Sorry. You're getting close but the water hasn't broken. You aren't dilated yet."

Bob and I were both disappointed. I shuffled out through the big glass hospital door on his arm. The hot asphalt of the parking lot radiated in the sun. I curled my toes to keep my sandals from slipping off my swollen feet. I'd never felt so awkward. Bob patted my arm sympathetically as we made the long drive from South Phoenix back home to Scottsdale.

Though inconvenient, the long drive to Dr. Hanss' father-friendly environment was well worth it to both of us. After consciously and deliberately dismantling my entire way of life to be a wife and mother, I was of no mind to be drugged, unconscious, and alone at the moment of birth. Bob and I had taken the Lamaze natural childbirth classes Dr. Hanss recommended. I was eager for the baby to come and Bob was eager to coach, to pass me ice chips at strategic moments, and to witness the birth of our child.

Two days after Mother's Day, Dr. Hanss decided it was time to induce labor.

Soon, I was in the delivery room, Bob at my side in gown and mask. Despite the childbirth classes of the last months, I was impressed by the vigor of the first contractions that unceremoniously grabbed my guts.

Uncertain as to what was coming next, but hoping for the best, I sat propped in three-quarters position on the delivery table, feet in stirrups in my elegant green hospital gown. The nurse, busy at the counter behind me, knew what to expect, but I needed some reassurance. "How long will it take?"

"To deliver?" She partially turned her head, speaking over her shoulder. "Oh, fifteen minutes."

When I was a girl I'd always thought that having a baby was like dying except you didn't die, but fifteen minutes? I could handle that. Just then, another contraction gathered force, rolling over my body like an ominous wave.

Bob, seemingly unaware, pushed a pillow behind my shoulders. I felt cranky. Why wasn't he having these pains?

"Nurse, this handle is too far away—" Another big wave hit and there was no holding back. My body was doing what was to be done, what women had done over the millennia, and it was totally out of my control. When it had rolled on through, I quickly spoke up. I needed to find out more before another contraction hit.

"Nurse, how many pushes do I have to go?"

This time she leaned over me, grinning. "Probably twenty, since you asked. If I tell you five, it'll probably be more." She tinkered with the handle on the table. "How's this handle now?"

I knew she was distracting me. As I mumbled something, she moved down to the foot of the delivery table. "I'm going to wash you off. It'll feel a little cool." Cold liquid made contact with my hot genitals and ran down between my thighs. I gasped.

Bob chuckled annoyingly. Ignoring him, I talked to the nurse instead. "It's ok. It feels good."

She was still into her "let's-distract-the-little-mother" routine. "Are you folks from here or are you from Chicago?"

Bob replied, "We're from Scottsdale."

Easy for him to be breezy when I'm doing all the work, the cranky voice inside sniffed, and he wasn't even accurate. I corrected the faulty information. "We lived in Chicago a year before we moved here, in Lombard. What made you think we were from Chicago?" Curious, I stretched to look at the nurse behind me at the counter again.

"The way you talk."

The conversation went on between Bob and the nurse. His voice was casual, as though nothing special was going on. "We're Midwesterners, actually, from Wisconsin."

The nurse picked up his cue. "Where in Wisconsin?"

Another wave was forming in my gut. Neither Bob nor the nurse seemed to notice. I began to wonder if my immense stomach and I had disappeared.

"Lake Delavan and Prairie du Chien. Shirl's from Prairie du Chien. I'm from Delavan—"

I gasped for a deep breath, interrupting his travelogue. What had I been told about pushing? Didn't matter. My body was way ahead of my brain. I heard myself let out a grunt as I pushed on the stirrups and pulled on the table handles, body tense with effort.

Dr. Hanss quickly slid to the stool at the foot of the delivery table and started giving me instructions. "Raise your head. That's a girl." In the middle of a push, I could only grunt a reply. My body said, "Push, push." This was no time to tarry. A little explosion of breath erupted from me. The doctor was right there.

"Don't make any noise, just keep bearing down. You can quickly let your breath out, when you need to, but take another breath right away. And keep pushing."

I nodded, not able to spare the breath for words. The wave was here. I needed to ride it. I pushed, pushed, then mysteriously, the contraction was gone. Surprised, I heard myself let out a long "Ooohhh" in relief.

Bob took my hand, "Boy, are you strong, honey." I looked at his shining eyes above the surgical mask. He wasn't so bad after all, but I didn't have time to explore my new line of thought. Cold antiseptic swabbed on my unsuspecting and not-so-private privates startled me to attention. In the strategically placed mirror above my head, I could see a flash of color on my bottom.

"Hey, I'm technicolor." Before any more chat, another wave hit me. I got ready, but then, the tide turned. The contraction was gone, and I realized I was drenched in sweat. What would my body do next?

"I feel hot. Bob, do you still have that washcloth? Wipe my forehead." He leaned over me, damp cloth in hand.

"Sure, honey." He began wiping, oh, so gently.

"Hurry," I barked at him, "before I go into another contraction. Get my hair back." My neck was wet with sweat. I could feel it trickling down under my long hair.

Like a recruit saluting a sergeant, he snapped to attention. "Right!" I was slightly mollified. It was the least he could do under the circumstances. I had my hands full here.

When another contraction hit, I held my breath, pushing, forced into a long silence by the effort. Dr. Hanss' voice came to me through the red color behind my closed eyes. "That's a girl. Keep it comin'! That's great. Keep it comin'! The baby's right there."

I had no idea. All I knew was that an inevitable force was moving through my body without my having one thing to do about it but breathe and push. All I could do was lean into it.

When the contraction eased, Dr. Hanss grinned up at me through my wide-spread thighs. He gestured to the mirror above the table with the syringe in his right hand as he gently touched me with his left. "You can look now. I'm going to put a little novocaine here, just in the right spot. Ok? Easy, just like an exam. Now, you'll feel a little pressure as I find the right spot. A little needle stick—" I flinched. "Easy, just a little pressure as the novocaine is injected." His voice was reassuring. "That's going to numb—"

I lost the rest of it in another big wave. I held my breath, pushing, pushing. I could feel the blood going to my face.

Dr. Hanss' voice drifted over the wave. "Keep pushing. Go ahead. Push down real hard."

I complied. Everything in me, my entire being, lent strength to that push, that bearing down. My push and his voice were all that existed in the universe.

"Superb! The baby's right there."

Finally, the contraction was gone. I let up, gasping for one great lung full of air.

"Good. Relax now, relax. Shall I put the rest of the novocaine in this side?" His reassuring voice asked my permission for his every move. I suddenly understood why a woman could fall in love with her obstetrician, the one man on the face of the Earth of any good at all when you needed him.

I emerged from my fantasy long enough to wonder what was going on. I turned to Bob, perched on a stool by my right knee. "Could you see the head when I pushed?"

"I think so. You can watch the mirror."

"I'm busy doing other things," I snapped.

Dr. Hanss overheard and chuckled. "She's busy working."

Then another wave silenced me, a big one. I pulled on the handles, held my breath to push, let the breath out in a burst, panted two quick pants, then pushed again.

A rapid stream of excited instructions tumbled out of my coach. "Thatta girl, pull back on those handles. Take a quick look, and I'll show you the baby's head."

Bob's voice in the background registered a full octave higher than normal, more a squeal than a statement, "Oh, Shirl, here it is, Shirl!" All I could hear was my own grunting. I hadn't known my body could push so hard. Just as I began to wonder if the push would ever end, the contraction left, a wave dwindling off into a feeble eddy. I caught my breath, slowing down.

"Yes. Just relax."

I opened my eyes, released from the red haze of effort. I suddenly wondered about my new child. What had I missed in the mirror? "Does the baby have black hair?"

"A little bit." The conversation was lost in another contraction.

Although the red haze again silently rolled in under my closed eyelids, I was exquisitely tuned to the doctor's voice. "As the baby begins to emerge, I want you to pant. Just breathe the baby out slowly." He demonstrated a few pants. "That's the time to open your eyes and watch what's going on."

I was grateful for the words guiding me through this place of no return. "You tell me."

"I'll tell you. I'll talk with you."

A big wave washed over me, relentlessly advancing to its final resting place. I took a deep breath, some woman part of me knowing this breath would carry a child into the world. I pushed a huge push.

Dr. Hanss' voice rose. "Thatta girl! Keep 'em coming.

Push again. Come on. Push down hard now, thatta girl!"

I gasped and pushed again, feeling the energy and excitement in the room. Bob whispered, "Here he comes, Shirl." There was a small eddy in the wave, enough for me to grab half a breath.

I suddenly felt weak, soaked with sweat, hair, wet strings on my neck. "Pray for me, Bob."

He promised.

The wave was back, and somehow I was ready. Bigger than ever, it carried me away, in the red haze. Then Dr. Hanss' words broke through, "Think about panting. Give a push, then look and see what you're doing."

Another voice—was it Bob's?—floated to me in a soft, half-whisper, "Beautiful, Shirl." What did he see?

The crest hit me, and I pushed, pushed, felt a shift, and took a ragged breath.

Dr. Hanss said, "Easy now, pant, pant. Look and see the baby."

My breath caught in a little gasp, then came out in a yell I hadn't known was waiting there.

But Bob's yell was louder, "Lookit, lookit!"

I looked in the mirror to see the head, shoulders, and body of my child painlessly, smoothly emerge from my own, baptized in my blood.

Bob's excited tenor was still an octave high: "It's a boy!" His laughter rang in the room. Then his voice turned sweet, "Ducky—" but our son's first cry drowned him out, a little squeak.

I knew it was a boy. I had to see him!

His hair was reddish, so was his face, but he was beautiful. He squeaked again. How could I comfort him, this precious child, startled by the first light he'd ever seen?

"There, there. Don't cry, little love." I felt a tear slip down my cheek. "He's beautiful." I looked up for Bob, but the baby cried louder. I cuddled my son to me, speaking softly. "Bob, look at his face. He's beautiful." My husband slipped his arm behind my shoulders, leaning for a closer look.

I was delighted and so was his father. "By George, a boy!" He laughed.

Dr. Hanss laughed, too. "Are you calling him George?"

"No, no," I protested. That would be worse than Duffy, Bob's first suggestion of a name for our son. I'd promised him the next one could be Duffy. As it turned out, the "next one" was a golden retriever.

"No," Bob's voice proclaimed to the circle of listeners centered on the baby in my arms. "This is Kelly Benedict."

Indeed it was!

5

It All Started with Grandma

PRAYER TO THE HOLY MOTHER

O Holy Mother,
Beacon of Darkness,
You call me inside
Behind the veil
To Your heart,
To Your womb.
I feel the hot breath of Your words
And know Your presence,
Your power.
Teach me to walk simply and surely
In Your holy way.
Teach me to trust the edge You draw me over,
To fall deeply into Your arms.

"September 28, 1987," I noticed the date on the page of the daytimer open on my knees. It was exactly a month ago today that I'd left Phoenix for Medjugorje and so much had transpired. Now, back in Phoenix, I sat across from my boss at the County Health Department, whose desk was piled with waiting projects.

I liked Mary. She was smart, honest, humorous, quirky, and endlessly analytical. I knew she liked me, too, though we were different. She analyzed and directed. As department planner, I served as her right hand, running meetings to strategize goals and objectives, to set timelines, and to track accomplishments.

Mary's graceful fingers brushed mine as she handed me several neatly typed sheets, my performance evaluation. I scanned it quickly, then focused on the last paragraph: "Shirley's career is limited only by her own goals."

I was relieved. The piles of work not yet caught up from my three-week absence must not be bothering my boss.

Sliding her chair back, Mary reached to the credenza behind her, then pushed a paper across the desk to me. It was an organization chart. "As you know, Shirley, the department is reorganizing. I'm going to need help in some positions we're creating. Would you be interested in running one of the regional offices?"

I swallowed. This was high praise, under other circumstances, a budding bureaucrat's dream. But now, so much had happened to me, I wondered how I could tell her.

It all started when Bob came home from work one night with a magazine clipping. "Have you ever heard of Medjugorje, Shirl?" He spread the article on the counter. I glanced at the headline as I pulled a hot pan of lasagna from the oven: "Mary Appears in Yugoslavia—Peasant Children Pray for Peace—A New Fatima?"

Just then, Kelly burst into the kitchen from the garage, T-shirt soaked with sweat. The boys had been skateboarding in the driveway for an hour. "Mom, come see my new trick."

The pan of lasagna was burning my fingers right through the hotpads. He didn't notice. He was already back out the door.

"My new ramp is so cool!"

Bob leaned out the doorway to watch as Kelly went airborne over the ramp.

Shaking my pink fingers, I eased the hot pan down to the butcher block, and squeezed past Bob to look. "Ok, Kel, one more jump, then let's eat." I was as sweaty as he was in the infernally hot kitchen, and dinner was ready. I had no time for visionaries just then either.

Next day, grateful to be home alone, I flopped down in my big easy chair. Bob had left the Medjugorje article on the coffee table, knowing I'd be curious. It was a little worse for wear, speckled with tomato sauce from last night's lasagna.

Luxuriating in the quiet, I picked up the clipping. Teenagers smiled at me from the accompanying photo. They looked normal. These young people had begun to tell their families and priests about visions of the Virgin Mary. At first, they saw her on a hillside near their small Croatian village. Then, Mary spoke to them. Ivan, the dark-haired boy in the photo, explained her message: "She asks us to pray, especially for peace."

The article went on, comparing the visions to those in Portugal years earlier: "As in Fatima, observers in Medjugorje watch the sun spin, pulsate, and radiate colors, especially during the time of the visions. The children say Mary appears to them daily as they pray the rosary."

I closed my eyes and snuggled down in the big chair. Visions of Mary? This story felt like old-time Catholic devotion, pre-Vatican II devotion, gone the way of incense, bells, and Gregorian chant. Even in convent days, the rosary had never appealed to me—too much repetition. Just thinking about it made me sleepy.

I plumped a pillow behind my head and closed my eyes.

Grandma Cunningham had told me many stories of the Lady of Fatima and Lourdes when I was a girl. Stories of miracles and healing, stories of the sun spinning in the sky, stories of the Lady asking children to pray for peace in the war-weary forties. She had so much faith.

My mind drifted to those long-ago days of childhood.

When I was six years old, statues that looked huge to me stood on the altar in Sis's room: Mary, Joseph, the Sacred Heart, and the Infant of Prague. I wasn't allowed to touch the small box of matches on the altar, but I loved to watch the candle sparkling in its red glass.

Grandma lit it, then leaned over to whisper in my ear, "Shirley, God answers the prayers of children."

I hadn't heard this in catechism class. I looked up at her. Her usually crinkling blue eyes were serious. She put her arm around me.

"Will you pray with me to Our Lady?"

Amazing as it was, this was a serious request. I'd do anything for Grandma. "What should I pray for?"

"For peace, for the end of war, for Sis to get better." I looked over at my bedridden young aunt sleeping quietly in the bed nearby. I didn't understand that she was painfully dying as nerves broke away from her spine or that only a miracle could heal her. What I did understand was that Grandma was depending on me.

Scrunching my eyes tightly shut, I prayed hard to the Lady for Sis. I could feel Grandma's warmth as I knelt snuggled by her side on the hard prie-dieu, knees aching. Even with my eyes closed, I could see the light of the flickering candle flames.

That was so long ago, but I still missed Grandma.

She died too soon. I was only fourteen, just starting to tell her about my boy friends and my first formal dance. She would laugh, tell me I was pretty, and to watch out for those Irish boys.

It delighted me to be at Grandma's house, a happy place, always full of laughter, songs, hugs, and sugar cookies warm from the oven. As I sat in my big chair remembering, I felt as warmly loved as I had then. In the quiet, a sweet peacefulness seemed to gently enfold me, like Grandma's arms.

Then, somehow, I knew she was with me. Her presence was strong. In all the years of missing her, I'd never before felt my grandmother's nearness like this. I didn't know what was happening, but I was sure it was real. Tears of gratitude streamed down my face.

I sat there a long time afterward, quietly sorting myself out. I didn't understand, but my heart was full of Grandma and her devotion to the Blessed Mother, as she always called her.

Whatever this un-nameable experience of mine was, it made Medjugorje important. I'd have to find the words to tell Mom and Jane about the visions. They had loved

Grandma, too, had heard her stories. They would remember those days. I'd be sure to tell them.

Next thing I knew, Kelly was out of school for summer. Bob and I, both tired after a long year of work, sorely needed a break. He was directing a busy senior center and I was planning programs at the Health Department. We agreed to use every day of the three-week vacation we had each accumulated, packed up Kelly, and locked the door.

First, we flew to Seattle for a boating trip with friends in the Princess Louisa Islands near Vancouver. Then, without returning to Arizona, we flew to Hawaii. Kelly and Bob bodysurfed the perfect waves, while I spent blissful days relaxing on the beach, nose buried in a frivolous novel. It was an expensive holiday, but needed.

Work began again soon enough. Sun-tanned and relaxed, I walked into my office, and sighed. Some welcome home! The file folders piled on my desk each represented a big project. Gritting my teeth, I slid into my chair and gave myself a pep talk: *Breathe deeply. You can do this. It's time to buckle down.* Before I opened the first file folder, my phone jangled. The avalanche of calls from folks stalled on projects because of my vacation was beginning. Resolute, I stood and grabbed it.

"Shirley, is that you? I wasn't sure if I had the right extension in your big department." I held the receiver away from my ear and looked at it in amazement. This call, I hadn't expected. It was my sister, Jane.

I stuttered. "Jane! yes, I'm here." I could tell by her tone nobody was dead or comatose, but if she had ever called before, it certainly wasn't to the office. In the sixteen years I'd lived in Arizona, I'd learned well that the phone lines ran

Jane

from Arizona to Iowa but not from Iowa to Arizona.

"I'm just surprised to hear from you. What's up?"

Her voice was clear. "Shirley, I'm going to Medjugorje, and I want you to come with me."

I couldn't believe my ears. I sat down carefully in my chair, listening as she went on.

"I signed up with a tour out of New York and got the second to last space. If you call right away, you can get the last one."

I was speechless. I'd never gone on a trip with my sister in my entire life, hardly had gone to the Dairy Queen with her, much less a pilgrimage out of the country.

Jane's husband was a hog farmer. In 1987, pork prices had crashed. Neighboring farms were being foreclosed. Willie Nelson sang to raise money at Farm Aid concerts.

Decent, honest farmers we knew, despairing that they'd ever be able to repay bankers, hung themselves in their barns. Jane's houseful of kids and many debts meant she didn't get away from the farm often. When she and Tom did take a break, it was for an overnight in a nearby town to visit a fair or flea market, and have shrimp dinner in the local café.

"When does the tour leave?"

"In ten days."

I sucked in my breath. "Wow, Jane. I'd love to go but this is my first day back in the office after being gone three weeks. I've used all my vacation time for the year, and all my money. Our budget can't stand another big whack. Did you say $2,300?"

I could hear the disappointment in her voice. "Well, think it over for a few days. Maybe you'll change your mind."

I gently placed the receiver in its cradle and sat looking at it. Where did Jane get the money for a pilgrimage to Yugoslavia in the middle of the farm crisis? I had a million questions.

That evening, I recounted the story to Bob, shaking my head. "I'm so frustrated. Why did this invitation have to come now?"

He sat at the kitchen table, sorting through a handful of mail, mostly bills. "We haven't got our vacation paid for yet. I'm really sorry, honey, but this is the worst possible time."

I felt like crying. "I know. If the timing wasn't so bad, we could have found a way."

Next morning, it was still dark outside when I climbed out of bed. Bothered by Jane's call, I hadn't slept well. She was a little girl in grade school when I left home. I loved her so much, but I was always gone, never even living in the same state. I'd missed watching her grow up.

Needing some strong caffeine to start the day, I wriggled my toes into my bedroom slippers and schlepped through the sleeping household to the kitchen. It was still dark, the eastern sky overcast. I measured extra coffee into the coffee maker, then settled myself with my journal.

I was sad, missing a sister I seldom saw, whose world was so different from mine. Once my notebook was open, the words rushed onto the page as if they had been dammed up in my mind: *"God, why do You hold out to me what I want so much and can't have? This trip could be a way to get to know each other now, as adults, both of us wives and mothers. An opportunity to spend time together, just the two of us. A luxury we've never had on family visits surrounded by parents, kids, and husbands."*

Brewing done, the coffee maker went silent. I filled a cup and read the rest of the words I'd scrawled, sadness rising in my throat: *"We might never have this chance again, and this is a spiritual pilgrimage, not just a vacation, which is all the more reason I want to go."*

As I scribbled on, my sadness turned to confusion. Why had the unexplainable visitation from Grandma pulled me into the events in Medjugorje? Why had this chance to go arisen so suddenly, only to be stymied?

I remembered a video I'd seen of the teenagers during their vision. They were focused on something the camera couldn't record. I'd taught high school long enough to know how unlikely it was that a half-dozen kids could fake a trance that long, and then somehow all come out of it at the same time. They couldn't succeed in misleading their families, the priests, the psychologists who had studied them, and the throngs of pilgrims over the years since the apparitions began. No, the kids were in an altered state.

Picking up my pen, I came back to the question, Why did I feel so moved watching that video? It pulled me to some inner terrain without a map, and now, I really didn't know what to do with it. My eyes drifted to the early morning haze rising from the pool outside.

Then, something whispered, gentle as leaves fluttering in an unseen breeze: *If Mary is appearing in this world during your lifetime, and you can go, you should go.*

Longing for Grandma, my sister, and the Holy Mother herself suddenly bubbled up, flooding me with tears. In that moment, it occurred to me: If my grandmother's presence could break through my consciousness, certainly the Blessed Mother could break through to those teenagers in Medjugorje.

My questions about money, my backlog of work, and what I would tell my boss gently dissipated into a quiet sureness. This was a simple matter of priorities. I knew I had to act without delay.

Later that day, I walked into my boss's office to request some time off. Looking surprised, she glanced up from the monthly reports on her desk to gesture me to a chair.

"I know I'm just back from vacation and work is piled up here, but I have a chance to go to Yugoslavia with my sister."

Mary knew about Medjugorje. I'd told her about the visions over lunch one day. She nodded thoughtfully. This was a stretch for my analytical boss, but she had sometimes spoken to me of her powerful dreams. Hoping something of my story would resonate with her, I took a breath, summoning courage to go on, but she spoke first.

"I see this is very important to you." She looked at the department deadlines circled in red on her calendar, then paused, gathering her thoughts. "Ok. Take the time. Go with your sister."

I started to thank her, but she stopped me. "Don't worry. We can wait a little longer on your projects. I don't know what these visions mean—"

Just then, her phone rang. She spoke a quick greeting, then covered the mouthpiece. "I need to take this call. You can tell me later when you'll be back."

I felt as if I had suddenly stepped off a cliff into a free fall, and my face must have showed it. Mary grinned, waving me out the door. "Send me a postcard!" And so, the pilgrimage began.

The sky was dark outside the airplane's foggy window. It was getting late. I rubbed the glass with a Kleenex and peered out at murky clouds. After a delayed departure from Phoenix, we'd been flying several hours. We should've been close to New York by now, but I still couldn't see city lights. A twinge passed over my stomach. I didn't want to miss my connection to Amsterdam, the first leg of the trip to Medjugorje.

My musing was cut short by the pilot's voice over the intercom, sounding anxious. "We're expecting turbulence, folks. I've turned on the 'Fasten Seatbelts' sign. There are heavy thunderstorms, approaching Kennedy. Please be prepared for some bouncing."

Just what I needed! I nervously snapped my seatbelt together. I'd probably miss my connection. I didn't know anybody in New York. What would I do if the group was gone? I muttered a quick prayer. "Ok, Mary. I'm here because of you. Help me out."

Suddenly, an image of Mary flashed in my mind. She

stood in the cockpit behind the pilot, bending over him, one hand on his shoulder, the other guiding his hand on the controls. Then she pointed through the clouds to a path of light in front of the airplane. The path led to a bright spot on the runway where the plane was to land.

Seconds later, the pilot's voice came back on the intercom. "Well, we got through that just fine, and we didn't have one bump! But here in New York, there's a lot of traffic. It'll be some time until we can land. We'll probably be circling for half an hour."

Groans rose from the seats around me. I glanced at my watch. We were running late, and the airport was immense. I didn't know where to find the international wing and KLM. Would I make it to my plane?

My worries were interrupted by the pilot's voice. "Good news. We've just been cleared to land. We'll be on the ground in a minute or two."

I let go the breath I hadn't noticed I was holding. Then, I blinked. Our flight left Phoenix late, but despite bad weather and heavy airport traffic, it was arriving early. How often did that happen? And, I didn't know what to make of my dream-like vision of Mary guiding the plane to safety. Although surprising, the vision had felt, in some odd way, completely normal.

In the airport, Jane and I had a great reunion of hugs and tears.

Now, side by side, snuggling under a fleece blanket on the giant airliner, I was eager to chat with this sister I hadn't seen in more than a year.

"So, Janie. Tell me everything. We haven't talked since I let you know I could come on this trip."

She turned in her seat, settling in, then reached for my hand. "Oh, Shirley, when your letter came saying you'd come, I was more thrilled than on any other day of my life, including my wedding day!" I thought back to that summer so long ago, trying to recall the details of her wedding. My puzzlement must have shown.

Laughing, Jane prompted "Remember how surprised I was when you showed up? I couldn't believe you cut short your own honeymoon in Europe just to be with me!"

Of course. Now I remembered. Our plans had already been made when she set her date. Bob and I quickly agreed to fly home a few days early for the wedding, but we kept it a secret to surprise her. "Honey, I would never have missed your wedding."

She squeezed my hand again. "But this is even better." Her happiness brought tears to my eyes. I was glad to be with her, too.

Over the next hours, oblivious to our thirty-seven tour companions, we burbled together happily, catching up on my news, her news, and family news.

Then Jane's smile faded. "Shirley, I'm worried about Ray. He's been sick so often lately." A small line formed between her eyebrows. "I'm afraid he's really hurt his health."

Ray, our stepfather, had recently been in the hospital. When our mother married him, Jane was in grade school and I'd been at St. Rose three years. Ray had a drinking problem Mom hadn't known about when she moved to his dairy farm with her three kids.

"I'm sorry to hear about Ray, but how is Mom doing?" She'd already been widowed once, and I had gone through it with her.

"Well, it's on her mind. She sees he can't eat much. The other day, she told me he looked gray."

"That's not like Ray. Remember Mom telling us about him coming in for lunch all flushed when they lived on the farm?"

She smiled, "Yes. She thought it was sunburn. He kept things so well hidden."

"I wonder how long it was before she suspected he was red in the face from drinking. He never acted drunk."

"Probably when she started finding empty bottles." Jane was digging for something in her purse. "You knew about that?"

I nodded.

"But here, Shirley, I want to show you something."

She handed me a small, black, leather pouch.

"Last week Mom asked me to take one of Ray's suits to the cleaners. I checked the pockets and found this rosary. Actually, I found five. I was surprised he had so many. Anyway, I brought this one along. Do you think we can get it blessed in the Church of the visions?"

I opened the pouch. Black beads strung on a silver chain tumbled into my hand, crucifix glinting in the light. We'd both heard stories of rosaries mysteriously turning gold at Medjugorje. I handed the rosary back to Jane, not sure how I felt about all that. "At least we can pray for him and for Mom, for our family."

Finally, we were in Dubrovnik. Stiff and tired after hours of sitting, I shook myself. It was a relief to get off the plane for a stretch, but we were quickly loaded again for the last leg of our trip by bus.

Revived by a cup of coffee in the airport, I looked out the

window. Dubrovnik's small airport was just outside the walls of the old city.

"Jane, look at these red-tiled roofs and white buildings against the blue-green of the sea. Isn't this beautiful?"

She leaned across me, peering into the late September afternoon. "Yes. And the trees are so colorful. Look at all the reds and golds."

When the bus turned away from the city to a mountain road, we could see the sheer drop to the Adriatic Sea, and the Dalmation Coast with its many inlets and fiords.

Jane sat back in her seat. "Shirley, does this look like Greece? Weren't you there in fall?"

I looked out the window again at the swimmers on the beach, and the boats with their fishermen. I could see into the depths of the aquamarine water. "The coast does resemble Greece, but this landscape is more lush." Just then, my eye caught movement on the mountainside nearby. "Jane, look, quick. It's a herd of mountain goats!"

Our companions in the seat behind us had overheard, "Where? Where?"

In a holiday spirit, I called across the seat, hoping they'd see, too. A rising note of excitement filled the bus as we craned to take in what most of us were seeing for the first time.

Then, at sunset, we turned inland, leaving the steep mountains of the coast for the farmlands surrounding the village of Medjugorje. Long grasses undulated in the light breeze as the bus rolled over the straight, paved road angling through tranquil fields. Purple shadows of approaching night fell across the hills.

Our tour director, Diane, spoke to us in the newly quieted bus. "Let's pray a bit on this last part of our journey."

Rosaries clicked as we pulled them out of purses and pockets. Soon our voices rose and fell over the even purr of the bus motor.

"Hail Mary, full of Grace . . ." I'd prayed it daily for years in the convent. Familiar as daily bread, the ancient prayer was as repetitive as I remembered.

Ray's black beads dangled from my fingers, swaying with the movement of the bus. "Holy Mary, Mother of God," the phrases repeated, first on one side of the aisle, then on the other side. "Hail Mary, Holy Mary . . ." somehow, this time, I didn't feel lulled to sleep at all. The words were soothing and quieting, comforting in their rhythm, yes, but under that, to my surprise, an intensity was building. I was touched, the tears in my throat finally flooding out the words of the prayer. I looked around. On both sides of the aisle, my companions were dabbing their eyes.

Something out of the ordinary was breaking through to all of us, something I couldn't account for. It reminded me of my dream-like vision of Mary on the jet, but this time, I wasn't alone. Something was breaking through to all of us, something like a mother's presence.

Soon, it was dark. I drifted into a light sleep. Only when the big tour bus ground to a stop did I groggily come to, rubbing my eyes. Where were we?

Outside the bus, all was in darkness. I squinted at my watch: 11:30P.M. Then, headlights appeared on the road. No village was in sight. We were parked in open country.

One by one, cars drove into the field, surrounding us. Without a word, our tour director scurried down the aisle and left the bus.

It suddenly struck me that I was in a very unlikely situation.

This was a land of ancient feuds between Croatians and Serbs. It was nearly midnight and we were somewhere on a dark, isolated road in the middle of Yugoslavia, a communist country, among strangers.

Jane was asleep beside me. I poked her, "Wake up. I think something's wrong."

She sat up and stretched, leaning into the aisle, then quickly turned to me. "Shirley, our driver just climbed off the bus."

She twisted to look out the window. I hoped she could see him in the headlights outside. "He's there, but he's unloading our luggage." She sounded scared.

Stay calm, I told myself. *There's safety in numbers. No one is taking you or Jane or your worldly belongings anywhere you don't want to go.*

Just then, overhead lights came on as Diane clambered back on the bus. She smiled, facing us. "Didn't want to wake you all. As you remember from the pilgrimage fliers, there are no hotels in Medjugorje."

I whispered to Jane, "Did you remember that?"

She silently shook her head no. Diane continued, "Your hosts from the village are here to take you to their homes. You'll be staying near the church." Someone interrupted, calling to her in Croatian from the darkness. She answered briefly, then turned to us. "The driver says your luggage is loaded now, so find your carry-ons, and let's go."

What a relief! Our seasoned tour director had assigned our lodging—this one to this house, that one to that house—and even sorted out our luggage. As Jane and I stepped off the bus, smiling strangers waved us to their sedan.

After a short drive, we pulled up in front of a small, stone house, windows ablaze in welcome. We hauled our suitcases through the front door, to be greeted by the hearty aroma of fried chicken and homemade bread. Jacov and Shima allowed us a brief glimpse of our room, a front bedroom on the first floor, before hurrying us across the hall to their cozy dining room for a midnight supper.

Husband and wife smiled at us, nodding wordlessly as they went back and forth from the adjoining kitchen to the table, carrying plates and bowls of food. They spoke Croatian, no English.

I looked around at the sparsely furnished but immaculate home of our hosts and whispered to Jane, "I hope they'll let us help once in a while."

She whispered back. "Me, too! I'm not used to being waited on, and this is so much work!"

Shima was back, ladling vegetable soup into our dishes. Jacov gestured for us to sit at the table piled high with fried chicken, french fries, tomato and pepper salad, and homemade bread. We lowered our heads as he made the sign of the cross, softly murmuring a Croatian blessing. The hospitality of that midnight supper warmed not only our stomachs but also our spirits.

Next morning at dawn, Jane and I were awakened from bleary-eyed slumber by vigorous singing that seemed to be just under our window. Since we'd arrived in total darkness, we had no idea where we were in the village. We didn't know that Jacov and Shima lived just a short walk from the hill of the first apparition! The Lady of Medjugorje, like the Lady of Fatima, the Lady of Lourdes, and mother goddesses of many cultures, had shown up in a mountain grove with water nearby. Our lodgings were on the road between that mountain and the village's large church.

Hoping nobody could see me in my flimsy nightgown, I pulled the curtain back from the window.

Morning's early light sparkled on the bright steeple of St. James Church rising over the tile roofs of the nearby houses. Then I spotted the source of our wake-up call.

"Jane, look at this."

She crawled across the bed, poking her head under a corner of curtain, then sucked in her breath. "There must be twenty-five people out there!"

Women in long, black dresses and babushkas, and men in dusty suits and hats walked together on the way to church, rosaries dangling from their hands. In between decades, they sang, "Ave, Ave, Ave Maria."

Tears filled my eyes. "I've never seen anything like this before! Those people haven't been told they have to go to church. They're out there walking around at dawn because they want to."

We watched until the villagers wound out of sight down the dusty road.

That first morning, after breakfast, Diane gathered all of us in the churchyard for a little history. "The local authorities were uneasy when large crowds started coming to the village. They asked the priest to have the children pray in the church, not on the hillside where the apparitions had been taking place. That's why everyone goes to church every night. After Mass, the rosary is recited. During the prayer, you may notice a flash of light. Pilgrims sometimes see it right before the recitation stops. The children say that Mary is talking to them then."

I turned to look up at the immense church wondering why it been built in this tiny, out-of-the-way village. The local population was sparse, and I knew from our drive through the countryside that no other settlement existed anywhere nearby.

But that night when I arrived for Mass, to my surprise, the church was packed. Even the aisles were filled with locals and visitors. It tickled me to think that if the Holy Mother herself had provided the blueprint for the place, she had under-estimated the crowds!

Resigning myself that there would be no place to sit, I found space to lean against the sweaty wall as bells signaled the start of Mass. I stretched for a glimpse of the altar, but all I could see was the throng crowded around me.

Given my preference for solitude, I wondered if I could even begin to pray here. Then, curiously, despite the bobbing heads, the jostling elbows and shoulders, the creaking benches and kneelers, the reverence of my companions quieted me. To my right and left, voices prayed in languages I didn't understand—Croatian, German, Italian, and French— sibilant whispers rising and falling in the vaulting space. Then, from the altar, the priest began singing in Croatian. His commanding spirit created a palpable energy in the place. Language didn't matter. It was as if I had picked up the haunting melody of an unforgettable song I'd known all my life.

When Mass ended and the rosary started, I noticed the young visionaries were in the balcony. Their voices led the prayer as it alternated like chorus and verse from one side of the church to the other. The same sense of connection with my companions and some other reality that I'd felt on the bus swept over me again.

Suddenly, at a flash of light in the church, all the praying voices fell silent. Although I didn't see Mary as I had on the plane in New York, I felt her presence. She seemed to be gently and powerfully holding us all: the children in the choir loft who actually saw her and heard her words, the pilgrims crowding the church, and me. Somehow, the boundaries between us all collapsed. My heart knew we were connected, that we were one. The experience was beyond words but reminded me of the whiteout snowstorm of my day with Grandma so many years ago. This was a different kind of whiteout. I hardly moved or breathed.

Only when the woman next to me crowded past to leave did I realize three hours had passed since I'd come to the church. I'd lost track of time, despite my stiff legs, tired back, and discomfort in the humidity.

I rubbed my eyes and lowered myself to a seat. As the aisles emptied, the sea of bobbing heads no longer obscured

Sis

my view of the sanctuary. I could see the graceful statue of the Lady of Medjugorje for the first time since I'd entered St. James. Her extended arms seemed to invite me across the front of the church until I was kneeling at her altar. And then, it happened all over again: the sense of being held, gently enfolded. I closed my eyes in the presence of the Mother to hear what her silence was speaking to me, to deeply inhale her fragrance, the fragrance of roses.

Their perfume reminded me of Grandma's story of roses:

Sis, my aunt, had fallen critically ill in her small bedroom with the altar. Early one morning, Ella, Grandma's closest friend, came to the door with a pot of soup, knowing her neighbor had been too busy to cook. Once inside, she looked around and said, "Oh, Florence. Where are the roses? They smell so sweet."

Grandma flew into her arms, crying. "Oh, Ella. There are no roses. Sis just died."

As I knelt there, eyes closed, I prayed to the Lady for Sis, for Grandma, for all those I loved. It was a long litany.

Finally, an acolyte at the nearby high altar began to extinguish the candles, one by one. Realizing it was time to go, I stood, for one last view of the Mother's statue, banked with flowers. To my surprise, many looked like they were silk, but that couldn't be. I'd smelt roses. I reached to touch them. The first bouquet was silk, the next was plastic. There were no real roses on Mary's altar!

Surprised and humbled, I bowed to the figure of the Holy Mother in the nearly darkened church, then, found my way out, filled with awe. Whatever I had ever expected or hoped for was lovingly confounded by surprises at every turn here at this place made holy by Our Lady. This was clearly other territory. I'd had no idea Spirit could take such a powerful grip of the likes of me!

Next morning after breakfast, Jane and I set out to explore the village.

Two men in work clothes passed us on the road, tipping their hats.

Jane raised her eyebrows. "Well, that's different. At home, you get a wolf whistle from two guys like that." She turned to look at the backs of the retreating men. "They didn't even ogle us."

I turned, too. She was right. The men continued on their way.

We did, too, circling around a small park to walk down a street where several houses were under construction. One front door stood open, displaying grocery items. A small sign lettered in Croatian dangled from the doorknob.

Jane poked her head through the door, then came back outside. "Do you think this is a little neighborhood store?"

"Might be." A basket of apples stood just inside the door. I'd seen places like this in Greece. "Do you want to buy something?"

She eyed the toiletries lined up on a shelf behind the counter. "I could use some toothpaste." She stepped inside again. "There's nobody around. They must not worry about shoplifters. Well, let's go. Maybe someone'll be here later."

We swung off down the road, and Jane said, "You know, this atmosphere is kind of strange. Nobody seems to worry about stealing." She paused to look back at the open door behind us.

I waited for her to catch up the few steps between us. "I

know, and I'd wondered if we'd be the targets for theft, or even mugging! I wasn't sure how Croatians felt about Americans, but did you hear Fr. Svet's story last night?"

"No, what? I went to bed early."

"He said when the visions started in the village, the men stopped swearing."

"Huh! Maybe they stopped ogling and shoplifting, too." We grinned at each other.

"He also said there was no crime in the village."

Jane turned to look at me. "He did? That's pretty amazing. But can we trust the other tourists?"

"I don't know. But I did hear an announcement on the public address system that some stuff left laying around had been turned in: tape players, passports, even wallets."

By now, we were back in the churchyard. Sitting on a shady bench, I pulled off my shoe to empty out a pebble. Jane sat beside me, stretched her long legs, and turned to watch the crowds piling off a line of chartered buses. Three chubby boys in baggy shorts threw their bulging backpacks in a pile by the church wall.

Jane leaned forward. "Are those kids just wandering off?" The boys were already out of sight. Nobody seemed to be watching the backpacks.

I chuckled, "I guess Fr. Svet was right. No hooligans around here! We can relax."

The apparitions had powerfully influenced the people in the village. Although drawn to visit the site, I'd never imagined I'd see the Holy Mother myself. I didn't need to. Medjugorje itself was a miracle, one neither Jane nor I had heard about before the pilgrimage.

Next morning, I finally had a chance to hike the hill of the apparition, a small, rocky promontory about a half-mile behind the home of one of the visionaries.

Eager to visit the site, I joined the small group assembled behind St. James, glad to see Father Geoffrey, the lone priest in our party, among them.

Leaving the churchyard, we walked single file on a narrow path through some farmer's fragrant orchard, enjoying the warm morning sunlight. I ambled along, taking in the sweet scents of ripe apples, and wild yellow roses. Geoffrey walked ahead of me, swinging his broad shoulders. I could hear wisps of his conversation.

"When I arrived at the Dubrovnik airport, my rosary had turned gold. The chain, you know. The chain between the beads."

My heart skipped a beat. I had just met Geoffrey and didn't know him well, but I was powerfully curious. I coached the shy child inside me. *He's a priest. He'll be kind. Here's your chance to find out what this phenomenon is all about. He won't mind.*

I worked up my courage and hotfooted it right up to him as quickly as I could on the rocky path. "What happened? Can I see the rosary?"

Seemingly pleased that I'd asked, he smiled a crooked grin at me and brought the beads from his pocket. "The chain, medal, and crucifix were silver when I bought it at Lourdes last week."

They weren't silver now. The morning sun fairly glinted on that gold chain.

"I'm going to find a jeweler and see what I can learn about this metal."

My mind raced with questions. What would Goeffrey learn? Would the gold be commonplace to a trained eye, or would it be an unrecognized metal? If the gold was miraculous, what did it mean? What was this particular phenomenon all about?

Then I looked into Geoff's face. It was soft with tears and awe.

My questions suddenly seemed unimportant. This was God stuff, a gift.

We silently looked at each other for a long minute standing there on the sunny path. Then he put the rosary in his pocket and we continued our single-file walk.

Over our heads, birds sang a rowdy chorus in the apple trees of the farm orchard. As we passed, they quieted their noisy music a bit, just enough for me to catch a few of Geoff's words again, floating back on the morning air. He was bantering with Diane. It was something about the rosary. I laughed and called out to him across the few steps that separated us. "Well, Geoff, if you don't want the rosary, give it to me!"

With that, he turned, took two long strides to me, cupped my hand in his two large ones, and gave it to me. He flashed me a dazzling smile. "I feel that every gift I have received is given to me for someone else."

I felt like a five-year-old falling off the schoolyard swing! The wind was knocked out of me! Goeff's sudden gesture had so surprised me, I didn't know whether to laugh or to cry or to scream or to jump or to fall on the ground. I couldn't believe he was giving me his miracle rosary!

I looked at the golden chain and brown wooden beads in my hand, then back to his sincere face. He clearly meant it. He was not only willing to part with it, he wanted to.

That sunny morning in Yugoslavia, Geoffrey taught me something about gifts, about receiving them and letting them go, about passing good things on. It occurred to me much later that the rosary had come to me because I needed to learn that lesson. The lesson of letting go what is precious, of passing it on. Yes, it was touching to stand on the hill of apparition where the children first met the Lady, but for me, the lesson of gifts was an equally important miracle of Medjugorje, a miracle of the heart.

Winging our way home, as the plane flew over black expanses of international water, Jane and I talked into the night, sharing each remarkable detail of our pilgrimage. She hadn't seen Fr. Geoff's rosary. Handing it to her, I told her the story of the morning on the mountain.

She turned the beads over in her fingers as she listened. When I finished, she said, "Shirley, what does the Blessed Mother have in store for you? Do you know? I'll bet as you pray with this, Mary will guide you."

She'd read my mind. "I'm not sure yet." I looked at her, not moving. "Though I do know my life has changed."

"You're so lucky to have that rosary."

Jane bent to unwrap the package of gifts we'd bought for family and friends and began enumerating each one. "This medal is for Mom, this one for Sister Jean. This statue is for Betty." She suddenly went silent.

In the soft cabin light, I could see she was holding a rosary she'd just taken from its black leather case. It was the only one in a black leather case, the one she had brought from Iowa. The chain was gold.

"Jane, is that Ray's rosary?"

She looked at me, eyes full of tears, and silently nodded. When had the chain turned gold?

Lips trembling, she said, "I don't know. I haven't looked at it since my gifts were blessed."

Fr. Svet, a priest at St. James, had invited everyone to leave religious articles on the altar before the apparitions for Mary's blessing.

"Amazing! I guess Mary just goes to work unceremoniously. And, you know what? I have a feeling Ray's health might improve. That's what we were praying for in the first place, remember?"

She closed her eyes, holding the rosary between her palms as if taking in its power. "I hope you're right. I do think the most important part is the prayer." Then she leaned forward to looked at me. "But, it's hard to understand why these chains turn gold. Did Fr. Geoffrey have any theories?"

"Actually, he did have a theory. Geoff said he thought it was Mary's way of getting our attention. He thought everything going on there—the solar eclipse, the movement of the sun, and the glow around the cross on the church steeple— was meant to call attention to the Lady's message."

Jane held the rosary up to the dome light overhead, watching it sparkle on its golden chain. Her voice was soft. "Hmm . . . like God's neon. . . . "

Yes, the miracles of Medjugorje pointed to something beyond themselves. They were signs and wonders breaking through the ordinary, calling attention to a reality too powerful to be conveyed in words, like God's neon.

6

After Medjugorje

So, here I was, pilgrimage over, looking into the expectant eyes of my long-suffering boss who had just offered me a juicy promotion. How could I tell her what had happened to me these last weeks on this mind-boggling pilgrimage? Before I even left home, I knew my life would change, but I had no idea how much. I took a deep breath and launched in.

"Mary, I don't know how to explain, but I've just had an amazing experience."

She looked at me quizzically, cocking her head slightly.

"When I left for Yugoslavia, I didn't anticipate any of this. I truly appreciate the opportunity in the department, but I see now that this work . . ." I hesitated. What I now knew was that the work in the Health Department wasn't my call. Not now. "Well, it's not really who I am."

She looked truly puzzled.

I laughed, "What I mean is, I can do this administrative work, but . . ." I reached for words . . . "well, I guess I have more of a vocation than a career." My eyes filled. The truth of the words that had just come out of my mouth filled me with gratitude. "So, Mary, my job here needs to end."

I handed her a small, framed photograph of a woman standing in a bower of trees, arms uplifted. "Somebody gave me this in Medjugorje."

Mary lowered her head to study the misty image. When she looked back up at me, her eyes were moist. "So, you're like a kid whose mother called her home. Is that it?"

I nodded.

"Well, I understand, but I don't understand."

Suddenly, we were hugging each other, rocking side to side. Even if some of her tears were about the piles of work on my desk, still, I was grateful for my boss's understanding.

All I knew was that I had to be available for whatever God was cooking up. I couldn't miss the clarity that had dawned in me since the pilgrimage. Something powerful had burst through the surface of my life and the light was shining. I could see that my gifts were to be used, passed on, like Fr. Geoffrey's rosary. Whatever I'd done up to this time that had been successful, effective, and satisfying had been in line with my call. It was that simple. Those parts worked. The rest, the ones that came from my effort and not from the flow, didn't work. This breakthrough was an invitation, one I couldn't imagine refusing. God had plans for me. I didn't know what the assignment was, but I had to sign on.

Once relieved of my duties at the County, I checked in with an old friend, Fr. Brian. An affable Irishman, he was full of comical stories and sensible skepticism. Over my years in his parish, I'd served on his lay advisors' council and taught catechism. He'd even tried to hire me on staff before I went to work at County. As pastor at St. Pat's, he'd heard some wild tales about events in Medjugorje from returning parishioners and had been surprised I'd made the trip. He was eager to hear my take on the visions.

We sat at my kitchen table sharing the macaroni salad I'd hastily concocted for lunch. Brian listened as I poured out the whole story, from the moment I'd first read about Medjugorje and felt my grandmother's presence, to the flight home when Jane and I discovered Ray's rosary had turned to gold. We sat long at table as I finished the account.

Finally, he smiled broadly, "Well, Shirley, such a story! Sounds like the apparitions are real."

"I thought so, mostly because there was so much love in that village, Brian. It was like a family reunion, as if our mom had called us all home."

He sat back from the table, folding his napkin, but I had more to say. "And, Brian, I quit my job. I'm available to help you now."

His eyes widened as he reached across the bowl of left-over salad to squeeze my hand. "That's just music to my ears! I certainly do want your help." He pulled a notepad from his pocket, and began jotting notes to himself. "You have to tell this story to the women's group, and help with the Ministry of Care, the ones who take communion to the hospital and nursing home—"

As he was speaking, the phone rang.

After a brief conversation, I hung up and returned to the table, laughing. "That was the president of the women's group. She wants me to talk at their next meeting about Medjugorje! I think we've just had a confirmation." It was the first of many.

In Medjugorje, Fr. Jozo, the priest who first learned of the children's apparitions, later had visions of Mary himself. She instructed him to pray over the pilgrims. I was one of them, waiting in the long line for my turn to receive his blessing. When he covered my ears with his hands, without understanding Croatian, I knew well that something opened. I could hear with my heart. Then he had placed his hands on my shoulders. Again, despite language, I understood I was to help others carry their burdens.

Now that I was home and unemployed, it was time to begin my work of healing, of listening. It was time to start my counseling practice. I'd loved the informal counseling that always developed as I'd taught in Catholic schools, and the work I'd done with abuse victims as a graduate intern. Since finishing my MSW, I'd counseled inmates in the jail and a variety of clients at the retreat center. Now it was time to maximize this aspect of my training. I was willing, but had no idea how to go about finding an office. I mentioned my dilemma to Margaret, a friend who'd also visited Medjugorje.

Next morning after early Mass, she pulled me aside. "Shirley, you still looking for a counseling office? Meet Gabrielle! She has an extra room in her suite."

A willowy, blonde woman about my age stepped out of the row of chairs to greet me. To my amazement, her office was only blocks away from my house. We shook hands on the rent agreement, and I settled in. I hadn't even advertised when, in a flurry of activity, clients started to come out of the woodwork.

Several weeks later, I took time from my busy schedule to drive downtown. My practice had started so fast, I couldn't wait for the mail to deliver my new business license. I picked up the envelope waiting for me at the reception desk in the municipal building and swung out the door. Intent on hurrying back to the office, I was startled to hear my name called from the steps behind me. I turned to see a smiling woman I couldn't quite place.

"It's me, Sandra, from jail."

Of course. She'd run a support group at the county jail where we'd both worked. Some of her recovering alcoholics were in my job training program. We'd had many occasions to cheer each other up in the tough environment. I hadn't seen Sandra in the five years since I'd left.

"Sandra, you look great! You must've gotten out of jail. What're you doing now?"

She smiled, pulling me into the cool shade of a big mulberry tree next to the hot sidewalk. "You'll never believe it. I'm still in the clink, but we finally got some programs for women and I run 'em."

"Oh, I'm so glad." Women's needs had been seriously overlooked in the system. "And you're perfect for the job."

"Yeah, Director Anderson funded my job and the programs." That was good news. We both knew the insecurity of grant funding. "So what're you doing now?"

I stood there smiling. Here we were, two women in a city of two million people, out of touch for years. Yet, we'd crossed paths, and I knew I was ready to return to jail.

"Well, it'll take me a while to catch you up, Sandra, so I'll give you the short answer: If your inmates need a counselor, I'm available."

On the drive back to the office, I thought about how I'd first landed in jail. It was 1980, and armed with a brand new MSW degree, I'd applied to the county system. After screening, I had been called for an interview in the Corrections Department.

I was ushered into an office in a locked down area of the jail. The Corrections officer leaned forward to look me over, then snorted. "You look like you belong to Junior League. Why do you want to work in jail?"

I might have looked like Junior League to him in my navy blue dress and shiny pumps, but I'd watched my dad deliver sacks of groceries to families down on their luck because somebody was in jail. We didn't have much money and Dad worked hard to provide for us, but he had a heart for the underdog. I did, too.

I looked the lieutenant in the eye. We both knew my credentials went far beyond the job requirements of the inmate employment and training program, and I'd passed the drug screening polygraph without question. Like it or not, I was his new employee. I smiled at him sweetly. "I'm a social worker, officer."

Once on the job, I read the records of the young inmates vying for the few training slots available. Many were just over the legal age. I doubted that their rather minor infractions would've put them in jail if they'd been white and their folks could hire good lawyers.

I'd read the statistics in my social work texts. More kids of color were in jail than in college. Those statistics came to life day after day in my office as the inmates came for interviews. I listened to childhood histories of horrific neglect and abuse: the girl who'd been tied up and raped by cousins who finished the insult by peeing in her mouth; the shy boy who showed me scars on his arms and legs, inflicted by a drunken stepfather's cigarette. Some of these kids were homeless, in need of a roof and a meal, and had deliberately broken the law to get arrested, hoping to be safe in jail. They needed a chance. Rehabilitation and job training could be that chance.

But after a few months, it was a struggle to make the program work. Most Monday mornings, the training center would call to report a handful of my trainees absent. When I checked, inmates told me that when the school van came to pick them up, they were locked down for no apparent reason.

The disgruntled guard on duty would grin. "Never got any paperwork, Ma'am. No sirree."

Knowing I'd delivered it before leaving on Friday afternoon, I felt like Sisyphus pushing a boulder up the mountain only to see it roll back down.

I pulled into my parking space, setting a nearby yellow acacia bush dancing. This was a new day. I was ready for more boulders. It felt good to be going back to jail.

Since the jail had no counselor on staff, Sandra kept me busy. I soon got into the routine of visiting her inmates every week.

One sunny morning in February, after early morning Mass at the Casa, I had a good half-hour to while away before my drive across town to the detention center. A little quiet meditation in the garden before the day began was a welcomed luxury. Grateful for the Casa's hospitable bottomless pot of coffee, I poured a cup and headed to my favorite seat on the patio.

I'd no more than sipped the first mouthful when an elderly woman, carefully balancing her own coffee asked, "May I join you?"

Before I could reply, she'd seated herself beside me and leaned back to survey the garden and the sky. "Oh, this sunshine is wonderful." That done, she turned to me, sticking out her free hand. "I'm Sister Esther, just here a few days from Iowa."

I was chagrined to lose my privacy but had to grudgingly admit, I remembered February in Iowa very well.

"You must be like my niece," she said. "She knew enough to come where it's warm. She's lived here for years now, while I'm still teaching in the cold country."

I smiled, then our exchange, the polite conversation of strangers, lapsed into silence. Till then, I hadn't noticed how brilliant the sunshine was, even with sunglasses. Maybe Esther'd be quiet and I could meditate a bit after all. I closed my eyes behind the smoky lenses.

No such luck. She shifted on the bench, sipping her coffee. "I don't know why, but I want to tell you a story. . . ."

I squinted at her, rearranging my bottom on the not-so-comfortable wrought iron bench. "Oh?"

Esther looked at me as though her thoughts were elsewhere. "Do you mind? It's a story I usually don't tell."

Hoping her yarn wouldn't be too long, I gamely replied, "I'm all ears."

"Well," she began tentatively, "I've been a sister since I was very young. Always loved it, until last year."

True confessions from a sixty five-year-old nun? It had taken me years to talk about my life in the convent and when I did, it wasn't to a stranger. I eyed her with new interest.

"The trouble started when I was transferred to a very small rural school." She pushed her glasses a bit higher on her nose, as if about to look into things. "The two sisters teaching there had been together for years."

My companion looked like she should be ready to retire, instead of starting a new job, but maybe that wasn't an option in her order. "So, you were a newcomer?"

"Yes, and I hated the change. Those nuns were so clique-y. They were used to their routines and wouldn't include me. After a few weeks, I was so lonely, I thought I'd die. I couldn't go on that way." She swirled her coffee in its Styrofoam cup. "Well, Sister Victoria—that was my Superior—heard me out. Let me tell you, I ranted and raved, told her I deserved better and had always gone where I was sent." Esther shot me a quick glance.

I tried to imagine how Sister Maureen would have reacted to such a tirade. "Was your Superior shocked?"

She took a sip of coffee, then laughed. "Far from it. When I finally stopped for breath, she asked me one question.

'Esther, have you talked to God about this?'

Well, I was still so angry, I snapped at her: 'Yes, I asked God to move me.' But Victoria stuck to her question. 'No, that's not what I meant. Have you let God know how angry you are at Him?'

My mouth dropped open, but Sister Victoria just sat there looking at me."

She shook her head at the memory. I smiled, gratified to learn some things had changed in the convent since my departure. I remembered how much I'd needed a new assignment after Wisconsin Rapids.

Esther drained her coffee cup and went on. "The Superior told me she'd transfer me at the semester, but first, I had to talk to God about my anger. She actually sent me to the chapel right then and there. At first, I felt sheepish complaining to God, but I truly wanted to get out of that convent.

Once I got started, I let God have it. 'It's not fair. I've worked for You my whole life. Now I'm old. This is no time for all this trouble. I need friends. I don't deserve this.'"

She left off long enough to twinkle at me. "I just thundered. Got myself so worked up, I was actually crying."

Then she hesitated, looking at me appraisingly. "You won't believe what happened next."

Her voice dropped to a whisper. "When I looked up to the front of the chapel, Jesus was walking there, in the sanctuary. Jesus! Carrying His cross!

He looked over his shoulder at me and said, 'What would happen if I stopped now?'

Esther sat back in silence, eyes welling up. "I knew I was awake, but I didn't know what to say or do. I was stunned."

In a moment, she went on. "Well, I went back to that convent and those two nuns. Nothing changed. They still snubbed me, but the most wonderful part," she smiled through her tears, "it didn't bother me any more. I was at peace."

Just then, a car horn sounded. A blue Chevrolet pulled up in the parking lot. "Oh, that's my niece." Esther stood and waved, then turned back to me, her smile deepening the crow's feet around her eyes. "Visions and all, you can see why I don't broadcast this story, but it just seemed like you were supposed to hear it today. . . ." She gave my shoulders a quick hug and was gone before I could say a word.

As the car wheels crunched in the gravel, a trail of dust motes hung in the morning sunshine. I watched them settle on the jasmine vines climbing the garden wall, trying to absorb Esther's story.

The vision touched me, but what, I wondered, had prompted her to tell it to me, a complete stranger? Could such a vision have healed me enough to go back to Wisconsin Rapids after that tough year so long ago?

Still puzzled, I stood and stretched, emptying my cold coffee in the grass. It was time to go to jail. I guessed I'd never know.

Once at Durango, the first inmate on my schedule was Amanda, a slight blonde girl of nineteen who walked with a limp. Her pale face seemed to become even paler as she sadly recounted being abandoned in San Francisco by her parents when she was eleven to be picked up by a pimp who added her to his stable of prostitutes. She limped because of the leg injury she'd suffered jumping from a car to escape him.

Now in jail, she was enduring new torments. Amanda wept inconsolably. "The other women in the pod have been in jail together before and were here a long time before I was locked up with 'em. They don't want me around. They harass me, threaten me, and even beat me up when the guard's not looking. They're cruel. The only way I can get away from them is by going to Bible class once in a while."

I lost part of Amanda's recital as a sudden chill passed over my bare arms. I moved the box of Kleenex balanced on my knees to the floor, then faced the bedraggled young woman, pulling my metal folding chair close to hers.

"Let me tell you a story," I said.

When I finished, she sat in complete silence, eyes fixed on me without moving. Then she burst into heart-wrenching sobs, reaching her thin arms to hug me tightly. I rocked her, patting her thin shoulders, waiting for the storm to pass. Finally, her tense arms relaxed. She sat back, turning her mascara-stained face to me, lips trembling. Words wouldn't come.

She slipped her hand, damp Kleenex and all, into mine, blinking back tears, then choked out a few words, "I needed to hear that story."

My next visit to Amanda didn't really surprise me. She'd pulled her hair back neatly into a ponytail and sat tall as she told me what I expected to hear. The women continued to be cold and nasty to her, but she was able to be peaceful. "Like that nun you told me about, something inside me changed." Amanda dropped her eyes, then glanced at me shyly. "When I prayed, Jesus talked to me, too. And I've been going to Bible class twice a week."

As I drove home across traffic that afternoon, I wondered if I had entertained an angel. Sister Esther, a stranger, had come, delivered a story of visions, and without knowing why, I'd carried it to my next stop, then passed it on with miraculous outcome.

The next morning when I awoke in the pre-dawn hours, the previous day lingered in my thoughts. The strange synchronicity of Esther and Amanda seemed to be a gentle lesson about being in the right place at the right time, and paying attention.

I padded out to the kitchen for my first cup of coffee. Once the pot was perking, I wrapped my heavy bathrobe tightly around me and slipped out to retrieve the morning paper. To my surprise, Mother Teresa's picture was on the front page. She was here, in my city!

Mother Teresa's life and conversion had inspired me for a very long time. She'd explained herself so simply. She knew she'd been called by God. It changed her. She left her comfortable convent to serve the poorest of the poor, "Jesus in a distressing disguise."[10] Her generosity, born of love, deeply touched me. To encounter this saint was the desire of my heart.

I quickly spread the newspaper on the kitchen table to read her itinerary:

9A.M.—Meeting with priests at the cathedral; 10A.M.—Meeting with nuns at some school; 2:00P.M.—Mass with the deacons.

Was that all?

I scanned the columns again, frustration mounting. What about me? Wasn't I volunteering in the jail, the nursing home, the hospital? When would I get my turn? I'd long since accepted my status as an unnoticed, non-ordained woman, but it hurt to be left out again and again by the bureaucrats of my denomination who overlooked those quietly ministering behind the scene, not identified by the cloth.

I sniffed as I put the newspaper aside. *You, God,* I said to myself, *You just let it happen in Your church!* Disappointed, I went to my desk to check the day's appointments. Then, the phone rang. It was Sandra.

"The women's pod is in lockdown, Shirley. Can you come back next week?"

In a minute, there was another jangle. My 9:30 counseling client was sick, could we reschedule? That done, I put down the receiver and turned to a pile of paperwork. Before I'd read the first insurance form, a third call came.

The volunteer handbooks at church weren't ready. We'd have to wait till next week to review them. Another meeting was scratched.

Well, that did it. My day's appointments had evaporated. I'd have lots of time to catch up here in the office.

Then came the phone call I'd never forget.

"Would you like to see Mother Teresa?"

I couldn't believe my ears. It was a friend who volunteered at the Sisters of Charity shelter downtown. "Just bring a rose; it'll be your passport."

Remembering my earlier flash of anger, I'd dissolved into choking tears. God had heard my prayer after all. I wasn't left out, maybe by the institution, but not by God!

Just hours later, I was at the church with a small group of volunteers from Mother Teresa's shelter in Phoenix. The mobs I'd seen surrounding her on television were nowhere in evidence.

I entered, quietly seating myself at the end of a pew near the altar and looked around. About forty women were there, each holding a beautiful rose. A nun from the shelter stepped to the podium and invited us to place them in a vase at the Mary altar.

The next thing I knew, the slight figure of Mother Teresa came walking down the aisle, passing within my reach.

She stood in the sanctuary, a small bent figure, smiling beatifically, and began to speak. Her message was an invitation to each of us to serve each other, to bring the light of God's love to all those in our world. When she had finished, she beckoned us to come to her, one by one, to receive a gift.

I fingered the medal I received from her hand that day.

I hadn't been left out after all, but instead, God had gently taught me a humbling lesson of love. Would I ever learn to trust, to follow? Once again, I'd been guided to the right place at the right time. Once again, I'd been carried.

I'd have to tell Amanda.

7

The Unthinkable Becomes Inevitable

E ven all these years later, it still can't be told. Certain dark family secrets, once the storm has passed, move over into the personal ownership of the one to whom they belong. The long-standing secret that took away my choices and assumed that I didn't know what would be best for me is no longer part of my life. It is the property of my former partner, shrouded in privacy. And, of course, I understand. Sort of.

It was all about a secret that continued over the twenty years of my marriage to Bob, finally destroying it, because I was unable and unwilling to live within its confines. As is the case with every couple, our relationship danced between times of privacy and times of sharing, on the ever-shifting edges of autonomy and intimacy. I'd thought our dance went pretty well until the day the secret came out.

The Phoenix desert sweltered in searing heat the summer of August 1990. Heat radiated from the concrete and pavements of the city as we suffered blistering temperatures day after day, week after week.

One weekend, Bob and I escaped to our mountain cabin with friends for some relief. On Saturday, we hiked in the woods and grilled hamburgers. As the day ended, finally reviving, we sat long, watching the stars through the tall pine trees.

The next morning, I awoke strangely unsettled. I'd dreamed over and over of a huge mansion surrounded by a shaded lagoon and many pools on the rolling grounds of a great estate. I'd wandered from room to room, amazed to find it filled with treasures: ornate furniture, chests overflowing with silver, richly colored tapestries and jewels, all haphazardly crowded together. I was amazed to discover the mansion was attached to my everyday house. But once I left it, I didn't know how to get into it again, I couldn't find the entryway.

Sweaty with frustration, I rolled out of the tangled sheets trying not to disturb Bob. I would start breakfast; shake it off, I told myself as I pulled a robe over my pajamas. The helpless discontent of the dream gradually faded as I fried the bacon and scrambled the eggs. By the time we finished our leisurely brunch, it was 1:30 and our guests were eager to head back to Phoenix to relieve their babysitter.

"So great you could come. Drive safely now!" Bob's voice echoed in the pine-fragrant air as we leaned over the deck railing to wave our good-byes. The departing van crossed the creek and chugged out of sight.

"And now, for you, ducky." His arm snuggly circled my waist, steering me through the screen door, through the cabin's front room, and into the bedroom.

Dream forgotten, I laughed, tumbling into the big, unmade bed, pulling him after me. "Couldn't wait to get me alone, huh? Shall I shut the window so the neighbors don't hear us?"

Bob was already nibbling on my ear. He gave me a long kiss, then whispered, "Oh, I think I can stifle your screams!"

Our lovemaking was sweet merging, connecting like the coming together of two tides, mingling currents, until only one gentle flow remained. Afterwards, I lay warmly nestled in his arms, relaxed, basking in the glow holding us both, floating. On the surface of sleep, I opened one eye to find Bob studying me, his elbow propped on the pillow under my head.

"Shirl, I love you so much," he said, his right hand lightly stroking my arm. "More and more all the time."

I smiled, reaching up to give his neck a warm hug, but he pulled back. Startled, I twisted in bed to get a full view of his face. Over the twenty years of our marriage, Bob's frequent proclamations of love usually warmed my heart, but this conversation carried a chilling undercurrent. Something prickled inside me. Why was he so serious?

Bob started ominously, "I feel like I'm falling off a steep cliff, and there's no going back. . . ."

In that moment, the dance that was our marriage went over the precipice. His revelation stunned me into silence. Beyond anything my imagination could conjure up, it sent my mind reeling.

He saw the shock on my face and quickly continued. "I've never lied to you. There are just some things I haven't told you," and then he went on with his story.

"Bob, I don't get it. What do you mean?" I couldn't grasp what he was saying to me. How could he have held such a secret for so long? I thought we'd told each other everything.

He looked at me, eyes pleading. "I've been afraid to tell you all these years, but now, I love you so much, I want you to know all about me. I hope you can understand."

I couldn't take it in. The warm connectedness with my husband of twenty years was suddenly, terrifyingly shattered. It was too overwhelming. I ran for the bathroom, nauseated, my gut in a spasm of pain. I sat there, gingerly balanced on the toilet, my bowel draining until only water released from its wrenching contractions. Deep within me rose shuddering sobs. I was alone, bewildered, and stunned by the frightening unknown.

I needed something hot, a cup of coffee. With shaking hands, I pulled on jeans and a shirt and went to the kitchen.

The familiar space now felt strange. I was numb. I moved mechanically as though something inside me had blown a fuse. I watched my hand pour coffee into my favorite mug, wondering from a far-off place if I was in shock. It was Bob's father's mug with donuts drawn on it and the homey verse, "As you go through life, brother, let this be your goal. Keep your eye on the donut and not on the hole." What would loveable, old Ben, now dead these six years, have thought of all this? Then a worse question hit me. Suppose he'd known Bob's story all along? A new wave of nausea washed over me. Was even my trust in Ben to be shattered?

I stumbled out to the deck for air, leaned over the railing, and let the anguish in my stomach release into the greenery below. Finally, I went back into the cabin and shakily lowered myself into my rocking chair. Clammy and weak, I wiped the fine sweat from my upper lip with a fingertip, coaching myself, *Just breathe. Just breathe.*

Bob sat at the table in profile to me, knees held closely together, delicately chewing, crooking his little finger as he held a sandwich. I had often seen him sit just so.

Who was this man I thought I knew so well? The wonderment at this moment was that he could eat at all. And so peacefully. Was I crazy? I just didn't understand, but I couldn't talk yet. Not yet. Bob agreed we'd take a break and discuss things later.

Time passed in some surrealistic haze as we packed up and drove home. It was as though something internal, visceral, had dislodged within me. I felt like a zombie by the time I crawled out of the car. In the kitchen, Kelly stood in front of the refrigerator, glass of just-poured milk in his hand. He gave me a penetrating look, "Mom, what's the matter?"

What could I say to my seventeen-year-old son about the cataclysm that had abruptly turned my world upside down? "Just a little tired, Kelly. Just tired, that's all."

He turned to spread peanut butter on a slab of bread. "That's funny. You usually come home from the cabin all rested." The wound inside me tore further. I patted him on the rump as I hurried past him, hiding the tears I couldn't stop.

I'd often told my son that I'd tried to choose his father very carefully. I'd told him I'd wanted to give him a good father, the best I could find. And for all these years, I'd thought I'd done just that. Bob was a fine dad, always attentive to our son, an affectionate, sensitive, responsible, and involved parent. Now I was worried. What would this crisis do to my only son at the threshold of his manhood?

I waited that night until Kel was out of the house, out of earshot, before reopening the conversation with my husband.

"Bob, I can't grasp this. I thought we never kept anything from each other. I don't understand."

We sat on the plush, tan sofa by the fireplace in soft lamplight, turned toward each other, but not touching. On the sofa where we had so often snuggled together in the glow of the fire. The fireplace was now dark, in shadows.

Bob, hands clasped, sat on the edge of the cushions, head hanging down, looking at the tile floor between his feet. "I had hoped you could understand. I can see this really upsets you. Please believe me, I never intended to hurt you." He reached for my hand.

"But you have." I pulled back from him, tears spilling over. Part of me didn't want to hear another word from him, but another part quaked at what my imagination conjured up when I didn't know the truth.

His disclosure began. I was to learn more in many months of counseling ahead. That day, I began to wonder what I could believe from him after twenty years of dissembling.

It marked the beginning of doubts that continued for the rest of our marriage.

My voice rose. "I am upset. And terrified. I feel totally in the dark. What a trusting fool I've been!"

My words stung him. A red flush deepened his color. He slammed his palm down on the arm of the sofa, rattling me. "Shirley, I'd hoped you could accept this, but whether you do or not, I have the right to live my life as I wish."

His eyes were steely. Although he'd never turned it on me, I knew lots of pent-up anger rode just under the surface of this man who was turning into a stranger before my eyes. He was on a roll now, "And I never lied to you. I just didn't tell you everything. You know I'm not a liar."

I quickly got up from the sofa and strode into the kitchen, choking on the tide of molten anger I couldn't hold down. How could I have so misread him?

As I stood at the kitchen sink, a shudder passed through me. When we'd first met, I'd wondered if he really was as good as he seemed. Then I'd met Ben and decided Bob was the real thing, a good man, just like his dad. But Ben had a secret, too. I'd forgotten about it over the years. Until now.

In 1984, after his second wife, Millie, had died, my father-in-law spent lots of time with me. One day, not feeling well, he'd been resting on the couch and fell to reminiscing about his wife. He missed her, I knew, but the good-old days he recounted were only part of the story. They'd had their problems, too. I listened awhile, then asked him if he knew why.

He pushed his glasses up on his nose, looking at me with sad eyes. "Well, Shirley, Millie and I never lived together as husband and wife."

I felt my eyes pop open.

Ben glanced at me and sighed. "Yeah. On our wedding night, she sat on the bed to take off her stockings, and . . . well, . . . I just told her there wouldn't be any sex."

I looked at him in wonderment.

He swung his legs to the floor, and hung his head. "You know Bob's mom almost died when he was born. That's why he was an only child."

I'd heard that story from Bob and guessed she'd been injured giving birth, but Ben corrected me.

"No, it was because I never went near her again."

I was dumbfounded. He'd been that afraid he'd lose her? So afraid that he'd closed down at age thirty and never made love to his wife again?

When I told Bob the story, he said it was news to him. I'd forgotten about it over the years, but today it returned with a vengeance. I'd always thought Bob was just like his father . . . but both were men with long-standing, surprising secrets. Family secrets! Why? Why?

I slowly turned the faucet and watched the tumbler fill. My mind reeled at the new significance. After a long drink of water, I retraced my steps into the family room.

Bob sat on the edge of the sofa, hands clasped, looking at me, waiting. I lowered myself into the far corner across from him. He seemed calmer.

"Bob, I don't understand any of this. I need to talk to someone."

He shot me a glance, "A counselor?"

I nodded. Unable to read his reaction, I hesitated, knowing I needed to proceed with caution in this unknown territory.

He dropped his eyes back to the floor and sat silently for a long moment, then leaned back with a sigh. "I know you want me to come with you, and I will. But not now. First, I want to go away for awhile."

"Go away?" Another shock.

"Yeah, to California. I need to know how I really feel before I can do any counseling with you."

I was stunned again, my comfortable security with him suddenly and painfully dismembered.

Finally, I drew in a long breath. "Well, if you don't know how you feel, you need to find out!" I blew my nose and asked, "How long will you be gone?"

Bob stood up in the darkened room. "I'll take my vacation time, probably a month or so. I should be able to arrange things in the office tomorrow. I could probably drive out Tuesday morning."

Tuesday? The day after tomorrow? So soon? At the thought, some other delicate piece tore away inside me leaving a bloody gash. I turned away, wiping my wet face with the palms of my hands. My mind raced to stay ahead of an avalanche of questions. Where would he go? What would he do? When would he know how he felt about me and our marriage?

Finally, I asked, "What will we tell Kelly?"

Bob walked to look out the French doors. Moonlight reflected on the dark surface of the pool. "Oh, just that I'm taking a few days off, some time to myself, like a retreat. You know. We've both done things like that before . . ." His voice dwindled into vagueness.

As I looked at his silhouette against the French doors, I wondered if *he* would dwindle off into vagueness, out of my life never to be seen again. It was too much for me. I burst into tears and ran from the room, frightened and alone, to our bedroom and what was to be the first of many sleepless nights.

Once Bob took off for California, Kelly knew, in that unspoken way of his, that trouble was brewing. As I drove him to after-school basketball practice, he nailed me in the privacy of the car. "Mom, what's going on? Why are you so sad? And so mad at Dad?"

I'd been waiting for his question, practicing in my mind what I would say.

"Kel, Dad and I are having a problem right now. It has to do with us, not in any way with you. It's very hard, but we're working on it, and I think we'll be going to a counselor when he gets home."

Kelly turned to look out the side window, giving me his back. "Well, fix it." His words were short, cold, angry. Before I could bring the car to a complete stop at the gym, he had the door open and, swinging his gym bag out ahead of his long legs, jumped out, the door slamming behind him.

My heart ached as I watched him trot quickly across the

parking lot to the boys waiting. Damn Bob anyway. Because of him, I could lose the affection of my only son. Why? Why? I wheeled out of the lot, brushing away my angry tears.

Later that night, I sat at the kitchen table, lonely in the quiet house, pouring over the newspaper. I couldn't ignore the frightening question in my mind: What if Bob disappeared, never to return from California? I had to make some practical decisions. I moved the yellow marker down the column, "Help Wanted: Professional/Administrative," then pushed the paper away. It didn't make sense. I'd given up my good job after my trip to Medjugorje, filled with conviction about the direction that I needed to take. Now this. The nice little box that was my life had been thrown on the floor where it shattered into a million pieces. How would I ever put it together again? My trust in Bob was ruined. Maybe I couldn't trust God either. *Where are You now, God? Are You gone, too?* The question hung there in the emptiness of the cold kitchen. Maybe He was. I laid my head down on my arms and cried.

Gradually, a peaceful quietness came over me. In the welcomed calm, I wondered if I had somehow put Bob in the place reserved for God in my heart. If so, I hadn't realized it, hadn't meant to. It was a new thought. Then, gently, causing no ripple in the sea of calm, the words came to me: *God is close to the broken hearted, the crushed in spirit He saves.*[11]

Yes, God was close, after all, reaching out to me in this moment of peace. The words strengthened me. This was the only moment I had to face. It would always be so. The past was gone, and, with God's help, I knew I could trust the future. My life would unfold, one manageable moment at a time. I could handle that, even if Bob took all our money and disappeared into another life. I wiped my wet face, picked up the newspaper, and told myself I'd be all right. I'd begin again.

Bob did come back from California, and sooner than expected, but my trust had been dealt a blow. He'd kept so much from me for so long that I doubted I'd ever know his true story. Confused and afraid, I asked him to move out while we worked on our marriage. For eighteen grueling months, we tried to break our painful stalemate in counselors' offices. According to him, there was nothing wrong, and I was making a problem where there wasn't one. He wanted to go on as he had for twenty years and even invited me to enter the private sphere he'd carved out for himself.

But my heart was broken. My pain was compounded by keeping the reason for it to myself in hopes of controlling the damage that had been done, of perhaps rescuing the floundering marriage.

What Bob defined as private, I experienced as secretive concealment. What I'd thought was authentic in my life with him was painfully undercut by doubt. Now as I searched my memories for clues, the pieces gradually came together. I had had intimations, but they were subtle and I'd discounted their importance. There were the strange phone calls for him that he'd explain were for some "other Bob McCauley." And then there were the times I'd feel he was about to say something to me, but when I'd ask, he'd say, "No, there's nothing."

I'd thought we were close, but he'd chosen to keep a secret I didn't know was there. I was thrust into the anguishing question: Was my entire marriage based on illusion?

The months rolled on, through the fall, months of lonely separation. I went back to work at County, in my old department, glad to have a regular paycheck, and glad, too, for the busy days that helped me forget my pain. But my empty weekends were a struggle, and as fall turned to winter, I dreaded Christmas. I especially worried about Kelly's Christmas.

Then Mom called from Iowa. "Shirley, would you like me to come out for the holidays?"

I felt like she'd thrown me a life raft, but was it too much to ask? Although she'd been widowed the year before, she didn't need companionship. My two sisters and lots of step-kids lived near her. "I'm probably not very good company right now. . . ."

"Don't you worry about that, honey. I'll see if I can get a ticket."

I hung up, trying to remember the last time Mom had come to Arizona. Ray had been in detox. Was it 1984, six long years ago? I couldn't remember. Although I was now fifty-one, and she was a ripe seventy-five, I needed her. My life was in shambles.

Once under our roof, Mom promptly dispatched the heavy mood. She unpacked Christmas presents from her bulging suitcase, caught us up on family news, and trounced Kel and me at four hands of rummy. We were a constant threesome for days.

Finally one night, my son reluctantly tore himself away from us for a ballgame at school, leaving us to our own devices. We decided to set out on a private tour of Christmas lights around the city.

"Here, Mom." I handed her a folded newspaper with street routes carefully marked in red ink. "You read the map and I'll drive."

"With your sense of direction, it's a good thing we've got

a map." She took the newspaper with a laugh and climbed into the darkened car.

"Never mind. Just find some Christmas music on the radio, will you?"

She fumbled with the buttons for a minute, then switched on the interior light to check the map. "Oh-oh, I think you should have turned left back there at the last corner."

"Big help you are. At this rate, we're more likely to see the Christmas star than these neighborhood lights."

Mom didn't miss a beat. "Just be careful, young lady! I'm still your mother." I grinned. It felt like old times trading smart remarks with her. Who cared if the unfamiliar streets only occasionally rewarded us with a twinkling display of Santa on a red-tile roof? We had fun as we backtracked and circled in dark neighborhoods wondering if the newspaper addresses were wrong, if the homeowners had simply pulled the plug on their displays, or if we were on the wrong planet. Only after I nearly got stuck in a long, one-way, muddy lane next to a canal did we decide to call it a night. We were hilarious as I backed out through tumbleweed and desert grass in the dark. The laughter felt good after months of tears.

Once home, I soon had the fireplace roaring. We settled in to toast our cold toes and sip hot chocolate.

Mom looked at me thoughtfully. "So, honey, tell me what the problem is all about."

I hated to hold back from Mom, we'd always been so close. I'd had lots of phone calls from her over the months, but had kept silent despite my painful need for sympathy, hoping against hope that Bob and I could work things out. I desperately wanted to salvage my marriage. My entire life was on the line.

And I had to think of Kelly. He didn't know why we were in turmoil. His dad had insisted he not be told. If Bob's issue got back to him through some clumsy family gossip and I hadn't told him first, my son would lose trust in me. I never wanted that to happen.

"Mom, I just can't tell you. We're counseling, trying to work things out. It's better that I not go into it."

I could see she was mad. She set her cup down on the edge of the fireplace, looking at me.

I started to cry. "Oh, Mom. Please."

She closed her lips tightly and shook her head. "Why can't you tell your own mother? I've never understood . . . all those years . . . all that bliss. Is this something new or something that has been going on all the time? Bob doesn't drink. . . ."

I knew she was searching her own experience for something awful enough to tip over my marriage, the marriage she had just sarcastically called so blissful.

Mom, Mom, the voice inside me pleaded. *Don't! Don't tear anything down.*

I couldn't stop crying. My heart ached until I thought it truly was breaking. If only she would take the few steps to me, just hug me. I needed comfort and love. But she sat stiff and angry.

"Shirley, I still don't know why you can't tell me."

I'd never felt so alone in my life, never expected my mother would let me down. Through my tears, it gradually dawned on me that no comfort would come from her. The realization pulled the plug on my sorrow. It ebbed away like water swirling down a drain, leaving me empty. I blew my nose and sat up straight.

"Mom, I'm sorry. I'm trying to save my marriage, and I'm

thinking of Kelly. He doesn't know what's wrong either. Please try to understand."

The conversation ended as a standoff. Unable to penetrate the wall between us, we went to bed silent and exhausted.

Mom didn't phone often after her visit. Her withdrawal compounded my loneliness. First, I'd lost Bob, now I'd lost my mom. Her silence made me doubly grateful for a call from my sister, Jane.

"So, how are you, Shirley?" Her voice came through crackles on the long-distance line.

"Surviving, I guess. You know Bob and I are still separated?"

Her voice was soft. "Yes. It's so hard to believe."

Yes, it was hard to believe. My thoughts flashed to the last conversation I'd had with Bob the day he moved out. He'd said, avoiding my eyes, "It seems that the unthinkable has now become the inevitable."

I'd snapped back angrily, "Yeah, thanks for ruining the rest of my life!"

Jane's voice broke into my painful reverie. "Shirley, this must be so hard for you. You made so many changes, quitting your job to start counseling and to work in a jail."

She was right. When we'd returned from Medjugorje, I'd been so clear about being called to change my work, so sure my new life was on track.

Jane went on. "Do you remember when we were on the pilgrimage, you thought something would happen?"

I frowned, holding the phone a little closer. "No, what are you talking about?"

"Well, . . ." she spoke slowly as if choosing her words, "One day on the trip, you said you thought that Bob and

Kelly wouldn't be in your life much longer. Of course, with Kelly growing up, that didn't surprise you, but you didn't know what to make of the part about Bob." She waited a minute in silence, then gently asked, "Do you remember telling me that?"

A memory dimly stirred. Yes, I had said that. It gradually came back. I'd told Jane about my vague intuition. At the time, nothing was wrong between Bob and me, just the usual ups and downs of married life, and he was healthy. I hadn't understood where the strange notion had come from. "Huh! Do you suppose it was a prophetic flash of some kind?"

"I wouldn't doubt it. God has to have had a big hand in what's happened to you. It's been so out of your control."

Bleak as all the upheaval was, it certainly was out of my control. Maybe God did have a hand in this somehow, some way. Maybe in the big plan, the task that Bob and I came together to accomplish was complete. The thought helped.

But, I was lonely and so hurt. When I let myself think of marrying again, I doubted I could ever trust a man enough to open up, doubted I could ever take that risk again. From the start, I'd known Bob's revelation was healthy for him. The only problem was, I could no longer be his wife. I was too injured by the question of what our marriage meant to him. Our bond had been broken in one terrific blow, and I wasn't capable of bridging the gap to meet him as mate again. I knew, too, how tough it would be for me to ever replace Bob in my heart.

The same problems didn't seem to trouble him. Shortly after our divorce was final in December, he told me his plans to marry again. He was married on Valentine's Day.

By Easter our divorce was four months old. The April morning was golden and balmy as Kelly and I arrived at the

Casa. Although relieved to have the divorce over, my sadness hadn't lifted. I hoped celebrating the glorious Resurrection liturgy at church would help.

The choir's Alleluias started off cheerfully enough, but before Mass was half over, across the chapel Kelly and I saw the back of Bob's head, his new wife at his side. Unbearable grief rushed over me. I might have expected he'd bring her here to the place we had known as our spiritual home for years, but seeing him with the tall brunette was a shock. Her hair tumbled to her shoulders in the same style I'd worn for years. I felt like a small leaf carried away in swirling torrents to be lost in the deep, leaving no trace.

I grabbed my purse and, blinded by tears, pushed my way through the crowd to escape. Kelly followed.

I'd tried so hard to protect my son from my pain, knowing he had his own, but I just couldn't hold it in any more. Once outside the chapel, I burst into sobs. He hugged me tightly murmuring, "It's ok, Mom. It's ok. We've still got each other."

After our Easter dinner together, Kelly left to spend a few hours with friends.

I rattled around in the empty house, trying to read, to do a few pieces of ironing. But as the interminable day wore on, I couldn't shake off my heavy loneliness. The deepest place in me ached as a painful refrain repeated again and again: *How will I survive my broken heart, my lonely life?* By evening, my sorrow was so overwhelming, I couldn't find words for it.

Nowhere else to turn, I sank down in front of the altar in my bedroom and my treasured icon of Christ. The gentle face before me rippled through my tears. Kneeling there in the darkness, all I could pray was, *Help, help.* Over and over, *Help, help.* Eyes sore and swollen from a day of crying, I closed them and prayed my nearly wordless prayer again, asking for help I was powerless to describe. Utterly alone, abandoned, and helpless, I truly felt there was nowhere else to turn.

Finally, with effort, I lifted my heavy eyelids. The small candle on my altar flickered in the dark room, then steadied. In its light, the icon seemed to change. I rubbed my tired eyes and looked again. The icon changed again. I blinked and squinted. As I studied what had been the face of Jesus, the features shifted again. It was as though many faces were being slowly projected onto the painting, one after another. First, a young face, then an old one. A female face, then a male. Asian faces. Spanish faces. Black faces. Brown faces. Some from other centuries. I rubbed my eyes again, but the faces continued to flash before me. Dozens of faces.

I closed my burning eyes, breathing in the stillness. Out of a profound quiet, the words came: *You can never be alone. I am always with you.* In the gentle silence, a peaceful presence radiated from the icon, comforting me in a way I didn't understand. When I finally looked again, the face of Jesus, suffused with light, gazed at me with love and healing.

My grief at the loss of the man who had meant everything to me slowly faded into gratitude. In that moment of prayer, a powerful healing began. My heart knew that the gentle Christ was with me, present in each one I would ever meet. I had God's promise, for this moment and always. I could never be alone.

Over the days and weeks that followed, hope returned, little by little. Like any wife who has felt betrayed, it took time, and I needed to understand. What had really happened to Bob and me, to our marriage seemingly made in heaven?

I'd studied spirituality for years, but not marriage, not intimacy. How did it all fit together? I needed to know what was healthy and what was blighted. I plunged into study, finding books and training. In a year's time, I'd tracked down the leaders in the field: Ellen Bader, Lonnie Barbach, Patrick Carnes, Fran Ferder, John Heagle, Harville Hendricks, Harriet Lerner, Roz Meadow, David Schnarch, and Joan Timmerman. I gradually found the answers I needed, and as I did my inner work, it began to spill into the outside world. I became expert in couples communication, conflict resolution, and especially the challenges of integrating spirituality and intimacy.

Although I was still working all week at yet another agency, on weekends I offered retreats on sexuality and spirituality. "With God, become makers of love," I invited. I had lots to say and many of my clients, needing the input, responded. It was healing all the way around. I definitely was teaching what I needed to learn, from my heart and gut.

The retreats were a huge success, but I was so busy. The weekend retreat work added another set of tasks and commitments on top of my forty-hour a week job and my small private practice.

What I hadn't counted on was the tremendous inner urging the retreats stirred up in me. I wanted with all my heart to spend more time on this healing work and to return to my practice full time. I'd never intended to let it go in the first place, but when the crisis with Bob hit, I thought I had little choice. Now, two years after the divorce, the old urge returned stronger than ever.

I took up the subject with my spiritual director. In the early seventies, I'd studied the Spanish mystics, Teresa of Avila and John of the Cross, with the kindly Carmelite and treasured the chances I'd had over the years to tell him what God was up to in my life.

Letting go of my day job became a topic of debate with Father Ernie. He wanted practical mysticism and urged me not to be rash. "Hang on to your salary and benefits, Shirley." I didn't like the advice, but I did share his anxiety. Despite the insistent feelings I had about retreats and counseling, I decided to wait, to watch for circumstances to develop.

Finally, one day, after a series of crises at the agency, I was frustrated. I'd been grappling for months with a tough project and wasn't sure the boss was behind me, so I asked. He was honest enough to tell me he wasn't. Despite fear and trepidation, I submitted my resignation. I recognized divine timing. I could leave. At last, it was time.

Then, I dreamed for a second time the old dream I'd had that day of crisis at the cabin. It picked up where the first one left off. I was home in my everyday house, still unable to get into the treasure-filled mansion, but this time, I didn't wake up frustrated. Instead, in the dream, I ascend a flight of stairs, stopping at a mirror on a door. I study my reflection for a moment, then walk through it effortlessly, finding myself in the heart of the mansion, finally among the treasures.

I understood. By reexamining the amazing complexities I'd lived with for a lifetime, I found the entryway and passed through to the spacious mansion and its abundant treasures. Looking at myself was the answer, not allowing myself to be confused and blocked in the darkness. Looking at myself was the way to the treasure within, and curiously, my reflection showed me the preciousness of *who I am* in my true identity!

My heart sang with joy as I awakened. I hadn't known I had so many elegant gifts yet to explore!

8

You Made Me Love You

A NEW SONG

Do you give us each other?
(No better partner for the pulsing music,
for the dance on risky freedom's edge.)

I discover love bounding in me,
Unconditional, unguarded, free.
Big enough to fluster fear,
Strong enough to give and be given (kindly),
Grateful only to pirouette
And bow
And be applauded
And received (at once fierce and grateful).

If this robust love frightens you,
I will hold it in the golden silence of my heart
Where it leaps and dances
And loudly sings, untamed.

The first time I heard Jerry's voice, I was sitting in my bedroom easy chair, bare legs propped up on the bed, trying to stay cool under the overhead fan. We'd played a little game of telephone tag that week after my ad appeared in the singles paper: "Professional woman, looks, brains, personality, spiritual and earthy (yes, they do go together, Harold!) seeks emotionally and physically healthy male 45-61, also spiritual, interested in dancing, movies, books, theatre, art, music, hiking, and committed relationship. No smoking, please. Light drinker ok."

By July of 1994, I'd been divorced a year and a half and was learning to be single, at fifty-five, after twenty years of marriage. I'd tried my luck at a few singles dances, nervously remembering I'd met Bob at a singles dance. This time, I crossed paths with engineers, retired military officers, and computer types, many obviously playing a game of professional single with no intention to commit. I quickly decided odds of meeting a compatible man would be greater if my minimum requirements were clear at the get-go. Singles ads were a viable alternative.

I balanced a yellow pad on my knees, cradling the phone to my ear as I took notes. I'd had some blows to my self-trust, thanks to Bob, but I could still size a guy up.

"So, you're a retired dentist?" I inquired.

A deep, smooth voice filled my ear. "Actually, I had to give up my practice. Eye injury. Yeah, racquetball accident." Before I could sympathize, he continued. "Can't really practice dentistry by Braille." A light chuckle punctuated his retort.

So, he wasn't yet retired. Likely this one was younger, then, than sixty-five.

My pencil moved across the page: dentist, humor, resiliency.

He had more to say, "I've been in Arizona about ten years, but my practice was in Michigan."

Memories of Northville flashed across my mind. Maybe we knew the same people. Maybe he'd gone to school in Michigan.

"Actually, my practice was in Bloomfield Hills, but I went to school in DC, Georgetown." He went on without prompting.

This one was eager to talk, to fill in details and sell himself to me, a good sign. I listened, continuing to scratch a few words on the pad: Georgetown, big name school. Catholic, too?

"Oh, yes, Georgetown is a Jesuit school. I went to prep and right on through. High school was all boys, of course. My sisters went to Immaculata Academy."

I knew what Jerry Smith was about, sight unseen. Georgetown Prep in the fifties was a school like Campion in my hometown. In another world from today's freak dancing, it was a school where watchful Jesuits chaperoned the dance floor, routinely disentangling teen couples too snugly wrapped around each other, slow dancing to "Love Me Tender." Jerry would be smart, mannerly, used to academic discipline, and I'd probably love his sisters. We'd have stories to swap about suspicious nuns checking our hemlines and commandeering sheet music like "I Get Ideas" from our lockers.

The last note on my yellow pad: "Catholic."

"So, when can we meet?" he sounded eager.

I hesitated. In the ritual of singledom, I had stayed to the cautious end of the continuum, limiting contact to phone chats only I could initiate until I was very sure the unknown stranger on the end of the line was not an axe-murderer, or worse.

"Well, where do you live?"

"Near Scottsdale and Shea. I just sold my house on Gold Dust. I'm in an apartment now."

Gold Dust? Wasn't that my friend Sue's old address?

"Sue?" His voice sounded incredulous. "Sue Joyce? Do you know her? I bought my place from her when I moved to Scottsdale."

Now it was my turn to be incredulous. Sue and Jack had reported each step of their real estate deal to us as it went through offers, escrow, and closing. The buyer had been a dentist from Michigan.

"Nice folks," Sue had said.

My mind was made up. "I can meet you for brunch in an hour. How about the Hearty Hen?"

He sounded surprised and pleased at the quick turn of events. "I'll be there. I look kinda like Santa Claus, beard, big guy . . ."

I recognized him right away, though he was dressed in blue denim and not red velvet that hot Sunday morning in July. As I approached the table, he stood up, sticking out his hand. Mine was tiny in his large paw. Next to his ample six-foot frame, I felt fragile, but somehow safe.

As the waitress placed steaming plates of bacon and eggs on the table, I reached for his large hand again. "Let's say grace."

Afterwards, dropping a napkin to his lap, he glanced at me approvingly. "You have a lot of self-confidence."

I looked up, wondering what he meant.

"Well, saying grace like that. You know who you are, and you're comfortable with it."

This guy was reading me! What I was like was none of his business until I got good and ready to let him know. I shifted in my chair, slightly unnerved, hoping to look nonchalant as I salted my eggs. "Well, I usually say a blessing, and I knew you were Catholic. So tell me a little about yourself."

The big man across the table carefully loaded his fork with eggs and chewed thoughtfully for a minute. "Ok. I came to Arizona in the mid-eighties. Had several different businesses: restaurants, a manufacturer's rep company, different stuff. Before that, I began my career as a dentist. I was young, in the Navy. Then, I went into the reserves and started to practice in Michigan."

It turned out at sixty-two, he was a bit older than the age I'd specified in my ad. I listened carefully for signs of evasion as he told his story. He'd been married twice, not once.

"Yeah, that had major repercussions on my finances."

It was too soon for any questions about that, but I appreciated his directness, and I understood. Finances had been a worry for me, too. Giving up a regular paycheck to start my private counseling practice was quite a leap after a two-paycheck marriage.

Jerry shook his head in wonderment. "You have even more confidence than I thought at first." He leaned across the table, smiling at me. "Shirley, has anyone ever told you that you have a great inner beauty? I can see your soul in your eyes."

I felt my cheeks flush. What was I supposed to say to that over scrambled eggs on Sunday morning, in full daylight, and the first meeting, to boot? But behind his heavy lenses, Jerry's eyes were serious. If this was Irish malarkey, he had the poker face for it. While I was still searching for an answer, he sat back, folded his napkin, and changed the subject.

"Let's see. What else? Well, the Smith family is full of

heart trouble. Both parents, my brother, and my sister. I'm ok, but I should lose some weight."

I grinned at him. I could spare a few pounds, too. He seemed to be leveling with me.

"Since you're Catholic, you're probably wondering if my marriage has been annulled." Another quick turn. And he was right. It did matter to me whether he was free to marry in good standing as a Catholic. I was.

"To tell you the truth, Shirley, the marriage hasn't been annulled, and I've felt like a leper since my divorce. Attitudes were pretty negative back then." A flicker of sadness passed over his face. I knew what he meant.

In the years following the Vatican Council, harsh judgment toward those with broken marriages was by no means in short supply. Fortunately, since then, the Church had instituted diocesan tribunals for couples seeking annulments. I'd taken advantage of the process and found as I worked through the months-long exercise of examining my marriage and its subsequent collapse, that my vows had been seriously undercut. According to church law, to enter a binding marriage, one must have full knowledge and make a free choice. I didn't have an important piece of information, and I didn't even know it. I'd wondered when I met Bob if he was too good to be true. I was skittish, refusing his attentions until I knew he was about to leave the priesthood. If I'd known about the secret that began years before I met him, I certainly would have run.

Jerry was listening closely. "I've heard some horror stories about annulments," he said.

I'd heard the stories, too, but that hadn't been my experience. I meant every word of my marriage vows, and intended to honor every promise I'd ever made before God.

The annulment helped me to resolve the pain and confusion of the horrific rupture that was never supposed to happen in my life.

I'd forgotten the conversation until a few weeks later. Jer called unexpectedly in the middle of the day, his voice excited. "Shirley, I've got some great news. My ex-wife has filed for an annulment."

I was glad for my new friend. I knew he wanted that. He'd told me he'd been going to Mass regularly despite the legalities. And, although I was still wary, the synchronicity of Jerry's annulment was not lost on me. Faith had been the mainstay of my life, always, especially during the turmoil of my split with Bob. Then, I'd felt my life was shattered. Now, I had to wonder if an unseen hand was at work picking up a couple of those splinters.

"Here's your chance to get things straightened out with the Church," I said.

He chuckled. "Yeah, this could be the start of something big. Hey, I'm taking off work early. Wanna catch a matinee?"

I glanced at my daybook. Why not? My last client had just left. I told him to pick me up in an hour. As I hurried home, the overcast sky released a few sprinkles onto my windshield.

When I heard Jer's car in the driveway, I was waiting. I swung open the kitchen door ready to run out, then stopped in my tracks. Jer didn't look well. He climbed out of the driver's seat, face as gray as the sky, extending his car keys to me.

"Sorry, Shirl, but I don't think I'm up for a movie, after all. Not sure I should even drive. Having some kinda spell. Would you mind taking me to a doctor at the Air Force Base?"

An anxious tingle shot through me. I reached to the

kitchen counter for my purse, pulling the door shut after me. "Sure. Jump in."

I nervously watched him as I headed off into the cross-town traffic.

He was full of explanations. "I want to be a big, macho guy, and I'm embarrassed to let you know I'm not. Dunno what's going on with my heart."

"Have you been to Luke before?"

"Oh, yeah. I have a doctor out there. . . ."

He sounded short of breath. I was confused but murmured something, wanting to reassure him.

I caught mostly green lights, and soon we were at Luke. I'd never been on a military base before. All the buildings looked the same to me, boxy institutional structures as gray as the day, but Jerry obviously knew his way around.

"Turn left. That's the clinic next to the hospital."

I parked in a space marked, "Visiting Retired Personnel," and followed him in to a portable building identified as Health Services.

The uniformed orderly on duty signed him in. "Right this way, Commander Smith."

They disappeared down the hall into an examination room leaving me alone in a long, narrow waiting area. Sitting on the lumpy beige leatherette sofa, I flipped through dog-eared copies of *National Geographic* and *Woman's Day*. I couldn't get his family's unhappy history of heart trouble out of my mind.

The orderly returned. "Commander Smith would like you to come to the exam room, Ma'am." Before I could ask how Jerry was, he turned smartly on his heel, expecting me to follow.

Once in the room, I found Jer stretched out on a table,

shirt off, tethered to monitors. His gray color scared me. Maybe he hadn't been taking care of himself so well after all.

A slender doctor bent over a machine straightened up to greet me with the courtesy of an officer and a gentleman, but then quickly returned to the squiggly printout in his hand. After a minute's scrutiny, he made some comments in medical terms that Jerry seemed to understand. I hoped it wasn't bad news.

He went on. "This looks pretty good, sir. I'll give you a copy to take to your cardiologist tomorrow. He can decide what tests you need. Looks like a little blip," the doctor nodded at me, "but it's best to be safe and get things checked out. You can get out of here now."

Jerry promptly pulled the monitors off his chest, and swung his legs off the table. "Glad to hear it. I'll follow up."

His bravado didn't fool me. I saw how slowly he moved.

He gamely grinned at me. "Can you reach my shirt?"

On the way home, Jer snoozed in the passenger seat at my side as the memory of him tethered to monitors, gray-faced and wheezing, replayed in my mind. Just how serious was his heart condition anyway?

As if reading my anxious thoughts, he asked, "Are you worrying, Shirley?"

Slowing for a light, I glanced at him and our eyes met. "Well, truth is, I *am* worried." Nothing shifted in his face, so I went on. "Your health problems scare me."

"I don't expect to be sick." He turned to look out his window, but not before I'd seen a small line appear between his brows. He repeated himself. "I don't expect to be sick. I'll follow up with the doctor."

I hoped so. The episode at Luke was unnerving.

As the months passed with no more heart scares, my worry slowly subsided. He was as good as his word in following doctor's orders, and he did seem better. Meantime, I discovered much about the new man in my life that pleased me. For one thing, he cooked. The end of a long workday often found me at his apartment watching as he fixed a tasty chop and wok dinner. Nobody else had cooked for me since my mother.

One balmy night after a feast of shrimp, snow peas, and rice, we decided to top it off with lattes at our neighborhood coffee shop. On the way, we passed a jewelry store. Jer pulled me to the window, pointing to a diamond on display. "What do you think?" A large, princess cut stone mounted in gold sparkled against black velvet.

I was dazzled! "Not bad! I do want a rock this time. You read my mind."

Jer and I had been circling each other at ever-closer range for about a year now, and my birthday was coming. By then, I'd certainly have settled my last niggling doubt, so I thought. But before I knew it—special occasions be damned—the ring was mine. Well, I thought, he was a bit impulsive, but the guy loved me. How much proof did I need?

The next night, I sat perched at his kitchen counter watching the light sparkle on my diamond, while Jer, apron wrapped around his generous middle, worked at the cutting board. Eyeing me as he scraped a handful of chestnuts into the wok, he smiled. "So, Shirley. Tell me something."

"What?"

He piled some mushrooms into a dish. "I know you love your ring—and I loved giving it to you—but I have to say, I'm a little mystified."

I looked from the diamond to his face. "Why?"

"Well, you seem so uninterested in trappings, and you are the original generic shopper."

I laughed, recalling a recent grocery store debate we'd had about the virtues of Grey Poupon compared to the store brand of mustard.

He chuckled, too. "The rock doesn't seem to fit with that. Must be something I've missed." He turned to rummage in the refrigerator. "You're indifferent to big cars . . ." He straightened up, bag of sprouts in hand, to look at me questioningly. "I could guess what the rock is about, but I'd only be guessing."

I spun around on the counter stool, reaching for my glass of ice water. Could I freeze the hot tears rising in my throat?

Seeing my turmoil, he reached across the counter, "And don't get me wrong," he tapped my wrist for emphasis. "It's not about the cost. I'm just curious."

His innocent question had reopened the old wound of the break-up with Bob, the old pain. I'd needed this beautiful stone to reassure myself I was loveable for the woman I was, just for myself, but I'd never explained. Of course, he'd wonder why I wanted a ring that plummeted his bank account into red zeros.

"Jerry," I swirled the ice cubes in the cold tumbler, "I hope you can understand this. The ring . . ." tears rose in my throat.

He turned, leaning his elbows on the counter, wooden spoon in hand, face intent.

I struggled with the unexpected rawness of my old doubts. Had I ever been loved in all the years of my marriage? Or had I only stood for something in Bob's mind?

I started again. "The ring is about me. Somehow, it tells

me that you want to adorn me as your woman, that you celebrate me as a woman. I can't tell you how much that means to me."

Jerry's quizzical expression faded into softness. He looked at me silently for a moment, then nodded. "I guessed right, then. And I do love you as the beautiful woman you are."

Stepping around the counter into his arms, I knew he understood the blow my femininity had taken. He understood. That was all that mattered.

Next day, over lunch with Bonnie, the night before was still fresh in my mind. Warm, Arizona sunshine streamed onto our table brightened by fresh, white carnations and greenery. It glinted on my ring. She leaned over, a broad smile starting in her gray-green eyes. "What's this? What's this?"

Heat rose in my face. "Yes, yes. I'm engaged, Bonnie, and to a very sweet guy. Jerry. You haven't met him yet."

She settled back into her chair, still obviously surprised. "How about that! Well! You deserve a sweet guy. And what a ring!" Then she leaned toward me again, hunching over the table on her elbows, eager for romantic tales from another "fifty-something."

"Tell me more. I'm dying to know!"

I suddenly felt like a fifteen-year-old. Why couldn't I talk to this good friend without blushing? I wondered. "Well, he's kind, funny, caring, and guess what? A good cook!"

"My God, a miracle. There must be *something* wrong with this guy."

I hesitated. Her husband, Jim, had been disabled with MS for most of the twenty-five years I'd known the two of them. Would it be painful for her to hear about Jerry's health? Her eager smile told me I could be honest.

"He's a great guy, but I'm worried about one thing, his heart. He's having some tests. You've lived with Jim's illness for a long time, Bonnie, and I know that hasn't been easy. . . ." My voice drifted off as she looked out the window for a long moment. I respected this strong woman, my friend. I waited, watching her face.

When she turned back to me, her gaze was clear. "You must be wondering what to do."

"I am. The ring was a surprise, I have to admit. I wasn't completely ready. If I were twenty or thirty, I wouldn't even want to deal with the health issue, but at fifty-plus, most of us have some problems. How important do you think is it?"

Bonnie reached across the table for my hand, her smile a thin curve. "Nothing to do with Jerry. I haven't even met him, but it can be difficult, Shirl. I was so crazy in love with Jim, I'd have married him no matter what. But it can be difficult."

A cold, empty feeling spread across my mid-section. Well, I'd wanted to know.

I lay awake that night, seeing Bonnie's concerned face in the restaurant, her words echoing in my mind. Coldness rushed over me again. Pulling the blanket over my shoulders, I curled up, hugging my legs, and questioned myself. Did I love Jer enough? Could I handle this?

A few days later, Jerry called my office, surprising me in the middle of the afternoon. "Shirl, I'm at the hospital. The doctor did an angiogram . . ." He took short breaths between words as he spoke. "And now, he won't release me."

The receiver felt heavy in my hand.

"He says I need treatment right now. I don't know if that means surgery."

I hadn't expected this. My insides were shaking. I heard

myself speak as if over the roar of a high sea. "I'll be there as soon as I can."

I raced across town to the hospital, grateful to be ahead of the rush hour traffic. A tall, blonde nurse ushered me into a waiting area. "Dr. Smith's in the operating room right now. His cardiologist will be in to talk with you in a few minutes."

Operating room? Was this an emergency? Her smile didn't calm the black tide rolling over me. "Can you tell me what's going on?"

"Mrs. Smith—"

"No, please! I'm Shirley Cunningham. We aren't married."

Jer and I were usually amused when strangers guessed from our gray hair that we'd been a couple for thirty years, but at that moment, it didn't strike me as funny. I bit my lip, wondering if I'd ever marry this man with the unstable heart, now apparently in crisis.

The nurse's surprise changed to sympathy.

"I'm sorry, this has to be tough for you, but to answer your question, the surgeon is placing a stent in Dr. Smith's heart." I was bewildered. What was a stent?

"You've heard of balloon angioplasty?" She watched my quick nod. "The stent is a new technology that works like angioplasty. It's a little tube that holds the blocked vessel open."

Strength suddenly drained from my legs. I sat down heavily in the nearest chair. My heart raced. This was just what I was afraid of.

Somehow I got through the worst of it, and in a few days, he stabilized. The day he was able to return home, I stocked his apartment with milk and bread and fed him chicken soup. By evening, when I was sure he was resting, I called Bonnie.

"Jerry's out of the hospital, but his car's still at the hospital.

I need to pick it up—" Before I could ask for help, she said she'd be waiting for me.

Although it was nine o'clock, the temperature was still 100 degrees when I pulled into Bonnie's driveway. Grateful for her willingness to step into the hot desert night and my troubles, I slanted the air conditioning vent her direction. "Hey, friend. Thanks for helping me out." The words caught in my throat. I hadn't talked about the storm inside me all these days, not since I'd sped to the hospital to find Jerry in surgery.

"We aren't even married yet, and I don't know if I can cope. . . ." My voice faded as the truth of what I'd just said dropped down into me.

The flickering dashboard lights reflected on Bonnie's worried face. "What does the doctor say about Jerry's condition?"

In the darkness of the car, my voice was a long drone as I recounted the story I'd given Jerry's kids, my family, and friends. "That the stent will help him. He avoided open-heart surgery with it. Scares the hell out of me, though."

She reached across the gearshift and rubbed my shoulder. Bonnie, long a caregiver, was reflective. "How old is Jerry? Sixty-something? Probably most men you'd meet would have health problems. So many have heart trouble."

I appreciated her realism. She knew I wanted to marry and heal, but my doubts were huge and circling like birds of prey.

Later, alone at home near midnight, I couldn't sleep. Questions flapped their ominous black wings in my head: Would any man I met need my care? Could I never resign the unwanted role of caregiver I'd had all my life? Would I never be taken care of, always be alone and scared? The black wings flapped on, reminding me that my work was solitary, that I had few relatives, that I was getting older, that life ahead would be harder, not easier, that my own health could fail as I worried about Jerry's.

I wasn't at all sure I could marry him. I had to talk things over with him, and soon.

The chance came a few days later. Jerry's cardiologist had urged him to walk, and I was eager to lend my support. We meandered through Scottsdale's green strip, an oasis created for desert flood control that extended through what had once been a horse ranch, but now was called McCormick Park.

Rounding a bend, I spotted a picnic table. Late afternoon sun slanted through the palo verdes surrounding it, creating lacy patterns in the shade. We sat under the graceful fronds where the air was cooler.

My stomach churned as I rehearsed what I wanted to say to Jerry.

As usual, his antenna was up. "You seem quiet today."

Early on, Jer's alertness to my moods had felt like an intrusion. Today, I was glad for the opener.

"You're worried about me, huh?" His eyes met mine.

I nodded.

He wiped the sweat from his forehead on his sleeve. "Not much I can do about it. I feel pretty good today."

It was now or never. I didn't want to lose Jer, but I doubted I could live with the hard reality of his bad heart. "Well, I'm glad this is a good day. But I don't know if I can cope. I'm not a good nurse."

When Kelly was little, he had asthma. First I'd be sick right with him, then worried, then impatient for him to snap out of it, then mad at myself for not being Florence Nightingale. Jer knew it; I'd told him all that before.

He took off his glasses, polishing each lens with his

shirttail. In the afternoon light, little lines of fatigue beneath his eyes, usually hidden by the heavy frames, looked deeper than I'd noticed before. He turned away from me, squinting through the lenses, checking for smudges. "I don't expect to be sick. You don't have to be my nurse."

My stomach tightened. A little cramp was starting high under the ribs on my left side. Was I making a mistake? Did I care enough about him to deal with his health problems? I didn't know. The questions unnerved me.

"Jer, I don't know how I feel about our relationship right now."

He leaned toward me, elbows on the table. Was it the afternoon light or was he pale? What if the stress of this conversation was bad for his heart? The cramp in my side turned into a painful spasm.

"Shirley, you've got to be sure." His face was earnest.

"I know." I looked down at the ring sparkling in the late afternoon sun.

He reached for my hand. "Don't even *think* about taking off the ring, please. I love you and it's yours, no matter what."

What could I say? He was a good, generous man, but I still had my doubts. I disengaged my hand from his. "I'd like a break for a while."

He sighed, keeping eye contact with me as he took a swig from the water bottle we'd shared. "How long a break are we talking about here?"

I couldn't look at him. I had too many mixed feelings, and just needed to get this over. "I really don't know. Please, give me some time."

And so the hesitation began.

I buried myself in work. The troubles of my clients made my own look small by comparison. I was doing fine. My love life might be a mess, but my work was right on track. That was important to me, very important.

Late one Friday night, I sat at my desk in the dim light of the den, sipping from my ever-present cup of coffee. The week's work was finally over. The weekend stretched out ahead of me, empty, as empty as the silent house.

I turned the mug in my hand, absent-mindedly eyeing the logo: *Workaholics Anonymous*. It came from my old boss, one of a long line of slave drivers I'd worked for, so I once thought. But now I'd learned better. My private practice had taught me who the real slave driver was. Yeah, work—the great anesthetic—I knew all about it.

Finally, the house was utterly still. I had no place to go. Nothing to do.

I eased my weary body up from the desk and into a big, soft lazyboy, usually reserved for clients. Curling up, I closed my burning eyes, noticing the ache in my back and shoulders. Jerry could always give such a good shoulder rub.

Suddenly, sadness washed over me, spilling into tears. I missed him, his sweetness, his concern. I missed him holding me in the night. All he ever wanted to do was love me.

I shook myself. Where was all this coming from? Hadn't I been doing fine without him?

Aggravated, I grabbed my cold coffee and walked into the living room. In the dim light, I bumped the coffee table, sending my precious dried rose bouquet flying in every direction. Unable to part with those flowers, I'd watched them fade into fragile vestiges of the once-magnificent rosebuds Jerry had given me over the months. Now I felt I could never part with Jerry, but I quickly bounced into my old doubts. Another man I'd dated, a diabetic, told me with an edge in his voice that I was indeed a "perfect specimen." Maybe it was too much to hope for a man whose health was as good as mine. Maybe I should marry Jer after all. Did I want to?

Wearily, I watched my thoughts double back over the same, tired questions. Finally, I told myself, *Just go to bed, sink into oblivion, just sleep your way past this tangle of doubts.* Sighing a long sigh, I turned away from the rose petals spilled there on the floor, red as blood.

Thanksgiving morning was brisk but glorious, sunny under a relentlessly blue sky. I'd just returned from church, purse and car keys still clutched in my hand, when the doorbell rang.

The florist's deliveryman smiled at me over two-dozen fragrant tea roses.

I stood in the doorway, watching his departing back, the calmness of my morning shattered by bittersweet pain. Hugging the flowers, I fumbled to open the card scribbled in Jerry's handwriting: *"Love is like a prayer. God will not ignore it."* The words blurred through my tears.

I closed the door, cradling the tightly furled buds gently in my arms. In the kitchen, I slowly unwrapped their tender stems and began placing them one by one into the crystal vase that had held so many of Jerry's flowers. Was love like a prayer? My heart warmed at the thought.

Kicking off my pumps, I walked stocking-footed on cool tile to the bedroom, carrying the precious flowers to a place on the dresser. Their beauty dazzled me for a moment as the rosebuds doubled in the mirror.

I suddenly wanted to see my ring. Careful not to jostle

the bouquet, I slowly eased the big middle drawer of the dresser halfway out to grope through my silky lingerie. Then, I felt the plush ring box. A tingle went through me. My ring! As I snapped the little box open, a ray of November sun danced across the diamond Jerry had been so eager to give me.

I slipped it on my finger. It rested there, an old friend come home. Silently, I welcomed its weight and whatever it might represent. I missed Jerry. I didn't want to, but I did. I missed his patience, his solicitude, his falling in love so fast and so hard. Hadn't he taken good care of me, watching over me with an off-handed Irish charm that I'd loved? I missed his easy smile, his dimples, his beard, the physicality of his big-ness, his warm hands, the chemistry between us.

I wiped my bleary eyes and slid into the bedroom chair, propping my journal on my knees. A warm feeling washed over me as I wrote *"Thanksgiving 1996"* on the empty page.

"I'm thankful for Jerry. He's part of the big plan for my life. His love is an invitation I can choose to accept. It's really a free choice I can make; to give and receive love every day."

I underlined the word, <u>choose</u>, then chewed on my pen. In my vacillation, had I been trying to protect myself from what might happen in Jerry's life, even from life itself? Could I really leave my fears and doubts behind? I wanted to. I wanted to believe I could.

A surge of energy seemed to flow through me as I put pen to paper again. *"How can I go wrong by choosing love? If I make that choice, won't God give me the strength to face whatever might happen? Sure, I'm not ready now, but if I go along, step by step, day by day, God will give me all I need when I need it."*

I sat back, closing my eyes in the silence. I knew I'd found the guidance I'd sought. There was no need to be frightened. The answer was trust. I could trust that Jerry had been given to me for his healing, yes, and for mine. I could accept him and choose to begin a new life.

My journal page was filled. I read the scrawled handwriting, amazed. Maybe now I was finally ready to learn how to really love.

I uncurled myself, stretched and padded to my desk in the den in search of stationery. On a sheet emblazoned with roses, I wrote:

"Jerry, Thanks for the beautiful roses. I knew I'd missed you, but I was surprised at the flood of feeling that came in the door with those flowers this morning. And, you're right. Love is like a prayer; God will not ignore it. Your love and God are definitely in my face right now.

I'm wearing your ring as I write this. I finally know I care desperately that you have a heart of love for me. How can I thank you for your beautiful invitation to love and be loved? I finally understand what it is to choose to do just that."

I stopped to wipe away my tears, hoping it wasn't too late for another chance.

"The most sincere hope of my heart is that you have not run out of patience with me. Please, Jerry, I want you back. I'm thinking of dancing with you. . . ."

The night of our wedding, tears glistened in Jerry's eyes as he led me to the dance floor. Our guests watched, anticipating our first swirl across the floor as husband and wife. But I signaled the musician. There were a few words to say first. All eyes were on me as I took the mike.

"I guess every last one of you wondered if I'd ever marry Jerry, I'd broken up with him so many times."

Jerry's son-in-law Dave clapped and called out, "That's for sure!"

"Well, this song is my explanation." Blushing, I cued the piano player, and opening my arms wide, belted out the old familiar hit from the forties: "You made me love you. I didn't want to do it . . ."[12]

Jerry's eyes were soft. I hugged my new husband as laughter and applause drowned out my last notes. The song said it all! After so many fits and starts, I was still dazed by the miracle of this wedding.

I'd entered the chapel on his arm, surprised at my own nervousness. Once there, in the soft candlelight, Jer stood waiting for me to speak, his face lit from within.

I'd written my vows with complete composure and calm, but when my eyes met his, tremors shook me. Our guests rustled a bit, then quieted until I found my voice.

"Jerry, I promise from this day forward, our lives will be spent together. I will be faithful to you and promise to always stand at your side in good times, and in difficult times. I promise to laugh with you, and to take a light view of our lives and our troubles."

My voice had trembled then, in the first of many pauses and hesitations. A vow to take trouble lightly? My heart knew well only God could have brought me to that promise.

Jerry, holding my hands, dropped his eyes to blink away a tear.

"I promise not to take myself too seriously, and I give you permission to tease me."

A gentle wave of laughter moved through the chapel. I

was sure our families and friends could easily imagine how much divine assistance I'd needed to lighten up from the fears that had almost kept me from the joy of this moment.

Looking into the circle of smiling faces gathered around us, my eyes brimmed with tears. Kelly quietly handed me a Kleenex. I took a deep breath, and despite my fluttering heart, spoke my final blessing to Jerry.

"Thank you for giving me the opportunity to choose to love. Thank you for inviting me to love you. Your love is a gift that teaches me a little more each day about the God who has so elegantly drawn our lives together. May the Holy One who holds us both, and to Whom we belong, bless you through me as we walk into the future together."

Those were the words. They had come right from my heart. I had really done it!

Now it was time to dance!

9

On New and Labyrinthine Ways

THE BLACK MADONNA

Woman of the garden,
You are black and you are beautiful.
The one the lover sings among the lilies.
The one enveloped by night under the stars,
The moon at your feet,
The aurora borealis your mantle.
You are mystery,
Coming from the deep, returning to eternity.
Regal, yet simple, of the people.
Close as earth,
Musky as a lover's breath in the darkness,
You hold me.
In the sightless dark, I awake in your embrace.
Living and moving safely in You,
Rocked in your womb,
You nourish me, guide me,
Without seeing or knowing,
Enfolding me in your warmth,
Like dark and fragrant earth.

You are my mother.

Airborne at last! The city of Phoenix quickly miniaturized as I squinted at the desert floor through the early morning sun glinting on the airliner's wing just outside my window. Finally, I was beginning my Black Madonna pilgrimage.

Since a trip to the Holy Land three years earlier, a vague yearning had stirred in me. The Mount of Olives, Mount Tabor, Mount Sinai, the high places of Jesus and Moses were moving but left me hungry. I couldn't explain even to myself exactly what was missing. I'd hoped Bethlehem and the Jerusalem sites where Mary had certainly stood would carry the balancing feminine power I'd found in Medjugorje, but they didn't. My spirit was seeking holy places of the feminine divine. I wanted to visit them, too, but where were they? Despite Grandma's many stories of miracles and healing, I knew the Catholic shrines at Lourdes and Fatima didn't attract me. My search had taken a while. I smiled to myself remembering the day it all began.

It was early morning. I was in the office with a full schedule of clients ahead, and a desk stacked with unread mail. I'd no more than opened my daybook, when the phone rang. It was a cancellation. Then, it rang again. Another cancellation. And again. Cancellation.

By 9:00 A.M. my calendar was completely clear. I sat looking at it, bewildered, until I remembered that other day my appointments had suddenly evaporated, the amazing day I met Mother Teresa. Wondering what marvel this sudden change of plans might bring, I decided just catching up on the mail would be miracle enough. The pile, mostly insurance forms and bills, was precariously balanced on the corner of my desk, a magazine on top. I grabbed it and headed to the coffee lounge. The paperwork could wait. Once settled with my first jolt of caffeine for the day, I flipped the glossy cover open. An ad caught my eye: Join Us for a Shamanic Journey to the Black Madonna.

Was this the pilgrimage I'd been looking for? Quickly scanning the information, I learned that the Black Madonnas were enshrined in Catholic churches in France and Spain, places familiar to me. I knew Chartres Cathedral had a labyrinth, but I didn't know it also had a Black Madonna. As I read, I wondered why these Madonnas were black. I didn't know then that the sites dated back to the Old Goddess era of 40,000 B.C.E. I hadn't thought about all the goddesses revered there from then until now.

Maybe I'd encounter the Mother's healing power at these ancient holy places as I had at Medjugorje. This was a shamanic journey, after all. Perhaps I'd be blessed by the mysterious presence of the feminine again. Since Mom died last year, I needed it more than ever. I'd promised myself to salute her and the Holy Mother with a pilgrimage. What better use for my small inheritance?

I returned to the ad. It left me wanting to learn more about the trip.

In small print at the bottom was an 800 number. Without another thought, I scurried back to my office and the phone. Flattening the magazine on my desk with one hand, I dialed with the other. Only as the phone rang did it occur to me to wonder what I wanted to know, what I could ask to get some sense of the pilgrimage.

A pleasant voice came on the line. After I'd explained myself briefly, she proposed I talk with someone else. "Ellen

Zweben is a psychotherapist in the Bay Area," she said. "She's made this trip several times."

Ellen was friendly, forthcoming, and knowledgeable. She answered the questions I had about the sites, then went on to say we'd be expected to prepare ourselves by fasting, meditation, and reading. The book list was extensive, dealing not only with the Black Madonna, but also with the ancient goddesses, the Gnostic gospels, the Nag Hammadi scriptures, and Jungian theory on the conscious feminine. I'd read some of the literature Ellen glibly rattled off, but hadn't known that the Black Madonna was a link to another time when darkness symbolized the positive, when it stood for much that was later rejected in modern times: the body, the feminine, indigenous cultures, and people of color.

Ellen went on to explain the logistics of the pilgrimage. We'd travel cross-country in vans for two weeks in a group no larger than twenty. While at the sites, there would be shamanic ceremonies and plenty of time for meditation.

This was getting closer to what I wanted to know. Maybe these were the holy places I'd been looking for. Were the pilgrimage, the ceremonies, and the meditation likely to be a way to meet the Holy Mother? I decided to ask.

"Ellen, what have you gained personally from your experience of the Black Madonna?"

She hesitated a minute, then softly replied: "I am no longer afraid of the void."

The void. Of course. The void, the dark night. The shamanic journey was about entering the dark night, encountering the unknown, what was not yet born, still in the darkness of the womb. The mysticism I'd so loved as a young nun had first invited me to what was obscured in shadow, beyond words, impossible to imagine, yet not to be feared. The Madonna's blackness suddenly made sense.

"Would you like a cup of coffee? A blanket?" The flight attendant's cheerful voice called me back from my reminiscing. I'd been so deep in thought, I hadn't realized the cabin was cold. I said yes to both offers and, in a minute, was gratefully tucking a blanket around my knees. A magazine fell out of its folds onto the seat. The headline stopped me: "What's Your Horoscope for Today, Gemini?" Still waiting for my cup of coffee, I scanned the article. One sentence leaped off the page: "What would happen if you simply embraced this new heretical thinking to see where it would take you?" I smiled. As a crone of nearly sixty, I'd learned to investigate all the paths that led to God. Was that heretical? No. The loss of the feminine divine was a real wound, and I knew well that I was on the mend.

I was airborne indeed, and ready to fly.

When the pilgrimage group assembled, I met China Galland, one of the leaders. While I wasn't quite sure why I was on a shamanic goddess journey, I could relate to China's experience of the Black Madonna. She'd walked two hundred miles from Warsaw to her shrine at Czestochowa, Poland. She'd been to Einsiedeln in Switzerland, to Loreto in Italy, and to Medjugorje. I'd read her book *Longing for Darkness: Tara and the Black Madonna*[13] and marveled at the power of her journeys. What we had in common was this interest in the Madonna, degrees in English, a Catholic background, and impressions of Medjugorje.

The rhythm of our pilgrimage included time spent in our

circle, China often providing the historical context for what we were seeing, and leading us in reflective journaling. She suggested we start by asking ourselves what the Black Madonna wanted us to know. My entry surprised me.

"What I want you to know is:
I am one. All you learn is related to me. There are many manifestations of my love and life and beauty and wisdom. In your living and your dying, you are bringing me to birth.[14] Know that by leaving the former house of prayer, you approach me in the darkness of the garden where all that grows and blooms is beautiful and connected to me and my life. You will lose nothing of the foundation I have already provided you, but now, your path leads in new and labyrinthine ways on which you meet me at every turn.

What I want you to know is:
Your body is sacred, a manifestation of me, made in my image, full of goodness, beauty, and life. Your energy flows from my creative energy and is part of all the energy moving in the universe. Gently let go of whatever you see that blocks that divine flow, and encourage all you meet to surrender to my divine love and leading in the same way.
Know that Jesus comes from me and is the revelation of my Light and Love. He taught that I am Love.

What I want you to know is:
You are being led. You know the darkness of the garden is full of fragrance. It is a safe and enclosed place, like the womb from which you came and will return, buried deep with the secrets of the Earth, your mother. Bless the darkness and

invite it. Enter eagerly with joy, trusting that as the light fades, mystery is revealed without word or thought, in beauty and wonder.

Release what needs releasing to enter the deepest place of beauty and love——the rose of Engedi, the rose of Sharon. Labyrinthine ways are a continual flow, and you will learn at every turn until you enter the rose. Remain in the center of the deepest rose, enclosed and embraced until you are called forth to bring the richness of my gifts to all in your life. Know that you are part of each one on your path."

When we read our journals in the group, the woman at my side looked intently at me. She spoke gently but clearly: "You are channeling the Goddess." Channeling? The word scared me a bit, until I thought of the great prayer of Francis of Assisi: "Make me a channel of your peace."[15] How often I'd prayed those words. Perhaps they were being answered here in a new way, as I opened to the power of the feminine, the mystery of the unknown, the beyond. Perhaps channeling was another aspect of prophecy. I'd have to think about it.

One of the first stops on our pilgrimage was the French village of Besse. A small stone church in the center of town was the site of one of the most ancient and primitive Black Madonnas I'd ever seen. A few shafts of light fell from the high windows to illuminate a startlingly earthy old crone in the shadowy church. My companions and I quietly took our places on hard wooden benches near the statue.

All was still. As time passed, the Madonna's darkness slowly engulfed me. I closed my eyes and fell off an edge into some unknown depth that seemed to expand into a great quiet.

Then, something called me back, some small movement. The return from stillness took effort, like swimming up through deep water. Finally, I opened my eyes. Crumpled on the floor in front of the Mother, was Brigit, the youngest woman in our group, apparently unconscious. Another of our companions, eyes closed, gently cradled her. John, one of the shamans, moved around Brigit, sometimes tapping a small drum, sometimes quietly whistling a few notes.

Peering around the dim chapel, I saw my roommate Jackie watching quietly. Others knelt or stood, eyes closed, hands raised in prayer. Standing in the row ahead of me, Allison trembled as she extended her arms toward Brigit.

The scene, completely silent except for John's occasional drumbeat or birdlike chirp, transfixed me. I remembered the feeling I'd had in Medjugorje when some of our group fainted in prayer.

Later Jackie and I returned to the hotel. My roommate was nervous.

"What was going on back there? Was that some work of the devil?" Jackie perched on the edge of her bed, brow furrowed.

I sat down across from her on the other twin. "No, I don't think so. Brigit was fine when she sat up. A little dazed maybe."

Jackie hugged herself in her heavy sweater, as though chilled. "But I never saw anything like that before. Have you?" Her question hung in the air as she settled back, leaning against the headboard.

I thought about charismatic prayer meetings and wondered if she'd ever been exposed to them. It turned out, she had.

"What was your experience?" I asked.

"Oh, they sang songs, I guess, and read the gospel stories about Jesus, and some women spoke in tongues."

"What'd you make of that?"

"Well, our priest said it was a kind of prayer. Said it was actually described in the Bible." Jackie had heard from her pastor about saints fainting in prayer, too.

"Charismatics call it 'being slain in the Spirit.' Sometimes it happens in prayer meetings. I think that's all it was with Brigit today."

Even though I wasn't too sure what had happened in the church, I didn't share my friend's uneasiness.

Jackie sat quietly smoothing the bedspread with one hand. "But what about John's dancing?"

I'd never seen a shaman in action before, but knew that indigenous healers used gesture and sound not so different from Christian priests with their own gestures, rituals, and chant. "I think it was supposed to be a blessing, or maybe a healing. I guess we're more used to incense and bells."

Jackie was quiet. After a moment, she swung her legs over the side of the bed and crossed to pull down the window shade, closing out the night. She spoke over her shoulder. "Well, ok. I'm sure there must be many ways we can bless each other."

I agreed. I'd felt the power of the Madonna myself that afternoon in the old stone church. A vision of golden gates standing slightly ajar had vividly unfolded in my mind's eye. Turning down my bed, I decided not to bring it up. Jackie had enough on her mind.

Our eventful pilgrimage continued. We visited many Black Madonnas in hillside villages, in out-of-the-way country churches and in the crowded cities of France, following the path of ancient pilgrims.

One rainy day, grateful I was not on foot as they had been, I spotted a roadside sign through the steamy window of our van. It announced that we had left France and entered Spain. Soon, immense mountains hove up from the floor of the plain, the mountains of Montserrat, the serrated mountains. I'd seen the Alps, the Rockies, and some respectable mountains around Arizona, but never anything like the mountains of Montserrat. The van chugged as we climbed higher and higher, each turn of the road revealing more rocky vistas, and more huge configurations. One range looked like a sleeping goddess.

Then, daylight was gone as the sun dropped behind the craggy boulders surrounding us. By the time we'd wound our way to the plateau atop the heights all was in darkness. Here the Benedictines had built their monastery centuries ago to honor the Lady of Montserrat.

Grateful to stretch after the long day of travel, I stepped from the van and looked around the monastery complex. It was like other Black Madonna sites we'd visited in tiny French villages hanging off mountainsides, except that the usual commercial distractions were nowhere in sight here. This high place was dedicated only to the Lady.

It felt good to move, to unload suitcases, carrying them to the third floor on the antiquated elevator. Once in our assigned room, I threw open heavy wooden shutters to let in the warm, fragrant night. A full moon shed its brilliance on a fountain murmuring in the garden beneath the window. I leaned out, craning my neck for a glimpse of what else might be seen in the darkness.

Leading to the left from the open space below was a narrow cobblestone street, dappled with moonlight. To my surprise, there, high on the church facade at the end of the shadowy street, stood a retinue of saints dazzling in floodlights. I pulled my head back in the window to check my watch. It was eleven o'clock, but it didn't matter. I was going to the church. I called over my shoulder, "Back in a while."

Jackie leaned around the corner, toothbrush in hand, eyes wide with surprise. No time to explain, I shut the door quietly between us and ran down the stairs. The blazing saints had magnetized me, filling me with a strange urgency to stand in front of them.

Once in the unlit street, I hurried along, grateful to see only one route in what I knew must be a complex maze of lanes and byways. Only when I'd arrived in the empty quadrangle of the church did I slow down to catch my breath. Smooth marble tiles paved the expansive plaza. Inside the high wall, statues of saints, eerily life-like in the moonlight, stood guard from shadowy niches, but it was the church itself that drew me. The conclave of blazing saints on its façade seemed to command, *Come, come to the Mother.*

I approached. On the threshold of the ancient shrine, I stood, hesitating, remembering the encounter with the powerful Mother at Besse. Despite whatever had drawn me down the narrow street from my room to the doorstep of Montserrat's Black Madonna, I knew I wasn't ready to stand before the Ancient Mother alone in the blackness. Somehow, I could sense the void.

A night bird swooped low over me breaking the silence of the courtyard with a single, shrill call. I turned and retraced my steps. In the quiet square, the only sound was the flapping of the bird's large wings as he returned to his place in the wild just outside the wall.

Next morning, as I threw open the heavy shutters once more, the monastery village was bathed in sunshine. Whatever had unnerved me the night before was gone with the daylight. Eager to complete my unfinished business, I wound my way through the twisting streets back to the church. This time, nodding to the saints at the door, I entered without hesitation and slid into the nearest pew. Immediately, my eyes were drawn down the long aisle to the silver adornment of the high altar, and then to the lofty heights above it. There, presiding in brilliance over the huge chapel, sat the ancient Lady of Montserrat. The statue was riveting.

Hardly glancing at the choir in the sanctuary, I heard, more than saw, forty black-robed monks singing office. Ornate tones of Catalonian Spanish carried the ancient chants. After Lauds and Matins, the monks left the sanctuary reverberating with glorious echoes of their prayer. In the silence that followed, I closed my eyes. I'd been staring at the Black Madonna statue for so long, I could still see the image. As it gradually faded, the stillness in the chapel deepened.

Then, there was a rustling around me. My companions were moving toward a side aisle, the entrance to the regal statue high above us. I quickly stood, eager to join them, to become part of the long line waiting to venerate the Madonna. On both sides of me pilgrims whispered prayers to her in languages I couldn't recognize, all the while reverently fingering rosary beads. Two by two, we passed through wrought iron gates held open by golden angels and then became part of a throng crowding a staircase flanked by mosaics of women saints. I climbed with them, impatient to kneel before the Madonna long known for her power to heal, wondering what healing I needed.

I thought of my mother, dead now nearly a year. I was here because of her. She'd never visited Medjugorje, but had been touched by the stories Jane and I told of our pilgrimage, stories of a mother's love and its power to heal.

Mom had always wanted to be a nurse. She brewed up home remedies never heard of by the neighbors. At one time or another, she'd tended every member of the family when they were sick. To the remedies and vigils, she added her prayer, never hesitating to invite the rest of us to pray, too. She was a good mom. I missed her.

Jostling along in the crowded stairway, I was too close to the phalanx of women saints surrounding me to clearly see them, but once I reached the antechamber to the statue, space suddenly opened. A glorious blue and gold mosaic dazzled me. It was St. Ann, the mother of Mary, my mother's patron saint and mine. Her arms spread wide, she welcomed me into the chamber of the Madonna.

The Black Madonna of Montserrat, Christ child on her knees, sat before me with one hand extended, holding the world. At last, I entered the space made holy by centuries of prayer and knelt to kiss her graceful hand. It was so life-like, like the sweet, warm, living hand of my own mother, so often laid gently on my cheek.

My heart skipped a beat.

I was five years old again, comforted in the pain of a raging earache by my mother's loving hand on my fevered face. *How could it be?* I knelt spellbound by that mysterious touch. Then, the dam holding all my tears suddenly burst and overflowed.

The tears wouldn't stop. As I wept, the painful loss of my mother, the woman who had loved me unconditionally for my entire lifetime washed over me. All year, I hadn't been able to grieve. I had tried, but couldn't. Now those frozen sobs racked me as the flood of tears continued. Finally, I wiped my eyes and groped my way down the stairs to a corner in the chapel below.

The year before, Mom's funeral had numbed me. Old family feuds had unexpectedly blown up into a whirlwind brought on by her death. For weeks beforehand, I'd struggled to find my brother, long alienated from us all. He didn't make it to her bedside. Then, I arrived in Iowa to find my sisters tangled in misunderstandings over the funeral. It was left to me to hurriedly make last minute decisions about the ceremonies of the next day. As contingents from all sides of the family gathered for the wake, funeral, and burial, I tried to straddle the differences among them, some left over from many years earlier.

In the stressful, surfacy politeness of the occasion, my grief and pain had gone underground. Then, very soon, Jerry, Kelly, and I flew back to Arizona, back to a hectic year of work for me, a year of numbness.

I sat long in the chapel, waiting for the storm of tears to abate. When I finally could look up to the Madonna, I knew she had healed me. My heart was content at last.

Visitors quietly came and went around me, murmuring prayers, while in the courtyard outside, voices were raised in familiar Marian hymns. Peacefully, I listened to songs I hadn't heard in years. Then, I startled to attention. A male voice was singing "Silent Night" in German! Why, on this hot summer day, would anybody sing a Christmas hymn?

I knew the answer immediately.

One of Mom's treasured childhood memories was her

father's nightly lullaby sung to her in German, "Stell Nacht." Every Christmas of my life, she'd asked me to sing the hymn to her, to remind her of her father. The yearly Christmas ritual between us became one of my treasured memories.

In that moment, in Montserrat, in the month of May, my mother's spirit was with me as much as she had ever been any Christmas of my life. I hadn't imagined it. An unknown pilgrim's song of mother and child that summer day told me she was with me, not gone after all. She was just behind the thin veil, close, very near, her presence gently comforting my grief. I sat long in my corner in chapel, remembering my dear mother and our last Christmas Eve together before I'd entered St. Rose so many years ago.

Finally I stood, ready to fill my pockets with the soggy tissue I'd littered in the pew. Just outside the basilica's heavy brass door in the sunny courtyard, water made delightful music, cascading from a fountain built long ago by the monks. China had told us that Montserrat, like other healing sites of Mary and the ancient goddesses, had a spring and well where water still flowed.

Delighted to find it nearby, I sat on the edge of the fountain trailing my fingers in the cool water, refreshing as tears. The day was cloudless, the breeze cool and fresh. If only my sisters could be here to share this magnificence. I wanted them to know the Madonna's healing power, as I did. Despite their differences, their grief was as painful as mine. They needed healing, too.

I fished the Madonna medals I'd bought in the gift shop out of my pocket. Each precious silver medal sparkling in my hand was unique, delicately beautiful, like my still sparring sisters. Stooping to dangle them in the fountain banked with flowers and red votive candles, I prayed: *Dear Lady, let these simple medals carry peace to my sisters. Show them the gentle care you've shown me. Heal their grief and help them to love each other.*

I knew in that moment that the medallions would help me tell the story of Mom's presence at the ancient shrine to Our Lady of Montserrat.

A few days later, we arrived in Chartres, the last stop of our pilgrimage.

During some rare free time, Jackie and I wound our way through the twisting streets from the Hotel de la Poste to the church. The great thirteenth century cathedral's entrance was protected by archways crowded with saints. Lit by sunset, they stood majestically in rows, immortalized by medieval stonemasons.

Noisy tourists soon interrupted our admiration, pushing us through the ancient doors. We flowed with the crowd to the Black Madonna Chapel and to the crypt under the church where a second Lady was enshrined. It was only on the way out that I glimpsed a labyrinth pattern in the stones of the floor, nearly hidden by wooden chairs. I'd known about this meandering path embedded underfoot in medieval cathedrals. It was an ancient meditation tool designed to carry the pilgrim step by step into prayerful surrender to the unexpected turns of life's journey.

I urgently wanted to walk it, though custodians were beginning to clear the church. I took my chance and entered the labyrinth.

On the edge of the first circuit, a strong pull of energy, not unlike the urging of the nighttime courtyard in Montserrat, drew me in. The energy was even stronger than I had thought. I suddenly remembered the words I'd written in my journal early in the pilgrimage: *"Now your path leads in new and labyrinthine ways on which you meet me at every turn."*

But the custodians were not to be delayed.

"Sorry, mademoiselle, we're closing now. You'll have to leave." Reluctantly, I turned away to find Jackie waiting just outside.

When night arrived and our leisurely French dinner at the hotel finished, we again wound our way through the streets, now empty of art students and tourists. I could hardly wait to return to the cathedral for our group's vigil, a private time of prayer. At the entrance, we greeted our companions, already gathered there in silence.

As the church porter opened the door, I stepped into the half-light, filled with awe. A gentle luminescence shone from the balcony but the ground level was dark except for the red sanctuary lamp shining steadily at some distance from us.

Our leader placed a fragrant bouquet in the center of the labyrinth while the rest of us lit votive candles and quietly arranged them around its outside circuit. Then, we sat on the creaking benches to remove our shoes, each sound amplified in the empty space by the vaulted ceiling overhead.

An expectant hush fell over us when Kathleen and Martha moved to the labyrinth's center. Martha, a gifted musician steeped in the lore of medieval music, broke the silence. "To begin our ceremony, we have a song for you. Medieval pilgrims sang it to honor the Lady on their walk to this cathedral, a stop along the way to Santiago de Compostela. Since that's in Spain, this song is in Spanish."

Martha's flute and Kathleen's voice echoed in the darkness sending chills through me.

As the last sweet note faded into silence, one by one, my companions, now barefoot, began their walk into the labyrinth. I waited and watched, touched by their reverence and the holiness of this sacred place. Then I stood, bowed profoundly at the entrance, and stepped into the labyrinth. This was the moment I'd been waiting for, to pray here in this ancient and holy spot created in medieval times, a place hallowed by centuries of prayer. I moved in a slow but steady pace, step by step, wondering what to pray for, and at the same time, grateful to savor the peace of this last stop of our pilgrimage.

I quieted in the restful silence until I came to the first swing of the labyrinth's circuit. I was already so close! Although I'd only been walking a short time, my unexpected nearness to the center surprised me, reminding me of when I was very young. There had been times then when I suddenly knew I was close to God. Here it was again, a surprise of the Spirit.

I continued my slow but steady pace, step by step, wondering what to pray for in the restful silence. Strangely, as the divine presence grew stronger, I became more and more aware of the cold stones under my bare feet.

Then, abruptly, without warning, I couldn't move. Mystified, I tugged a little, trying to lift my heel, then my toes, then the ball of my foot. I couldn't lift anything. I was held fast to the spot. I stood there a minute, confused, then, giggled. I was literally stopped in my tracks.

When someone stepped around me to pass, my amusement faded. Others behind me wondered why I wasn't moving. I gamely tugged again, but I was paralyzed, frozen in place. Minutes passed. I was nonplussed, made helpless by my unmovable foot! I puzzled over what was happening, helplessly fretting about how long I might be held immobilized.

The red sanctuary lamp winked at me across the darkness of the cathedral. Then, slowly, gentle words came to me: *Stay with Me. You aren't going anywhere unless I open the way to you. And wherever you do go, it's because I have opened the way for you. You think you are doing your life, but actually, I am.*

These were the words of a tolerant mother explaining something simple to a greatly loved but somewhat dull child. I was thunderstruck, but I understood. I was stuck to learn a lesson of surrender, of being led, of meeting the Mother at every turn. Some part of my heart gave way and, with it, my foot suddenly released!

Only weeks later after I'd returned home did I grasp more fully the meaning of this remarkable experience. Although I didn't want to be told I was a workaholic, I knew that after vacation, my sweet peace and balance typically went out the window with the onslaught of appointments, phone calls, mail, workshops, and retreats. I knew how to let go and relax into vacation, but I knew even better how to work my head off.

Curiously, after this trip, the sweet peace didn't go away. I observed it, watching for the shift to happen. It never did. I was released from the old intensity, finally free. I wasn't in charge. If the way was open, I walked through. If it wasn't, something else was planned. I'd find out what later.

I'd affirmed all the years of my private practice that there was a divine plan for my life and work. Now, I knew it in my gut. On the labyrinthine way that was mine, God hovered at every turn.

10

No Need for a Hurricane

I see a brown horse,
Coming very close, each pore of his wet
    nose, his bright eyes, his shiny coat—
What is not to love about this horse?
I climb on his bare back, my arms around
    his neck, his soft mane blowing in
    my face
As we gently rise, smoothly rise, easily rise,
    from the flower-filled meadow
Until we are flying, higher, higher,
    ever higher.

In the mist and clouds, my lovely horse
    brightens until he is white.
I hold tightly as we fly,
As he grows a horn, a jeweled horn,
As he champs his bit, a jeweled bit casting
    rainbow prisms everywhere.

We fly up, up, up through the clouds,
    through the mist, through the rainbows
To a castle, every turret and wall cylindrical.
The doors open before us.
We follow a long, red carpet leading to the
    throne room.
A king with long, white hair and beard sits
    casually on his throne,
One leg thrown over an arm of it,
    foot dangling,
His shiny cylindrical crown cocked
    crookedly over one eye.

He speaks: "Why have you come?"
I ask him for the rest of my life.
He gives me a jewel, an immense jewel.

Suddenly, I am back in the meadow with the
    brown horse,
And
I have the jewel.

N ow it's time to tell the story. It's time. I understand. The jewel isn't just for me, but for each one who asks for life, and is willing to attend.

Crisis, crisis. What do I do? Email my friend, Judy!

> *"This is probably not a good time for me to email you, but I saw the doctor today. I do have cancer and need surgery. It's a tiny little growth, stage one. No big deal. Not likely to be a problem. I should be grateful to the wonderful radiologist who found it at such an early stage. Who does this doctor think he is with his calm pronouncement that yes, indeedy, I do have cancer and should be so grateful it's not worse than it is? You get my drift. I'm not grateful. I'm pissed. They want to do surgery right away. I don't like getting my life jerked around.*
>
> *At best, I'll be out of commission for six weeks. What about my practice?*
>
> *I need to decide between lumpectomy or mastectomy, and pretty damn fast. Either choice will involve yanking out lymph nodes, getting zapped with radiation, and if I'm not lucky, going bald with chemo. Anyway, I'll be ok, but right now, I'm in shock. I need time to sort this out."*

I reread the message. The word "cancer" stood out like neon. Suddenly I was back in the surgeon's office sitting in front of his large mahogany desk, Jer at my side. My husband had insisted on coming with me to what I expected to be a routine appointment for results of a surgical biopsy done weeks earlier. The doctor opened my chart, spreading reports across his desk. "Fortunately, the cancer is stage one, less than one centimeter. . . ."

A sickening chill quickly spread through my mid-section. Cancer? Out of the cold, a fog rolled in between us, muffling his words. After what seemed an interminably long recital of medical facts, there was a silence. I realized the doctor had asked me a question, was waiting.

I tried to push through the haze, to push a few words through it. "Cancer . . . my father died of cancer. . . ."

Then Jerry reached for my hand, and my throat flooded with tears.

But the doctor's head was bent over the papers on his desk, face unchanged. He began droning again. "Lumpectomy . . . estrogen receptive . . . lymph nodes . . . mastectomy."

Wait, wait, the voice inside me wanted to scream out. *I'm drowning here. I have more to say, more to explain.* I looked around for a box of tissue on the big desk. Nothing.

The doctor droned on.

Did he even notice I was crying?

Then, the last question of his monologue slowly registered: "So, do you want a lumpectomy or a mastectomy?"

A jagged edge of anger cut through my haze. I sat back in the chair, gathering dignity around me like a ragged blanket. My voice was back. "Doctor, I will need time to understand this before I can decide."

I glanced at Jerry. He was pale.

I went on. "I was totally unprepared for this diagnosis. I'm sure I've missed about 80% of what you've been trying to tell me here. I had thought since I hadn't heard from you in three weeks that this appointment was just a check-up after a routine diagnostic procedure."

Closing the chart on his desk, the doctor folded his hands on it, looking at me, his gaze bland. "Well, of course,

I didn't want to leave such a message on your phone."

A flash of anger shot from my head to my gut. "I've never been sick a day in my life. I didn't realize that I would have to ask to be informed immediately about my test if you found cancer. I thought everything was all right."

His mask didn't slip. "Fortunately, the cancer is stage one . . ." the drone started again. "Less than one centimeter . . . slow growing . . . no danger . . ."

Had he heard what I said? Had he seen my feelings? He's sitting here like he does every day, probably thinking, "Oh, another emotional woman. Let's just cut off her breasts."

No!

Anger rose like a tide inside me. I stood up, clutching the referral form he'd given me to a radiation therapist. I was eager to end this cold encounter. "Thank you, doctor. I'll call when I've had time to think this all through."

My chilly exit was stopped at the reception desk. The clerk wanted an insurance card.

As I waited for her to copy it, Jerry whispered to me. "They're quick enough to be sure they get their money, aren't they?"

I gave a mirthless laugh. I'd come to this office expecting only routine medical service and now was leaving in need of a support group or cancer counseling, some kind of help. I scanned the counter for brochures, but there was nothing.

Jer and I stood in the hall, taking deep drinks at the water fountain. When he folded me in his big, warm bear hug, the sobs I'd been holding in burst forth.

"Jer, I'm just so shocked. I wasn't expecting this. This is too much. I need time to deal with this, but I have to go back to the office, and look at me!" I cried even harder.

He gently disengaged my grasp, holding me at arm's length, to get a better look. "Everything'll be ok, honey—" but I interrupted him.

"I'm just so upset. Did I tell you that I asked when I made this appointment if I should cancel the rest of my afternoon sessions?"

He raised his eyebrows. "No, you didn't tell me." His voice registered surprise, then annoyance. "I could've taken off the rest of the day, too." He consulted his watch. "It's three-fifty. Can you reach your client now?"

"It's too late." I felt around in my purse for a mirror. "My four o'clock is already on her way." A little ragged breath I hadn't known was there suddenly escaped.

Jer folded me into his big hug again, mirror, purse and all. I shut my eyes, relaxing into his warmth.

"It's ok, honey. You just fix up your lipstick. You look fine." He kissed my cheekbone.

Dazed but grateful he'd come with me, I numbly climbed into my car and returned to the office. Somehow, I got through the session with my unsuspecting client. When the hour was over, I closed the door after her. The familiarity of my little oak desk, easy recliner and sofa full of pillows comforted me. Sitting in the pile of the pillows, I wrapped myself in the cozy chenille throw I kept handy for clients.

The anger and fear of the afternoon were gone. I felt dead. Numb.

Just then, someone tapped on my door. Startled, I jumped up, smoothing the throw. Not wanting office staff to know what was going on, I cracked it open. It was Jerry. "I thought you had to go back to the office. What're you doing here?"

He stepped into the room, grinning at my surprise. "I did

go back." He closed the door and pulled me to himself in one move. "I told them I had to leave for the rest of the day. You need me."

Did I need him? I put my head on his shoulder. "Jer, I feel numb."

He straightened his arms, holding me back to look at me, then grinned and gestured to the sofa. "Do you want to talk, counselor?"

A mild terror arose in me at the thought. "No, no." I was used to battling my way through crises alone. "I'm ok. I just need some time alone to sort this out—"

My husband was unperturbed. "We'll do whatever you want."

He obviously had no intention of giving me time alone.

"Do you want dinner?"

"Oh, no." Nervousness trembled in my gut. "I couldn't eat right now." I needed a break, a distraction, to go on automatic pilot, not to think, not to feel, not to talk. A lifetime of crises suffered alone had built a wall inside me I didn't know how to reach over. Yet here was my good husband, sticking to me like a burr.

"Let's drive over to that furniture store on Bell Road, see if the bench is still there." After three years of marriage, we were finally doing some of the redecorating and re-furnishing we'd promised each other as newly-weds.

Jer squired me to his van in the parking lot. "We'll pick up your car later. We need to ride together for now."

"Well, at least let me drive." Only busy-ness could quiet the jitters spreading from my gut. I had to be busy, anything not to have to think. I heard myself chatter on, "If the bench hasn't been sold, we can measure it, see if it'll fit in the kitchen."

Later that night, too exhausted to sleep, I searched my bookshelves for a book I'd had for years about cancer patients. Finally, the blue letters on the tattered tan jacket caught my eye: *Love, Medicine and Miracles*,[16] by Dr. Bernie Siegel. I wiped the dusty cover with the sleeve of my bathrobe and headed for the kitchen. What did this doctor say about anger? I couldn't remember. Pushing a cup of water into the microwave, I paged through the book.

Was I abnormal? Was I hurting myself with this anger? The microwave dinged. I slid the hot cup across the counter, dropped a tea bag into it and sat down to read. Finding the section on anger, my eyes fairly vacuumed the words from the page. Yes, this was what I wanted to know. I was entitled to this huge, exhausting anger. Siegel gave permission. In fact, it was healthy. So was numbness. Normal, damned uncomfortable, but normal.

The clock said 3:00A.M. The pre-dawn winter sky was dark and overcast outside the kitchen window. Sitting back in my chair, I kneaded the tightness in the back of my neck, doubting I could sleep. I paged through the next chapter, then wished I'd gone to bed. It dealt with resentments and unresolved emotional issues. I closed the book, heart sinking. I got the distinct impression there was a reason I needed this illness, but I had no idea why.

I pulled a rug under my bare feet on the cold tile floor. After being so angry with the doctor, I was only partly willing to even ask myself these impertinent questions. Even now, I was still so angry, I refused to focus on it. No, I wasn't finished with my life yet!

Only when I gradually calmed down did it occur to me how many places I'd never been, things I'd never done that were now slowly slipping out of my grasp. So, was that it? Did I need cancer to give myself time?

It seemed a vague reason, giving myself time. To do what? I wondered. A little voice inside answered me: *Anything besides work—to paint, to write, to read, to meditate, just to be alone.*

No, that couldn't be it. The explanation was too easy. Maybe I had cancer because of something I didn't understand in myself, perhaps something to do with the way I'd pulled back from Jerry's support just hours ago.

Warming my hands on the cup, I took a sip, setting the tea swirling into a tiny tempest, a pattern of ripples. Had my life's tempests had a pattern, too?

I'd never thought about it before, but leaving the convent had been a lonely time. The nuns themselves shrouded such departures in secrecy. My family and friends, not understanding life inside the walls and hoping not to intrude, didn't ask many questions. I weathered the crisis largely alone.

Earlier, when my father died, I was a nineteen-year-old girl in a city away from home and family, with few friends close by. My mother's problems and needs over-shadowed mine. In the small space allowed for my grief, I had felt alone with it.

So what if I was used to bucking up, going it alone in those days? That was long ago. Surely, I'd learned otherwise in the long years of my marriage to Bob.

I paused to think about those years as slender fingers of first sun fell across the dog-eared journal in front of me. No, those were the years I'd written page after rumpled page in notebooks, pouring out my travail. Even then, I'd kept my feelings to myself when he'd lost job after job, not a rare fate for former priests working in parishes. It hadn't been easy going through career upheaval with him until he finally settled into social services.

Why had I struggled through those intense fears, frustrations, and sadnesses alone? To protect Bob? To support him? I sighed, chagrin surging through me at the fine line I'd drawn between my motives. Whatever it was, I'd left my own needs out of the picture.

Had I handled the end of the marriage and my divorce any better? Yes, I'd turned to counselors and a few close friends for support, but had largely kept silence, even with my mother. There it was, the same old pattern, toughing it out alone.

No wonder I'd pulled back from Jerry's support. I wasn't used to it.

I looked out my kitchen window now brightened with the gold of dawn, and decided to end that old stuff once and for all.

I had breast cancer, hadn't expected it, didn't want it, but here it was.

I had a big decision to make, lumpectomy or mastectomy. What woman could I turn to for advice? The answer flashed into my mind: my sister-in-law in DC. She'd had a bout with breast cancer less than a year ago. It was already 8:00 A.M. in the East. I eagerly dialed her number.

"Jerry phoned me from his office when you got the news, Shirley. I'm so sorry, but you know, my treatment hasn't been so bad. Sounds like you really could go either way, lumpectomy or mastectomy, depending on how you feel. I was so shocked at first, it was hard to sort out all the factors in a decision like that."

"I know. That's why I'm at such a loss. Do you know of

anything I could read? I've already found one book, *Breast Cancer? Let Me Check My Schedule*[17]—

Her laugh interrupted me. "Sounds like you! Well, for lots of information, *Doctor Susan Love's Breast Book*[18] is the best one I've found."

Her recommendation was all I needed to hear. That night, I stayed up late reading.

Over the next days, I felt calmer. Slowly, I absorbed the reality: I had cancer and needed surgery. With the realization came a great wave of sadness washing over the turbulent rocks of anger, eddying, flooding everywhere. I was drowning in a flood of loss I didn't understand. What was I losing? My beautiful breast? I hadn't realized I'd prized it so much.

One evening, Jerry and I sat long over the dinner table. He saw that my eyes were red from crying.

"Pretty tough day, honey?" he asked, voice soft.

"I'm so full of tears, Jerry. It was almost easier being angry."

He leaned across the table, taking my hand. "Do you remember that time just after we met when we took a dip in the pool together?"

I wiped my nose with a soggy tissue. "Sure. I thought it was odd that you'd been in the Navy but weren't any more of a swimmer than I was." I smiled at the memory. "What are you trying to do, distract me?"

He smiled, too. God, I loved those dimples.

"No. Do you remember anything else?"

I looked across the table to the pool just beyond the window, trying to recall. That night I'd been wearing a dark blue swimsuit with a ruffle across the top. "Oh, yes. You told me later you thought I was flat-chested."

His smile stretched into a wide grin. "That swimsuit wasn't exactly form-fitting. You never put your breasts on display, sweetheart. But I found out how wrong I was."

A new wave of sadness rolled over me, spilling into more tears.

He slid his chair next to mine, wrapping his arms around me. "You need to know, honey. I will love you and your lovely body with or without breasts."

I closed my eyes, taking in the truth of his words, and his warmth. "Jerry, I do know that. I really do."

He kissed my closed eyelids. In the darkness behind them, a delicate creature slowly crystallized. Was it a blown-glass unicorn? It seemed as if its chest had been carefully cemented, fused together, but now was broken again in the same delicate, easily injured spot.

I pulled back and looked at my husband. "I know you love me, Jerry, no matter what. It's just that I feel so fragile. This health thing I'm going through now has to do with that, not with you."

"Well, you are fragile," he kissed my neck, holding me close, and murmuring, "and so precious." Then he stood and drew me to him. "We can clean up here later. Let's go to bed."

I let him lead me through the house, wondering if I could break out of my sadness, if I could meet his passion. That it didn't take long surprised me. I found myself easily and sweetly carried by waves of heat to a place of peace and comfort.

Afterward, in contentment, I slept a little, then opened my eyes to find Jerry leaning on one elbow, returning my gaze.

I reached for his hand. "This would be so much harder without you." His wide wedding band was cold under my fingers. Suddenly my heart ached. He'd had so many serious heart episodes. Was this how it felt?

Jerry rolled back from me, lacing his fingers behind his head. "The first time I had a heart problem, yeah, I was scared." His eyes drifted to the ceiling overhead. Then, he looked at me again. "But you. This is all new territory for you. And breast cancer? That has to be a big hit to your sexuality, and you had one from Bob just a few years ago."

I pulled the sheets up around me. "You're right. I don't know how to do this. I don't know how to be sick." I suddenly remembered my mother saying she never worried about me, that I could take care of not only myself, but also nine or ten others. Yes, I knew how to be a caregiver, but I had something to learn about how to receive, how to be vulnerable.

I cuddled closer to him, nuzzling his shoulder. "Oh, Jer. I see now how you must've felt when you were sick. I'm so sorry. I just didn't know." I remembered the many fits and starts of our romance, breaking up with him, nearly losing him over his unstable health. Where was my compassion? Where was my love? In scant supply while superiority and self-concern marched boldly under a banner of "Good Judgment."

He reached out to smooth my hair. "You had no way to know, honey." He chuckled, "That's the trouble with you young chicks!"

Later, unable to sleep, I sat alone in the quiet house. In the echoes of our earlier conversation, I began to see the arrogance of my perfect specimen attitude. I'd thought of myself as young, energetic, healthy, sexy, and attractive. Yes, I'd long enjoyed the status afforded an attractive woman. Surely, this was part of my loss. Cancer was old, sick, and ugly. I saw my it-can-never-happen-to-me smugness with a shock of recognition. The smarmy stuff had hit me in the face before, I had to admit it. Until my marriage collapsed, I'd labeled divorced women as somehow inferior, the same way I'd labeled women with cancer, or for that matter, anybody seriously ill. There it was, painful to look at, but true.

Likely there were many old, unlearned lessons behind this new loss. Was there more? I decided there must be. Bernie Siegel challenged his patients to figure out not only why they had cancer, but also why the disease had chosen its particular location. So why did I have breast cancer? I asked myself. Was the disease some message about unforgiven injuries inflicted by Bob? Was it about some mother issue? Were today's tears the ones I couldn't find when Mom died? Maybe they were.

Exhausted from wrestling with questions, I trundled off to bed hoping I was coming closer to a few answers.

Next morning, I woke from dreamless sleep with clarity about one thing: I was facing surgery and needed guidance from experts. My doctor had been no help, but the staff at the mammogram center had always seemed supportive.

It was 8:00A.M. I swung my legs out of bed, wrapped up in my robe and hurried to the phone. A nurse answered. When I recited my unhappy experience at the surgeon's office, she quickly responded, "Shirley, you have to find a different doctor. Would you prefer a woman?"

A tear of relief slid down my check. "Oh, thank God! Can you suggest some names?"

She certainly could, and soon I had an appointment with a female surgeon specializing in breast cancer. A plaque on the rosy wall of her office displayed Artemis, the powerful virgin goddess, poised for the hunt, one breast bare, and to free her movement with bow and arrow, one breast gone. I knew I was in the right place.

We quickly determined that lumpectomy would be best. Since the growth was so small, my new doctor expected to easily remove it and find the lymph nodes clear of cancer cells. I was willing to face radiation as a safeguard.

Surgery took place on schedule. When I woke up, Jerry was at my bedside, a look of relief on his face. "You're ok, honey. The doctor says she really thinks she got it all. Your breast tissue looks good."

I was groggy, but reassured, and hurting! When I moaned, a nurse moved quickly to hook up an IV painkiller. "This'll help." Her voice soothed me as I drifted away into a dream.

I was with work colleagues on a beautiful, tropical beach, a wide-open expanse of sand and blue-green water. When they tried to enlist me in their project, I explained that I didn't have much energy for it just now, that I had a new job. In other words, I quit.

As part of my leave-taking, I sorted through a large, gray, metal desk, finding little of value. As I sorted, I realized I'd already thrown away information cards on previous students. Two drawers were full of tissue paper fluffs, perhaps party decorations. They could go. Then, I noticed the desk was washing down the beach in the tide. I hurriedly stabilized the two front legs on a cement curbing partly covered with sand.

Then, somehow, my lover was there. We were naked, or at least partly so, and very passionate. We wanted to go to our apartment for privacy, but the way was awash in the tide. Although not deep, the few inches of water across my ankles threatened to pull me off my feet. I struggled to get to the apartment door, which turned out to be the front entrance of the Casa, the retreat house I knew so well, though it didn't look like the actual place.

I woke up from the painkiller knowing the dream had been a gift.

Jerry, still at my bedside, listened to it carefully. Then his face brightened, "Sounds like we're going to Hawaii!"

"Well, an old Navy man like you will be right at home there. That gray metal clunker of a desk looked like government issue, too, no offense intended."

He chuckled, "None taken. Seems odd for it to be there on that lush beach."

I nodded. "And it's about to wash away. That could be about my work. I wonder if I've already let go of a lot. The cards about the students, and the little paper fluffs could mean that."

He crossed his legs, sitting back in the bedside chair.

"Well, I'd say this: you ain't letting go of much. Didn't you say you propped the desk up on something so it wouldn't wash away?"

"Doesn't sound like letting go, does it?" I paused for a moment. "Do you think this breast stuff means I need to give myself time for something besides work?"

He gave me a fake look of horror. "What? And not support me in the style to which I've become accustomed?"

I knew he thought I still worked too hard. I changed the subject. "What do you think about the lover part?"

He leaned nearer the bed, putting his hand on my knee. "I just want to know if we ever made it to the apartment."

I laughed, "I did make it to the door, but that will be dream number two. This sexy part had lots of feel-good energy, more than the rest of the dream. It was what led me though the water."

Jerry looked at me thoughtfully. "Why do you think the apartment turned out to be the retreat house? Does that stand for God?"

"Maybe, and the sexy feelings could suggest new life, something spiritual coming together. But what really struck me about this dream was the water."

He looked at me, a question on his face. "Why? Were you frightened?"

"No, but the tide surprised me. It was so strong in that shallow water, it nearly carried me away. I had to make a real effort to go against it."

Jerry stretched. He'd sat out my surgery and now my dreamy nap. "Well, honey, you're paying attention to a little pull of the tide. God doesn't have to send you a hurricane. And you made it through the water, right up to the front door."

He stood up, leaning over to kiss me. "You'll figure it out. I gotta go home and get some sleep."

It took a while to get the pathology report, and in the meantime, I fretted about the possibilities. What if the cancer had spread? The thought alarmed me. Would more surgery be needed, or worse yet, chemotherapy? I couldn't get used to thinking of myself as ill, but hesitated to believe the cancer was really gone. Maybe I was just arrogant, assuming myself somehow beyond the pale of ordinary mortals.

Day by day, the painful uncertainties of cancer pulled me to my edge, and there wasn't a thing I could do about it.

There'd been many such edges in my life. One of the first was deciding as a young woman what path to follow, then dealing with the anxiety of leaving that path, knowing I wanted children and marriage, but with no assurances or guarantees about what life would bring. Later, when my twenty-plus-year marriage blew apart, I faced another uncontrollable trauma. Now, this. I had no idea how to live through a health crisis. Other peoples' yes. Mine, no.

The worst exigencies didn't materialize. My lymph nodes were clear, and so was the tissue around the incision. By the time I'd healed from surgery and was on Tamoxifen, I'd decided to risk the dangers of radiation. At least it wasn't chemo. Scared but dutiful, I appeared at the clinic every morning. At first, I felt like an outsider among the women wearing hats, some of whom looked so pale and old. I desperately needed to keep a tidy distance behind my wall, and not become one of them. My hair was safe, at least.

Treatment began as the technician took measurements, carefully adjusting the calibrations of the huge machine suspended over my vulnerable nakedness. I tried to relax as she made small talk with me, while focusing the beam between points of dark blue tattooed on my breast. When she hurried out of the room, closing the lead door behind her, I was suddenly alone and panicky. I studied the shapes, angles, buttons, moldings, and shadows on the big hulk, now ominously humming above me. Gratefully, the treatment took only a few minutes.

I gradually learned to close my eyes. It was easier not to see the machine burning its way into my cells. There, in the quiet behind my eyelids, the Big Beam hummed, the only sound in the room.

To my surprise, as the days passed, the hum somehow became a song of angels. The Maria Angelorum chapel at St. Rose was full of angels. I'd never thought much about them except to admire their marble beauty, their white purity and grace. But now, gentle and benign angels seemed to truly abound, some scurrying in and out with the technician, some staying to hover around me.

Their song consoled me, but what I liked best was their wings. Somehow, the angels positioned their iridescent wings between the Big Beam and my delicate breast. Without opening my eyes, I saw the energy I didn't need deflected on those wings, becoming a stunningly beautiful rainbow of color. The powerful angels of Maria Angelorum chapel protected me.

Happily, I wasn't burned, but radiation sapped my energy. In the days and weeks that followed, life had to be lived simply. What I could do depended on reserves I found or didn't find in my recovering body. Although I heard from many friends and was grateful, I spent most days alone, quiet in an inner world, relishing the solitude as I healed. I kept my practice going, seeing a few clients in my home office, but mostly I journaled, rested, painted, rested again, then prayed, trying to accept what I could not change. But in the quiet tempo of those days of treatment, Bernie Siegel's pesky question about why I'd needed this illness tugged at me as the tide in my dream had tugged at my ankles. I still didn't know.

One sunny afternoon, Jerry and I sat on our warm patio, feet on the table, drinking iced tea. I repeated to him the troubling question that bedeviled me.

"Jer, do you think I somehow called this illness to myself?"

He looked at me silently for a long moment. "Do you remember that time you told me you felt like a big nipple?"

I'd forgotten that conversation, but now I remembered. He'd been sick. "Yes, yes, I did feel like a big nipple. Once I got past being scared about you, I was overwhelmed. You needed help. My clients needed help. Everybody in my life needed me—my sisters, Kelly, my friends—but there was nobody that I could turn to."

Jer rearranged his feet on the table, moving them out of the warm sunshine.

"Guess I didn't time that heart episode very well, huh?"

I breathed a silent prayer, reaching for his hand. "Oh, darling, don't take that on, please. We both know you couldn't time what your heart was going to do."

He laced his fingers between mine, resting our hands on his knee. "It's guy stuff, I guess. I just want to be able to help and support you all the time, honey." He swished the ice cubes in his glass and took a gulp of tea. "Anyway, you were frustrated, that's for sure."

"Well, I was drained." I giggled at the image suddenly flashing in my head. "One big, drained nipple!"

He laughed with me.

"Jer, you honestly did scare me, and all of that was before I resigned as assistant mom to my sisters."

Jerry was still smiling. "That in itself had to feel like commutation of a life sentence."

He was right. It had felt good to let my sisters know I needed their support and love, a few returns on my emotional investments with them over the years. Maybe I'd underestimated the heaviness of my oldest sister role, especially on top of everything else going on in my life.

"I think they're weaned now," I said.

I could see there had been changes. Long distance calls actually came from Iowa to Arizona these days, not just the other way around.

"That sun is getting hot for me, too." I wriggled my feet closer to Jerry's on the shady corner of the table, and squinted into the brightness beyond the patio's shade. At the edge of the pool, aloe blooms gracefully swayed in the warm breeze. "It's hard to think about problems on a day like this."

Jerry leaned back, closing his eyes, nodding agreement. "Well, we're just trying to figure things out." The ice cubes in his glass clinked with his movement. "Speaking of people who need you, how're things with Kelly these days?"

My twenty-something son had been living with us the last while, economizing as he finished school. "He's just tickled to graduate, and I'm darn glad you two have gotten along so well."

"Hey, gives me somebody to watch sports on the tube with." He raised his nose and his tea glass, crooking both little fingers. "I can't spend all my time at art movies."

"Just be careful, sir. It's not too late to have a miserable afternoon."

He laughed. It was a light moment, but we both knew we'd made a challenging adjustment with Kelly on board.

His expression sobered. "It'll be hard for you when he moves out, and I don't completely understand. Maybe it's because Kelly is an only child that you two are so tight. It's just different from my family."

A host of feelings rose in me. Yes, I loved my only son intensely, and I fully intended to stand at the side of this good husband. Certainly there was enough love for both.

Just then, the gate clanged open and Kelly swung in, one shoulder weighed down by a full book bag. "Hey, nice life relaxing on the patio while the rest of the world works!"

"Ok, smarty pants! If you're working so hard, how come you're home in the middle of the day?"

Grinning, he smoothed back a tousled forelock. "I've got some good news. The apartment I've been looking at is available now, starting the first of the month, and I'm going to take it."

The news caught me off guard. Jer voiced my question. "So you're not waiting until graduation?"

"No, I get a discount on rent if I move now, and it's just a few weeks till I'm out of school." Then he saw my face. "Mom, the place is only a couple miles away."

I turned to pour him a glass of tea from the pitcher on the table, hiding my quick tears. Here it was, his final launch into adulthood. "I'm glad for you, Kel, just surprised."

He took the tea, watching my eyes. "Mom, I'll drop by."

"I know you will, son." I took a quick swipe at my damp face and returned his gaze. "We'll make it a point to get together often."

Satisfied, he sat back. "You guys really helped by letting me stay here. I couldn't have made it otherwise."

Not wanting to be thanked, Jer spoke up. "I was just telling your mom how much I needed a jock like you to watch basketball with."

Kel laughed. "Yeah, she's not much of a jock." He took a sip of tea. "But, hey! We all got along pretty well, huh? Except maybe for the time I ate the last piece of Jerry's pumpkin pie, but"—he turned to me—"didn't you train me to finish up the leftovers?"

Jerry piped up, "Must've been a parenting error."

Kelly went on. "If I didn't eat the stuff, we'd have to mail it to starving children somewhere." We all laughed. "Anyway, I think it's cool that the pumpkin pie deal is the worst thing that happened around here."

My son was right. I looked from him to Jerry. "I'm just lucky my two favorite men like each other." I felt a twinge at my own words. I'd miss seeing this kid every day. Of the many roles I'd lived, motherhood was especially precious and now, that role was changing.

When Kelly was really out, to forestall my blues, I went into action.

I'd been splattering the walls of my small, windowless, ironing room for the last year, painting my way through some unknown inner world. Now I had the luxury of a spacious room with a window. I bought an art table and chair, assembled them and, abracadabra, I had my new art studio! Next, I covered the walls with my paintings—free swirls of vivid blues, yellows, and purples.

Stepping back to survey the wildness that had somehow sprung from my paintbrush over the months, I was eager to paint more. I sorted the bottles of paint lined up on my desk: teal, lavender, bright pink, dark pine. The colors vibrated with energy. I couldn't wait to start.

Hurriedly filling my water jar, I settled myself before a large, stiff sheet of watercolor paper ready for the paint to come to life. Then, suddenly I didn't feel like painting. Surprised and confused, I sat in my silent art room, gazing at the blank paper before me.

Then something came to me: *Portraits. Do pencil portraits.*

"No," I argued with the quiet thought. "I know how to do that. I can control the pencil. I want to *paint*. Paint gets out of control. I want to break out of the fetters."

Never mind, the urging continued. *Just draw. Do Grandma Cunningham.*

The only photo I had of Florence Cunningham was Mom

and Dad's wedding picture, both sets of parents flanking the bridal couple. I loved that shot of Grandma wearing the large, lacy hat that matched her dark elegant dress.

Just draw.

The feeling grew stronger.

I knew exactly where to find the picture. I sharpened my pencil and began.

The drawing that emerged amazed me. I sat perched on the stool at my drawing board looking down at my grandmother. Though I hadn't drawn a portrait in years and

Grandma Cunningham

thought I was rusty, this vibrant drawing was possibly the best of my entire life. It spoke to me of the many drawings I'd so proudly offered as a child for her unfailing praise so long ago.

All these years, that little girl who loved to draw had been locked away, neglected and languishing. Heaviness ached in my heart. Why had I allowed work to push her out of my life?

As I sat studying the drawing of my dear grandmother, gratitude washed over the heartache. The little girl who loved to draw was still alive, after all! Grandma had set her free.

Next day, I photocopied the drawing and mailed it off to Judy, my childhood friend. She remembered cookies and milk at Grandma's house on our walk home from St. Gabriel's grade school when we were kids.

When my envelope reached her, she called. "Shirl, the drawing looks just like your grandma, and it has such life, such presence. I hope you don't mind, but I showed it to Beverly. You met her last time you were here. She's quite intuitive."

Why would I mind? I'd wondered what Judy would see in the picture and was curious about Bev's reaction, too.

After the phone call, I carefully thumb tacked Grandma to the corkboard above my art table. Maybe it was her looking down on me like a guardian angel that made it easier to follow the prompting to draw more. I dug out the wedding picture again. Soon, portraits of my mother and father smiled encouragement at me from their place on the wall near Grandma.

Day by day over the weeks of my recovery, the urge to draw returned again and again. One face after another appeared on the blank white sheets in front of me, effortlessly, as if they had been politely lined up, waiting for me to release them with my pencil. Why was I drawing all these relatives, my maternal grandparents, and even Ben, my father-in-law? I didn't know. As the urge came to draw yet another relative, I simply drew. Gradually it occurred to me that when the last face arrived, I would have twelve portraits, enough for a calendar. I called Judy.

"Isn't this odd? Here I am, the inveterate planner, and it just dawned on me that I could make a calendar of these drawings. I'll have twelve."

Her voice was amused over the phone line. "Great idea. You're learning to free-fall, huh? A real departure from working all the time. . . ." Her voice dwindled off into silence. Then she spoke, "Shirl, I'm remembering the story you told me about walking the labyrinth at Chartres."

Electrified by her words, I sat up straight at my desk, a big a-ha surging through me. The labyrinth had taught me I wasn't going anywhere unless God opened the way. And when I could move, it was because God was in the lead. "Wow, I hadn't made that connection."

"Well, my friend, sounds like this art stuff is about being led. And what's more, I'd say the way is wide open!"

I began to see my encounter with cancer and the time of my recovery as a gift. I knew I was changing, learning to slow down, to trust, and to surrender. I still wasn't sure why I'd needed the illness, but some part of me knew that more than my body was healing.

Then, I had a dream.

It was time to talk to Judy again. She was in the dream, and in it, she was a psychic.

She chortled. We'd both been raised Catholic, but in recent years, she relied on her own ways of knowing.

"There was another psychic in the dream, too, a woman named Margolis."

"Margolis." She repeated the name. "I think there's a movie star named Margolis."

I rolled the name around in my head, too, then snapped to attention. The words my ear had heard were "My goal is."

Judy let out a long breath. "Whoa! 'My goal is!' Yeah!"

I chuckled at my clever dream-maker, and then went on with the story. "Well, Margolis is tall and beautiful with dark hair and eyes. She's wearing colorful, rather exotic flowing clothes."

"Hmm. She could be your alter ego, Shirl. Do you know where you are in the dream?"

"Well, before I meet Margolis I'm in that big house that comes up every so often."

"You mean the mansion full of treasures?"

We'd talked about dreams often. Judy had a good memory for mine.

"That's the one, but this time, the rooms have all been cleared out, except for one where large vases are displayed. When I object that the vases belong to me, the people in charge apologize and give them to me."

Judy sounded thoughtful. "That's a change. That house was packed full before. What do you make of it?"

I scratched my head. "Well, I'm still seeing clients, but I have slowed down. I guess there's a kind of new space."

"Yes, the room is empty, the vases themselves are large, and you own them. Maybe that means there's plenty of space for you to fill."

I didn't doubt it, but I did wonder what would fill all that room.

"Anyway, I meet Margolis in a hall, in a group of people. She ignores the others and deliberately comes to me. She embraces me, looking deeply into my eyes, then leads me to a quiet place. Once there, she tells me life is changing, that I'm beginning something new. I already know in the dream that she's talking about my work, my art, and the portraits. Then, she leads me further through more hallways and doors into her inner sanctum. It's filled with dancers, men and women in leotards of all colors. I dance, too.

She tells me, 'You're freer than you used to be, but still not completely free. You're still following the old pattern.' Then as if checking up, she places her hands on the crown of my head and says, 'Oh, lots of energy. Good!' She sounds surprised, but I'm not.

I tell her, 'It's my path. I'm willing to go there.' She listens closely, then asks me to repeat it."

"Quite a dream, Shirl. What do you make of it?"

"I know it's important, but right now, I'm not sure. I guess I'll have to live with it awhile."

A few days later, an email arrived from Beverly. I knew Judy had told her about my bout with cancer and now, she'd seen my drawing. *"I don't want to offend you or intrude, but this may be important for you. I'd like to give you the name and phone number of a medical intuitive I know in North Carolina. And, by the way, your drawing exudes energy. Have you considered dialoging with your grandmother through it?"*

I read her message again, then printed a copy and flopped in the big chair in the living room, my thinking chair, to read the message a third time.

Questions floated in my head. What was Beverly really saying to me? Had she intuited that the drawing had already spoken to me, albeit without words? Who was the woman she suggested I contact? Should I follow up on the lead? Though

I respected intuition, I wasn't always sure what to do with it. Consulting psychics was a no-no where I came from. Turning inside, I closed my eyes, and quieted my mind to pray.

Gradually, the answer gently arose: This whole chain of events had arisen from Grandma, and Beverly had approached me in a spirit of love. Love is of God, the greatest power in the world and always trustworthy. I smiled, thankful for the guidance and decided to call. I hopped up from my easy chair, the exact spot where I'd been visited by my grandmother so many years before, and went looking for the phone.

A soft voice with a pleasing southern accent answered on the first ring. "Hello, Shirley, I've been expecting your call." Beverly had said Petrina was an intuitive with a wide view. I wasn't sure if someone had told her I might call or if this was her wide view.

Her laughter tinkled like small bells in my ear. "Beverly said you might call for a reading on the phone. Too bad we can't meet in person, but Arizona's a long ways away! And here I am, a complete stranger to you. Let me tell you just a bit about myself. I have a degree in psychology, training in yoga, and I work with the body-mind-spirit connection."

I was reassured. This was the approach I used with my own new counseling clients. Bev had told me Petrina's husband was a physician. I guessed it was fair to assume she'd have good judgment.

After a few pleasantries, Petrina began her intuitive work by asking me to relax and breathe deeply. In a moment, she spoke. "Your body is completely clear of cancer, Shirley. I see you don't fear it, because—on some level—you know your body is clear."

I took in her words. On some level, I did know my body was clear.

"You don't fear death, either, for that matter. What you fear is that you won't do what you need to do, accomplish what you need to accomplish, to be whole and complete."

I sat back on my heels. How did this woman know the deepest fear of my heart was to fail to accomplish what I had been sent into this life to do?

The fear of not living out my call had propelled me into then out of the convent, into then out of marriage, and now was stirring the neglected artist and who-knew-what-else inside me. I sat up, leaning my elbows on the desk to listen intently to what Petrina had to say.

"So, now, breast cancer. The breast, of course, for a reason." She was silent for a moment. "You are being held down by masculine energy. . . ."

"Does that have to do with my work?"

To my surprise, she said slowly, "No, but have you been divorced?"

That again? Hadn't I completed my grief and my anger? Hadn't I forgiven and healed? I thought I had. I'd even married Jerry—this couldn't be about him! I admitted I'd been divorced some eight years earlier.

Petrina was silent another moment before she spoke, "No, I think the male energy has to do with your first husband. There's something heavy and dark about him that's holding you down." She paused again. "Yes, the darkness is about him. It's his."

Bob? A wave of resistance rose within me. I didn't want to reopen the old turmoil. But I did want to know why I had breast cancer. There was no escaping; I had to ask myself the hard question: Was the old hurt still unresolved, even now?

Petrina's voice interrupted. "Have you forgiven him?"

"I thought I had." What if I haven't? The possibility frightened me. What would that mean for my healing and for his?

My attention drifted away from her voice to a time when after nearly two years of marriage counseling and several separations, Bob and I, each deeply hurt, were locked in a standoff. I was exhausted, disheartened, and angry. At that juncture, Bob had asked to meet with me, hoping to make me see how harmless his secret keeping had been. But I was too traumatized. I doubted the marriage could be salvaged, but felt such a meeting surely would deal the deathblow. I'd hardened and refused.

Now, here on the phone with Petrina nearly ten years later, I didn't have to ask myself if I could accept him as another human being without judgment. My hardness had melted. I knew I could. Was that what was called for?

"Shirley, if you think you could meet with him in a spirit of unconditional love, it would be very healing for both of you. He needs to know you are ok, that he hasn't hurt you. He wants to hear that from you."

I gently placed the receiver in its cradle and sat quietly looking at it, thinking things over. Was this another part of the reason I had cancer? The question still bedeviled me.

Finally, I decided to call Bob.

He was surprised to hear from me, especially when he heard I wanted to meet. "Mind telling me what brought this on?"

I heard both warmth and wariness in his voice. Taking a deep breath, I began. "I know you were terribly wounded when I left. I'm very sorry for that, for your pain."

The sigh from his end of the line told me that even now, he was still not healed.

"Bob, I know you never intended to hurt me. From the beginning, I knew it was good for you to open up the part of your life that needed fresh air. I understood that." I swallowed a sob that suddenly shook in my throat. "It's just that I couldn't deal with it."

He was silent as the moment stretched out. My anxiety mounted. Maybe this call hadn't been such a good idea.

Then, he spoke. "So you want to meet, hoping we can forgive each other now."

I breathed a sigh of relief, "Yes, that's it." It was so important he understand. I needed to be sure my thoughts, feelings, words, and actions all lined up, to be sure I was completely straight with myself and everyone in my life, and to find true integrity of spirit. Otherwise, how could I heal? How could he?

"What changed? You absolutely refused to meet before. Why is it different now?" He waited for me to answer.

Of course, he would have reservations with me, a reasonable voice inside me offered. *Look at all that has gone before.*

"Well, it probably took these ten years of healing to get to this place. Bob, I want you to know I'm willing for both of us to get over our split up."

He made no objection.

"You know I'm dealing with cancer."

He murmured sympathetically.

"We need to be straight with each other for me to heal."

This time, his voice came through clearly and immediately. "Absolutely, Shirl. You need to heal. I'll help anyway I can."

I knew those words came from his heart.

A few days later, I drove across town to meet him. I'd wondered if my past sadness and anger would return, but from the moment I laid eyes on Bob in the café lobby, I felt only a shy curiosity, as if meeting an old friend after a long separation in which we'd both changed.

The hostess seated us in a corner booth made private by a row of potted palms. At mid-afternoon, the place was quiet except for faint piano music and the distant tinkle of glass and silver.

Bob smiled at me over the menu. "It's good to see you, Shirl, and good to see you looking so healthy."

I returned his smile, taking in the blue eyes I knew so well. In that moment, I was glad I'd come.

Just then, a chubby, red-faced waitress hurriedly swung past the potted palms. She breathlessly sloshed water glasses on the table, and with no further ado, demanded our order. Bob's eyes crinkled with amusement at the flustered woman's insistence. He flicked a quick glance at the menu, then at me. "Hey, cherry pie. Your favorite."

"Sure, I'd like that. Make it ala mode." I shrugged the sweater off my shoulders, holding my face serious.

While he studied the menu, I glanced at his tanned face. The worry wrinkles were a bit deeper than I'd remembered. Well, time had passed. Maybe they were new.

Once he announced his choice, the harried waitress bustled off, relieved to have that over.

I caught a faint hint of after-shave as my companion leaned across the table. "How're you feeling?"

"Doin' ok. I'm tired by evening, but I have energy in the afternoon." Six weeks of radiation had drained my reserves more than I cared to admit. "I feel more like my old self every day."

He studied me with steady eyes. "Glad to hear that."

I returned his gaze, pleased at my own calm, pleased it hadn't wavered under his concern, hadn't wavered in this meeting, the very thought of which had so terrified me in the past. Sitting with him was easier than I'd expected. I decided to get to my agenda.

"Bob, the reason I'm here is to ask your forgiveness for the pain I've caused you."

A clink of dishes alerted us that the waitress was about to round the potted palms again. We fell silent as she served us, waiting until she backed away.

"Do you think now she'll let us talk?" We both chuckled.

Returning to my question, Bob made a disinterested stab at the pie in front of him. "I forgave you a long time ago. I'm more concerned about whether you've forgiven me. You were the one who was angry and wanted to break up. I never wanted that damnable divorce."

He'd often pointed that out to me in our painful confrontations. Now I heard his words without shame. I knew they were true, and I accepted them, owning no blame, knowing I had had to leave, difficult as it was. This peace was new. And I was grateful.

"It's been a long road, but I honestly don't hold any judgment toward you, not now. I've forgiven everything, and I'm sorry I judged you then." I reached across the table for his hand. "Can you believe me?"

A tear glistened in the corner of his eye. I knew his answer.

I took a deep breath, relieved. "And, Bob, you always said there was nothing wrong with what you were doing. I feel now like I'd like to have the whole subject come out of the shadows. I'm in some kind of creative surge and I'm thinking of writing my story. I think it could help others who have their own struggles. Would you care if people knew?"

His face stiffened. "You mean you want to write about my private business?"

"Well, I'm just trying to put myself in your shoes. I know you think it's harmless—"

He interrupted me. "No, absolutely not."

"Ok," I answered softly, feeling confused, but quietly detached. I didn't understand, but I wanted to respect his feelings.

When we left the café, standing in the parking lot, he hugged me, red-eyed. "Be sure to take care of yourself."

Slipping into my car, I rolled down the window, shifted into reverse, and waved one final wave. As I wheeled into traffic, I was still calm as the moment I'd arrived. With the sun setting at my back, I pulled out from behind a truck, smoothly accelerating on the open road.

Bob had to live out what he had to live out. It wasn't up to me to judge him. I could live with the bewildering questions. Psychology offered answers on one level. My training gave me one perspective, a diagnostic, judgmental perspective. But a larger mystery remained. What quirk of fate made it necessary for us to lose each other? Was it some unexplainable karma? I didn't know. I'd never know, never be able to penetrate the darkness. All that mattered in the moment was our mutual forgiveness and healing. My heart knew I'd released him in a new way. That was the miracle of my lunch with Bob. I smiled. Cherry pie would always be my favorite.

11

"Who Are You Besides Who You Are?"

I dream I have a baby boy with dimples. He is beautiful, and my heart overflows with love for him. I am thrilled with this child, thrilled without measure to hold him for the first time. For some reason, I haven't held him until now, in a crowd at the back of a large, old-fashioned church. It is Christmas.

As I look to the altar, I see white curtains where the statues usually stand. These curtains aren't drifting around loose; they're hung on rods, fastened down top and bottom. Because the church is being remodeled, the statues are on the floor near the altar. The largest among these solid gold statues is St. Sulpice. A Franciscan priest I know strides down the aisle toward us, obviously upset that the statues aren't on the altar. As I call him over to see my baby, I notice his robes are a lighter shade of brown than the usual Franciscan habit. When he sees how wonderful the baby is, he stops complaining, but starts grumbling again when he goes away.

I understand, after the dream, that the big old-fashioned church is my life, my way of belief, and it's being remodeled, although it has happened unobtrusively, over time, and parts of me aren't used to it yet.

The curtains tell me, "It's all over. It's curtains now for the old ways." The statues, although still valuable, have lost their place of prominence. They are "old pieces," only symbols, not the real thing. The baby is the real thing. In the joy of what is newly born in me, even the mantle in which I'm clothed lightens up.

This is a dream of love, a dream of great sweetness. The new life, kissed by angels, arriving on Christmas, is the real thing. The real thing comes from inside.

After the dream, I saw many connections. As a young woman, I'd learned the lessons of spirituality from my mother. Mom's prescriptions weren't always perfect. "Be good, go to church, listen to the priest." Ever the good daughter, I'd lived and breathed Catholicism, not noticing how my mother's rules had confined me until after her death.

Then, after the estate settled, I happened on a book, *A God Who Looks Like Me* by Patricia Lynn Reilly.[19] I circled it, curious but wary. Was it really God stuff, the feminine images and woman-affirming language of prayer and reflection proposed by the author? My heart knew the reality of the feminine divine as if it were a home left long ago but never forgotten. The powerful experience of the Black Madonna pilgrimage had pulled me far beyond my mother's religious strictures, but my gut quivered.

Patriarchy's male images of the father and savior had been so pervasive. The theology, intellectual underpinnings, and male priesthood of Roman Catholicism emphasized the masculine, often overlooking feminine aspects of divinity and the gifted roles of Eve, Lilith, Mary Magdalene and even Mary, the mother of Jesus.

Yet, I knew first-hand that Chartres, Besse, and Montserrat were hallowed by the unmistakable presence of the Mother as surely as Medjugorje. But was the Black Madonna's power, the power of the Ancient Goddess, the same as Catholicism's Queen of Heaven? The pilgrims I'd met in Yugoslavia stood on holy ground with their shared Christian faith, but my companions on the shamanic journey were diverse: Buddhist, Jewish, Christian, Shamanic, and New Age. The Mother didn't care. Despite our differences, all of us had been gripped by Her. The question of whether God could look like me was a big one. I'd returned from the pilgrimage, wrestling with how I could ever integrate the undeniable experiences of those weeks into my beliefs. If I couldn't, the cost might be high indeed. I decided to keep my inner turmoil to myself. It was only later that the pieces began to fit together.

When I discovered another pilgrimage, called "The Goddess Gate," offered by my former community, the Franciscans, I began to understand. Cecilia Corcoran, FSPA, was leading groups to Guadalupe and other sites of indigenous goddesses in Mexico. I slowly grasped that I was walking through discontinuities and continuities, and that I was safe. I was not only on safe ground, I was on holy ground. Even Mom would approve.

It wasn't long until I was off to Mexico. Jean, another FSPA, was one of my companions. Sharing a seat on the tour bus, rattling down a dusty Mexican road, we remembered each other from thirty years earlier.

"So, Shirley. Where do you live now?"

"Arizona. I've been in the Southwest for years. And you?"

"Twin Cities. I'm a parish associate." Almost as an after thought, she added, "And I do some intuitive soul work."

In these days of priest shortage, lots of nuns filled in as associates in parishes, but Jean's casual after thought made my ears perk up. Despite my training as a counselor and spiritual director, the term, "intuitive soul work," was new to me.

Her eyes sparkled as she turned sideways to face me in the seat. "It's just a label that doesn't scare anyone."

She paused, looking out the window at a tumbleweed blowing across the winding road ahead of us. "As I sit with people in spiritual direction, images come to me. At first I didn't say anything . . ."

I jumped into her pause, full of questions. "But then you decided to? Why? What happened?"

Jean met my eyes and laughed. "The images didn't mean anything to me, but when I told one woman, she said, 'Well, I'll take care of it.' It was only the middle of her session, but she got up and left."

I chuckled, imagining how I'd have felt. "You probably thought you'd offended her."

Her voice dropped to a whisper. "Oh, I did."

"So what happened?"

Jean reached into her backpack, pulled out two apples, then offered me one. "In a few weeks, the woman came back. She told me she'd decided the images meant she should act on something she'd ignored for a long time." Jean polished the apple on her knee, then took a bite, and sat silently for a moment, as if chewing on her thoughts. "To my surprise, she solved a long-time problem."

"So then you started telling other clients about what you picked up about them?"

"Yes, since it seemed to have helped her so much."

I bit into the juicy red apple. It was my turn to chew on a few things. Here was a mature, well-grounded religious woman from my own former community, using inner vision to guide people while she worked for a Roman Catholic parish. Although Jean would never make the comparison, I thought of Padre Pio, the Italian mystic who knew what those who came to confess had to say before they said it.

I crunched thoughtfully on the last bite of apple. I'd heard years ago, on some retreat, that mysticism was for everyone, part of the normal growth of prayer, a side effect.

Cracking the bus window, I pitched my apple core to the wind and turned to Jean. I had to know what she'd pick up from me. She agreed and suggested I write out some questions ahead of time.

A few days later, we met in my room. We sat knee to knee in chairs near the open window, enjoying the warm afternoon breeze.

Jean lit a candle, said a short prayer, then took my hands. "So, Shirley, what's your first question?"

I went immediately to my deepest concern. "How can I grow more? I mean, spiritually?"

My companion closed her eyes, taking a deep breath. Then she spoke. "I see an odalisque resting on a bed of flowers and feathers."

I sat up straight. It had to be Margolis, the mysterious psychic I'd dreamed of months ago while I was undergoing radiation.

Jean wanted to know all about it.

"At first, I was puzzled by her name, then I understood it as 'my goal is . . .'"

Jean chuckled softly. "Clever play on words."

"Yes. My dream-maker does that." I went on. "In the dream, Margolis led me to her inner sanctum where she showed me dancers and invited me to join them. I did, but no matter how hard I tried, my dance repeated the same little pattern over and over. Margolis reassured me I was more free than in the past, but said I wasn't as free as her dancers yet." Tears sprang to my eyes. I hadn't expected another visit from Margolis!

Jean's face was softly lit in the candlelight. "Amazing dream. Was there more?"

I closed my eyes to remember. "Yes, she placed her hands on the crown of my head and said, 'Lots of energy here.' I told her, 'It's my path. I'm willing to go there.'"

Jean nodded. "So you *are* willing to open up your energy?" Pausing, she looked at me closely. "I think the odalisque has the same message as your dream. That as you relax and loosen up, the intuition and spiritual growth you want will come. That it's time to let go, to make less effort. Do you think so?"

I nodded, remembering being stopped in my tracks as I walked the labyrinth. Was the odalisque connected to my uncanny paralysis at Chartres, too? It seemed to be, and I'd already discovered less effort meant more freedom.

After a pause, Jean brought me back from my reverie. "Do you have another question?"

Still pondering what more the odalisque meant to teach me about my old dream of Margolis, I sat up and reached for my notebook. My next question had to do with work. As I'd slowed down after Chartres and cancer surgery, new creativity had seeped into the free hours in my day, but I wasn't clear about how art and writing fit with my counseling work.

Eyes closed, Jean pondered only a moment. "It's as though a river is flowing along. As it flows, it becomes turbulent, taking some of the shoreline rocks and grasses with it." She stopped, opening her eyes. "Do you recognize that kind of energy in your creativity?"

I was startled. That was exactly how energy pulled me along as I painted and sometimes, when I wrote.

She looked at me thoughtfully. "It may be important to use writing and art as your spiritual practices now. You're not used to thinking of them that way, but perhaps they are becoming your true work."

Art as a spiritual practice? Jean didn't even know about the pencil portraits that had ushered in visitations of my

Dancing Goddess

grandmother and parents. She didn't know about the paintings that had preceded them either.

I'd played with paint and charcoal pencils as long as I
could remember, but always with a starting point of careful
observation. My walls had long been hung with paintings
and drawings of women's faces, faces that caught my eye,
sometimes nuns, sometimes Native Americans, sometimes
fairy queens drawn by other artists. Then, one day, out of

Corn Mother

thin air, a goddess, hair swirling, spontaneously danced across the expanse of watercolor paper before me, spiraling in rivers of blue and eddies of green. I told Jean about it.

"Once this goddess danced across my page, I couldn't miss her. I fell in love with her. That day, I realized I'd been creating images of the feminine divine for years even though they weren't part of my Catholic way of thinking."

The little nun listened intently. "So, for the first time, without planning or looking at anything else, and despite what you believed, this image simply appeared before you?"

It was such a relief to finally tell the story and sort it out.

"Yes, and then, it was as if a door had opened. I began to see more faces while I meditated. The first was a woman whose eyebrows and hair were on fire."

Jean's eyes popped wide.

"Yeah, I was impressed, too, but when I tried to paint her, a different image appeared instead." I slid my chair back, reaching for my purse on the stand behind me. "I've got a picture here somewhere." It was the first in the packet of photos.

She glanced quickly from the snapshot to my face. "She looks like Corn Mother."

"That's what I thought."

"What'd you make of that?"

"I was mystified. I'd been on the Black Madonna pilgrimage by then, but still hadn't figured out how shamanic and Native American beliefs fit into my ideas."

A bird's call echoed sweetly from an arbor of roses outside our window. Jean smiled at me, "But here she was, nevertheless—Corn Mother."

I leaned forward, eager to tell the rest of the story, needing to finally understand. "Yes, and after that, I felt such an urging,

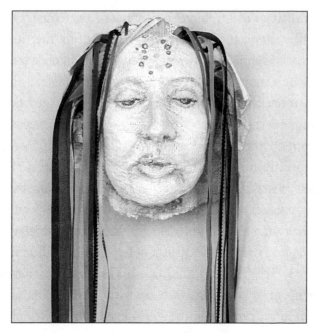

Feminine Divine

Jean, to create what came in meditation. It was strange that the paint arranged itself almost as if it had a will of its own, not at all like the careful work I'd done in the past. And, Jean, *then* I made a mask, the first and only mask I'd ever made."

I remembered the strange energy that propelled me to it. "I didn't want to do a mask, but it bothered me, for some reason, like a pebble in my shoe."

Jean chuckled, shaking her head.

"Finally, I asked Jerry to get me some tape, the kind that hardens after it's all wet down and formed."

"Surgical tape? The kind they use for casts?"

"That's the stuff. I had Jerry cover my whole face with it, just leaving little air holes under my nose."

I took a long breath remembering what it had been like

as he'd spread the tape over my eyes and mouth, walling me in. "While I waited for the mask to firm up, I went into a trance. It was eerie. Then, when he peeled the mask from my face, . . ." My voice drifted off.

I'd been jarred the first time I saw the mask. It was hard to describe, even now. Rifling through my packet of photos, I spread them on the stand beside us, sliding the shot of the mask toward Jean.

She picked it up, holding the picture delicately by its edges to study the blue green eyes, and narrow blue and yellow ribbons for hair.

"The face of the feminine divine." The little nun looked up at me. "She appeared so unexpectedly. What did you discover through this artwork?"

I thought for a moment. "My biggest discovery was the energy surging through me. It felt like your turbulent river. I still don't understand it." I searched Jean's face as if I'd find words there.

"And, I guess I learned not to expect or plan, but just to open up to whatever is going on, even when I don't understand."

"You learned something about accepting, simply letting things be. Shirley, it seems to me that the odalisque, the river, your dream, and your art are all of a piece. As you relax, your energy moves freely. I think now your spiritual life and your work are one and the same."

I was relieved and amazed. She understood what was still very amorphous to me.

I soon had occasion to think more about my talk with Jean. Shortly after returning from Mexico, while browsing in a bookstore, a book fell open in my hands.

... Making art was the most surprising ecstatic form I had ever discovered. . . . I never knew that the simple act of making something could be a doorway to religious experience. Every day I would stand in front of my drawing table, look at the empty page, consider . . . [what] I was going to work on that day, and begin. Hours later I would emerge from what seemed like a journey to another land, a trip that made me lose track of time and space, allowing me totally to merge with my material. It was only the fact of evening—the darkening of the light—that would cause me to end my work for the day.[20]

I knew what this was about. Years ago, before the Blessed Sacrament at St. Rose, I'd lost track of time and space in prayer many times, and I'd long understood that any activity could be an encounter with God. I made the connection: painting and drawing had taken me to the same quiet, inner timelessness.

The author went on:

. . . We must let ourselves express what is inside us, even if it makes us afraid. . . . As the lines unfold into pictures that weren't intended by the ego-consciousness, the person doing the drawing begins to see something in the picture. Sometimes it's perfectly clear, a representational image that anyone would recognize . . . other times, it's just messy lines, taking an abstract shape or form, but with a particular feeling or meaning to the artist. . . ."[21]

I knew the dancing goddess and the mask had arrived almost of their own accord. I closed the book, holding my place with one finger, to look at the cover: *Shakti Woman,* by Vicki Noble. I'd never heard of her and had only a vague notion that Shakti was a Hindu goddess, but the passage was a revelation to me. I was at once startled and reassured to discover someone had words to describe what had tenuously floated into my awareness. What I couldn't say but could recognize had been made explicit.

I decided to take Jean's suggestion seriously. Eager to see what would unfold, I began spending time each day not only drawing, but also writing, with the intent to come closer to this Holiness within.

Writing wasn't new. My closet shelves were lined with dusty scrapbooks from school days, brittle with age. Their yellowing pages were filled with stories and poems, the very first a proudly titled word picture in childish ten-year-old script, "Snow Queen." Piled on the scrapbooks was a lifetime of journals. Over the years, I'd often written daily, filling dozens of notebooks, reflecting on my life and the meaning of events, feelings, and relationships, but always for my own enlightenment, not to share with others, not for publication.

Now as I sat to write each morning, what had been introspection changed to another process, something I didn't recognize.

Then, as if on cue, I had another dream. It was brief and to the point. Jesus appeared. He asked only one question: "Who are you besides who you are?"

I answer, "A writer." I am mildly disappointed. I want the answer to be "An artist," but I say to myself, *You've never dreamed of Jesus before. This is important. You have work to do.*

It was a dream I had to notice.

Within days, I began writing my entire life story with the urgency of a river torrentially carrying away whatever was loose in its path. This wasn't like my old journaling, but I was resolved to keep going even though I didn't know where the fast current was taking me. Jean's images and my dream had worked on me. Although I didn't know the vastness of the world I had entered, I was ready for more.

My chance soon came. Judy called. "You said you were interested in learning more about intuition. We're giving a workshop here next month." Without hesitation, I signed on.

The day I arrived in Durwood Glen, the other participants were already gathered. Despite my eagerness, I didn't know exactly what to expect. Judy eased me into the group, introducing me to Marguerite. Her tight, warm hug, lasted a few beats longer than I'd anticipated. Then, she stepped back, dark eyes sparkling, to push a few escaped tendrils of curly gray hair back into place in the luxurious upsweep that framed her heart-shaped face. Judy had told me Marguerite's gift was helping people shift their energy. I didn't know what that meant, but I'd surely felt hers in that welcoming hug.

Toward the end of the workshop, my turn for a one-on-one session with Marguerite came up. We slipped away from the group to a quiet parlor in the back of the house. Dispensing with small talk, she seated herself on a wing chair next to the couch, and waved me over. "Stretch out, Shirley, and let's get started."

As Jean had begun that day in Mexico by encouraging me to relax, so Marguerite asked me to center myself. I quietly closed my eyes and took some deep breaths. The only sound in the room was a gentle sighing of wind through trees just outside the open window. Soon we both were still. The silence seemed to expand, filling the room. Behind my closed eyelids, the rhythm of my breath was soothing, peaceful. I floated, relaxed and tranquil.

Then Marguerite spoke. "Shirley, I want you to imagine a shoreline. Go there, to the water's edge."

As she spoke, I found myself at the pine-shaded mountain lake near my summer home, its still, green water reflecting the granite crags surrounding it. I climbed up the lichen-covered boulders eager to perch on the largest one for my favorite view of the lake. To my surprise, it had become an altar. I knelt down before it, awed by its size.

Marguerite spoke again. "Place here, now, on this altar, your willingness to surrender anything from the past that may hold you back from the newness God has for you in this moment."

I was willing, but what did I have to release? I asked myself. Hadn't the wounds of the past been healed? What did I have to surrender? Stymied, all I could do was wait quietly with the questions.

Then, rising from some sure place, came the words of an old prayer: *Receive my liberty, my memory, my understanding, my entire will . . . give me only Your love and Your grace. . . .*[22]

A hot tear trickled down my cheek. Yes, I'd release everything, not just my wounds, but also my ego, whatever could be in the way of this new thing God had for me, this great love. I promised.

Although I hadn't spoken, I knew Marguerite, silent at my side, understood my tears. As if in response, she whispered, "There is a gift for you on the altar, Shirley. Look for it."

At first, the flat granite slab appeared bare except for a few pine needles and oak leaves skittering across it in the breeze. Then vaguely, there did seem to be a gift on the altar for me. A maroon fountain pen, an ordinary fountain pen. It was the old-fashioned cartridge kind, now obsolete, an insignificant gift. I was disappointed.

Then, quietly, a little voice asked, *Why a fountain pen?*

The voice answered itself immediately: *To write, of course.*

With that, a huge dam burst, releasing a deluge of memories and feeling. When I graduated from high school, my father gave me a pen and pencil set. I saw the shiny maroon set in its white box in the middle of our lace-covered dining room table where I'd left it for weeks. I was hurt. Graduation was the first important milestone of my young life, but my father hadn't known me well enough to guess what might please me. He hadn't cared enough to ask, hadn't tried to give me a meaningful gift.

I remembered the night before graduation, too. Mom and I had driven around town for hours, the little kids finally asleep in the backseat, waiting for the house to be dark and quiet so we could creep into bed, finally safe, as my father slept off his mean drunk.

I'd resented the chaos my dad caused while I grew up, and I'd resented his dying when I was nineteen, abandoning me.

I could see him again in the hospital bed, reaching a feverish hand to me, tears in his eyes. I will remember his words the rest of my life. "Shirley, I never got to know you."

I'd kept a stony silence though angry words burned inside me: *That was your fault. I was here.* That night, he died.

Then almost without pause, another rush of memory washed over me.

It was Christmas. I was still in high school and editor of the school paper. Dad had called me into the kitchen to unwrap a big box on the table. It was an unthinkably extravagant gift, a typewriter! He'd pulled me to his lap where I could read the note left between the rollers: *"To the best little girl in the whole world, Love Dad."*

Remembering, my shoulders shook with sobs. *Oh, Dad,* I cried out inside, *why did you have to leave when I needed you so desperately? I was only nineteen.*

After a moment, Marguerite rested her hand lightly on my arm, calming me. I took a ragged breath and glanced at her through my wet lashes. Her eyes were closed, but her head was tilted, face attentive as though listening to something far away. It was a moment before she spoke. "Shirley, your father's spirit is here."

The words sent a thrill through me.

"He's saying to you, 'I know you now. And you are the best big girl in the whole world.'"

Then, like a whisper to the heart, I heard my father's voice.

Yes, Shirley. Now, tell the truth. Tell your truth. Tell your story. With that, he handed me the old-fashioned fountain pen, so long lain idle.

A wave of gratitude enfolded me, like an eddy of warm, ocean water, flooding over all that was past. Now I knew! He had loved me. He had seen who I truly was. My father's gifts—the typewriter, the pen—had recognized me. He did know who I was, his beloved daughter, a writer. I finally understood, finally, finally. At last, the pain of so many years ago could release and dissipate.

A soft wind at the window ruffled the curtains at my side. Stretching, I sat up on the sofa and smiled at Marguerite. I knew my old resentments were drifting away on the breeze. Truly, it was time to write.

One morning, just weeks after my encounter with Marguerite, I settled myself at the kitchen table for a quiet moment over a cup of coffee and the newspaper.

Jerry shuffled up behind my chair, still in bathrobe and slippers, and bent to kiss me on the neck. "What are you reading, sweetheart?" Over my shoulder, he read the headline: "Psychologist Offers Seminar on Talking with Angels." A statuesque blonde seated on a tall stool smiled up at us from the paper spread across the table. "Some cute gal talks to angels?"

I looked at him over my glasses, "Pour yourself a cup of coffee and never mind the cute gal!"

He chuckled and sat down, reaching for the carafe between us. "What I mean is, another cute gal talks to angels?"

I grinned. "Ok, you're off the hook. Have some orange juice."

He craned his neck, reading the article. "Dr. Doreen Virtue left her practice to write and teach about angels after they saved her life in a car-jacking." I angled the newspaper toward him and leaned to read, too.

"Hmm . . . Christian, clairvoyant . . . been on talk shows. I've never heard of her."

Jer sat back, pouring the orange juice. "Me neither." His eyes drifted away to the pool sparkling in the morning sunshine outside our window. "Makes me think of Ed Mitchell. Remember him?"

I nodded. In the fifties, Jer had met him in the Navy on an aircraft carrier, before Ed's career as an astronaut.

"One of the smartest guys I ever knew, and then that thing happened to him in space, something spiritual."

I'd read about it. He called it an epiphany.

"Yeah, I think he gave up his scientific career because of it. Or at least, changed direction." Jer leaned over to look at Dr. Virtue's photo again. "Hey, this gal is coming next weekend, and her conference is right down the street. Wanna go?"

I'd met a few angels along the way. It sounded like a good idea to me.

When we arrived Saturday morning, though we were nearly half an hour early, the hotel parking lot was jammed. Jer held the van door open as I climbed down onto the hot asphalt. "Do you think all these people are here for our seminar?"

He took my elbow, steering me toward the conference center. "If so, Dr. Virtue must be good, keeping folks in town in this heat. We could be in the mountains."

The auditorium was as packed as the parking lot. We stood in back, looking for seats. Then Jer pointed, "There's two." I followed him into a row in the middle of the hall. As I sat down at his side, he gave a quick glance around. "Must be 300 people here, easy."

I nodded. Subdued piano music announced the arrival of our speaker. As the crowd quieted, Dr. Virtue walked to the dais, her soft, aqua skirt gracefully swirling around her. She seated herself and began, without notes, to speak to the large crowd as easily as though she were alone with each one of us.

She told her story simply, a story of faith and spirit. Then, she assured us the angels and our departed loved ones were close and eager to help us as they had helped her. "We need assistance, but there can be blocks in the way of the loving help they are so ready to give us. Take a minute and think about what yours may be. Perhaps fear? Sadness? Anger?"

As she ticked off the possibilities, I took notes, then thought of the maroon fountain pen, and the pent-up anger I hadn't known I had. My dead father's encouragement had dispersed my old resentments as surely as his urging, "Tell the truth, tell your truth," had opened the way for my writing.

Doreen went on. "Fear, particularly, can hold you back

from the full use of your gifts, from accomplishing your true life purpose and all that your life is divinely intended to be." Her voice was clear and even. "Many angels are here now to help you release these fears. Remember, your deceased loved ones are among them. Let's think for a minute what fears you need to release. Fear of success?"

I hastily jotted that down. Yes, on some level, I feared success.

"Fear of criticism?"

That definitely had held back my writing and even the idea of publishing. I had to admit it.

"Fear of ridicule?"

Yes, another yes.

"Fear of putting the raw stuff out there, fear of vulnerability?"

I recognized that one with a cold chill. It was the fear that had kept me in the safe zone all my life, maintaining distance from family and friends, insisting on privacy to a fault. I wondered if it was affecting my writing even now.

Doreen went on, "Fear of money? Fear of having it? Or fear of not having it?"

I winced. Another tender spot! I'd always lived below my means, justifying it as frugality. I suddenly knew the fear writhing under the surface of my money habits was the same fear hiding behind my private-person persona.

I stopped writing. Where had all this fear come from?

Looking up from my notebook, I was startled to see Doreen staring into my eyes across the sea of heads between us. Maybe I was mistaken. Maybe she meant someone else. I glanced to my right and to my left, but she smiled widely. "Yes, I mean you. There's an older woman with you. Are you aware of her? She's very close."

At her words, I froze in my seat feeling a presence just behind my shoulder, the same presence I'd felt that spring day in the Madonna chapel at Montserrat while strains of "Silent Night" in German had so surprised me. No words could get past the lump in my throat.

Doreen asked, "Is this your mother?"

I nodded.

"She's telling you, 'I want you to succeed, honey. I *want* you to. . . .'"

I knew this was about the litany of fears I'd just uncovered, especially my fear of success.

As the day went on, Doreen came back to me again and again. In that crowd of 300, I was the only one she came back to three times, always with a message of my mother's closeness.

That night at home, I turned to my journal, trying to understand all that had happened in that unrepeatable day. Was it really ok with Mom if I wrote my book, described my new vision, moved beyond her simple life, venturing even beyond where my own life had ever gone before? Was it really ok to follow where it led? I remembered Fr. Goeff's message of so long ago, "Every gift I have has been given to me for someone else."

Was my life a conduit of wisdom for others?

Searching for a blank page in my dog-eared notebook, I fumbled across words I'd written only a few days earlier: *"You are seeing that your fear is deeper than you thought, but I have brought you here with great love. You are being born. — Your Mother."*

Then, it all clicked. I knew my life story wanted to be written as urgently as a baby wants to be born. There was no holding back this new life, neither my work schedule, nor my financial fears. The joy that had surged through me today convinced me that from her place on the heights, my mother's spirit had indeed spoken, and her message was about more than the book. It was her blessing on the spiritual remodeling underway within me. With that assurance, it was curtains for the old stuff. I was ready to surrender to the powerful birth pangs gripping me.

I was finally ready to trust beyond my fear. I even could trust what I didn't know I didn't know. I understood. My inner and outer lives were now carried by a creative force and the river was flowing.

EPILOGUE

EPILOGUE

—*If Only We Attend*—

TIME TRANSPARENT

It is silent there, and still.
In that paralyzing Presence,
Time becomes transparent, on the edge of now.
Eternity slips through uncomprehending fingers.

Is it darkness? Is it light?
Being has no dimension, has no hue.
Only the blurred outline of a whisper is there,
Not seen, not heard, but known.

Ungrasped, but wholly known,
Infinite Love gives.
There, in the silence of that Presence,
An illuminating embrace.

All of us are capable of becoming illuminati. In fact, it is our call, so that the eternal light may come into the world, as the light of Christ came so powerfully, long ago. Mostly, we walk in darkness, but in flashes we are enlightened that our lives are gifts from God.

Both the light and the darkness, of my life and yours, are meant to illumine us and others, as our paths have been lit by those who have gone before us.

The light is very near, and it is eager to reach us through the thin veil of our consciousness. The light presents itself over and over again, waiting for our attention. Oh, the value of the attending.

All connections are made because we have attended. Only through attending can the outpouring of light flood through the aperture that is our soul. Only from the inside can the floodgate be opened to allow divine luminosity into the world, to illumine our lives and the lives of all.

So, how are we to attend to this light? By gently listening to our own inner spirits, by slowing down, sitting quietly, journaling, allowing dreams, recollections, and imagination to emerge. All of us are artists, creating our own lives, but how seldom we stop to look at what we are creating.

When I am watchful and attend, though, I begin to see the Holy in all my affairs, great and small. And by my loving attention and welcoming, this Goodness truly flows into my life more and more, using me as I was created to be. Mysticism is not mysterious. It is the stuff of every day life.

I think of my computer. Day after day, I sit down and plug into what I already know how to do. It's only when I need to use some other function that I take a step in learning. Much more capacity is at my very fingertips than I realize. I see how I have run repeatedly through a small, well-trodden part of the maze, not opening to the vast expanse of intricacy and potential that is at my fingertips, at the entry to my heart.

It is only when I realize that I don't know what I don't know that I can learn. This humbling and difficult place is the very edge off which I must fly to learn wisdom in my life. Every moment steps into a new moment, never here before. All is continuously created anew, yet I catch myself holding to stale, old thoughts of should's and mustn't's.

Spirit catches me unaware and hurls me into the unknown that I may gloriously learn to fly. I gradually learn to trust the precipice, to fly beyond my little imagination, beyond to where Spirit so eagerly leads, always whispering, "There's more. There's more."

Giving birth taught me something of these mysteries. In the sweat and pain of labor, I learned on some level I couldn't have been told what I didn't know about myself. It was a knowledge beyond any Lamaze class, beyond any book on sexuality, a knowledge only my female body could bring. I was pulled into a new part of life with an inevitability that was impossible to resist. Labor thrust me into the unknowns of motherhood as it thrust my child into the harsh light of the delivery room, unexplored territory for each of us.

All is connected. The new life of that moment arose from a death. The life choice of a young woman, stricken with grief at the death of her grandfather, ultimately led to the birth of the child.

All that happened in the years between is part of the mysterious connection, too. Living among the nuns, I learned, unwillingly at first, to let go of my own agenda, to attend to whatever was next, at the sound of a bell. I slowly grasped a great truth: The Holy One is to be met at every turn, not simply in those times and places I'd arbitrarily chosen.

I didn't know then, but I gradually learned that I was not to deify even my guides, even the setting of religious life. I learned that God was truly everywhere in the garden. There was indeed no angel with flaming sword at the gate into or out of the convent.

God gradually broke down many little walls I'd constructed. First, I'd refused to think of myself as a nun, until it was no longer possible to resist the powerful yearning. Then, I'd refused to think of myself as an ex-nun. But in that safe haven of celibate women, as I let go of the feminine trappings I'd loved as a girl, paradoxically, the wall I'd constructed around my heart's desire to marry, to be a mother, came tumbling down.

More little walls were broken down in the years that followed. I'd been called into and out of the convent, called into a time of single life, then called into marriage and motherhood. The coming together in marriage taught me a spiritual reality about union that I hadn't expected. But the big surprise came as I sat nursing my lovely baby.

Bare-breasted in the warmth of human flesh against human flesh, I fell into deep states of prayer. My spirit was nourished as my body nourished my baby. Wonderment at God's close touch in the midst of so much sensuality made a big crack in the fortress I didn't even know was there. A fortress closing off Spirit from sexuality.

Other immense walls came down as my long-held identity as a good Catholic and life-long wife was released, painfully calling me out of my marriage. Only then did I recognize the judgments I'd held toward others suffering the loss of a marriage.

Eventually, it took cancer to show me more of my judgmentalism. In illness, I joined the ranks of the broken, saw the condescension I'd held toward those who were physically ill, perhaps dying, and in the dissolution of these judgments, Bob was also freed from the curse of my blame.

Such powerful touches of Spirit always leave an aftereffect of greater appetite. And so it was with me. I'd hungrily chased what I couldn't have imagined ahead of time. Following what I didn't understand became easier.

The rapture of an encounter with my grandmother's spirit led me eventually to Medjugorje and its lessons of the Mother. At the time, I was still numb to the wound of patriarchy, only partially aware of the great loss I'd suffered, but even so, my healing began. As Mary lovingly enfolded me in her embrace, it became clear my gifts were for others.

One of those gifts was listening: I could hear beyond words to the heart. Another was courage: I could open my inner world to others, standing in my own truth with new confidence. In those days, Mary carried me easily into the use of these gifts, guiding me to gently sidestep my denomination's restrictions. She also gradually drew me beyond patriarchy's Father God to the Great Mother. I followed the powerful and gentle Mother into a darkness where I could be taught.

Little did I imagine that the call of the Ancient Mother had the depth I would later discover among the Black Madonnas. An immense piece of wall fell down on that pilgrimage. I saw how I'd walled out other traditions, the spirituality of ancient times and places, restricting the light to only one window, a Catholic Christian one. What I didn't know called me strongly into the void, into the depths of womb-like darkness. But as life soon teaches the child, so it was with me.

I learned that there is indeed one stream, but many places of access, many pools and wells, many springs and outpourings. And so I was led to understand the Buddhist Tara, to grasp the gift of Iannana, to ponder the lessons of the ancient Venus of Willendorf, to study the goddesses within every woman—Hera, Aphrodite, Athena, Artemis, Demeter, Persephone, Hestia, Brigit, Coatlicue, Sophia, Shekinah, even Shakti, the mysterious Hindu Goddess. All were voices, faces of the multifaceted reality that we call God, names among the many names with which that Holy One is called.

I discovered that Native Americans spoke of Dawn Star, their prophet's name for the spirit they recognized as Jesus when the missionaries introduced Christianity to their world.[23]

I found parallels everywhere in the traditions that honored the ancestors. I discovered that angels, emanations from God, are ever at my side. The spiritual world, as real as everyday life, is crowded with helpers. The Catholic tradition names them the communion of saints. And, I understood from the drawings that flowed from my pencil onto the walls of my home, that these helpers were at my side, eager to comfort and guide and heal me.

Especially through the unexplainable encounters with the spirits of my own family did another wall begin to crumble, the wall that fear had built around intuition. Many years ago I sat writing as I am doing today, allowing inspiration to flood out onto the page. Because my God then was still a God of judgment, I had a fearful encounter with a denied part of myself, a part in shadow. My fear was so great that I retreated from the powerful voice of intuition, closing off a part of my spirit's potential. It was safer to hide behind religion, but as I kept chasing God, the Holy One coaxed me to pay attention to those little nudges more and more. And so I learn to attend to the gift of intuition, opening to the path Spirit intends for each of us, reminding myself over and over that I don't know what I don't know.

My life is gradually convincing me that there is more to it than I have dreamed. We are all mystics, and when we quietly allow it, we see images as in a dream. They arise from a deep place in spirit and psyche and emerge through the imagination. Some are captured in paint or clay: the Venus of Willendorf, the cave paintings at Lascaux, the Black Madonnas, and the images from ancient art in all times and places and cultures. Images from Hildegard of Bingen's visions seem somehow akin to Vicki Noble's art and its connection with Shakti, and to my own visions, as well, of the three faces of the feminine divine.

These are the messages of salvation calling to each of us through the depths of our own human spirit, the inspiration of that Reality we name God.

Curiously, another tradition has offered me a rich gift on this path: the Eastern tradition of yoga. Only recently have I learned to attend not just to images and voices but also to the subtleties conveyed by my body as I move or sit mindfully in asanas, yoga postures. Only lately have I learned to attend to thoughts and feelings as the whisper of the True Self, not different from the voice of inspiration, my angels, or Spirit. All is one and all is real.

Science can now explain how this "one reality" works.

That we are all connected is the premise of modern physics. Quantum theory explains that all of reality is but one energy. One field of energy connects our subjective intentions to what we think is separate, the objective world. Thoughts and feelings have the power to create because they are part of the energy pervading the universe.

All is energy and we are influenced by and influence each other more profoundly than ever before understood. Jesus told us that He and the Father are one, and we are one in Him. Let us finally hear and understand that despite our various doctrines, when we enter deeply into the spirituality at the heart of all religious traditions, we join one another and are freed from the illusion of separation. This is the royal road to peace.

Terrorism has recently awakened us to reality—we live in a global community. Let us finally recognize that we *are* one family on this earth, sharing our humanity and spirit. Let us recognize our unity, in truth, and offer our energy in prayer together, joining our intent for the good of all. Then let us act. Let us build the bridges to understanding, love, and peace so sorely needed in our diversity.

So who am I now? One who has been gently taught that God is love and all is connected. My mind stumbles on it, forgets it, loses focus, but the task now is to wake up more quickly and stay awake longer, attending to all that comes to me.

I am a writer, amazed at the web spinning out from my fingers, creating something where nothing was before, like Spider Woman, creating a world from within herself. And so it is in all our lives when we attend and follow our true purpose. God spins out into the world beauty and gifts, something wonderful from nothing.

I am a writer, one who willingly opens the channel for the Light that has poured through my life to pour through my fingers, to the keyboard and onto the page, to illumine the path of others. My call, and yours, is to be taught by our very lives, each equally valuable, equally complex, equally full of light—if only we attend.

References

1. Dom Gaspar Lefebvre, OSB, "The Burial, Liturgy of the Dead," *St. Andrew's Daily Missal* (New York: DDB Publishers, Inc., 1962), p. 1,588.

2. Matthew 16:26.

3. Francis Thompson, *The Hound of Heaven and Other Poems* (Boston, MA: International Pocket Library, 1936), p. 11.

4. Soeur Sourire, "Entre Les Etoiles," paraphrased from the original French, *Dominique* (Philips Records, 1963)

5. Ronald J. Wilkins, *The Emerging Church* (Dubuque, Iowa: Wm. C. Brown Co., 1975), p. 205

6. Bob Dylan, "The Times, They Are a' Changing," *The Times They Are a' Changing* (M. Witmark & Sons, Columbia, 1963).

7. Pete Seeger, "We Shall Overcome," *The World of Pete Seeger* (Columbia Records, 1974).

8. Jim Morrison, The Doors, "Light My Fire," *The Doors* (New York: Elektra Records, 1967).

9. Published by Andrew Scott, Inc., "Dream the Impossible Dream," also called "The Quest." 1965. Originally appeared in the musical, *Man of La Mancha* (Original Broadway Soundtrack: Kapp, 1965).

10. Mother Teresa, *In the Heart of the World* (Novato, CA: New World Library, 1997), p. 55.

11. Psalm 34:19

12. Patsy Cline, "You Made Me Love You," written by Joe McCarthy and James V. Monaco (Broadway Music Corp., 1940).

13. China Galland, *Longing for Darkness: Tara and the Black Madonna* (New York: Viking Penguin, 1990).

14. Bernadette Farrell, "God Beyond All Names" on *God Beyond All Names* Audiotape (Portland, OR: OCP Publications, 1991), Tape says: "In our living and our dying, we are bringing you to birth."

15. Barbara Calamari and Sandra DiPasqua, "Prayer of St. Francis," from *Novena: The Power of Prayer* (New York: Penguin Books, 1999), p. 61.

16. Bernie Siegel, *Love, Medicine and Miracles* (New York: Harper & Row, 1986).

17. *Breast Cancer: Let Me Check My Schedule*, edited by Peggy McCarthy and Jo An Loren (Boulder, CO: Westview Press, 1997).

18. Susan Love, *Doctor Susan Love's Breast Book* (Reading, MA: Addison-Wesley, 1990).

19. Patricia Lynn Reilly, *A God Who Looks Like Me* (New York: Ballantine Books, 1995).

20. Vicki Noble, *Shakti Woman* (San Francisco: HarperCollins Publishers, 1991), p. 159.

21. Ibid., p. 170.

22. Anthony F. Chiffoll, "Prayer of St. Ignatius," *At Prayer with the Saints* (Ligouri, MO: Ligouri Publications, 1998), p. 136. (Ignatius of Loyola)

23. Brooke Medicine Eagle, *Buffalo Woman Comes Singing* (New York: BallantineBooks, 1991) pp. 238-240.

Anderson, Sherry Ruth, and Patricia Hopkins. *The Feminine Face of God: the Unfolding of the Sacred in Women.* New York: Bantam Books, 1991.

Artress, Lauren. *Walking a Sacred Path: Rediscovering the Labyrinth as a Spiritual Tool.* New York: Riverhead Books, 1995.

Ashton, Joan. *Mother of All Nations.* San Francisco: Harper and Row, 1989.

Baldwin, Christina. *Life's Companion: Journal Writing as a Spiritual Quest.* New York: Bantam Books, 1990.

Barasch, Marc Ian. *Healing Dreams.* New York: Riverhead Books, 2000.

Baring, Anne, and Jules Cashford. *The Myth of the Goddess.* New York: Arkana Penguin Books, 1993.

Bodo, Murray. *Tales of St. Francis.* New York: Doubleday, 1988.

Bolen, Jean Shinoda. *Crossing to Avalon.* New York: HarperSanFrancisco, 1995.

———. *Goddesses in Everywoman.* San Francisco: Harper & Row, Publishers, 1984.

The Wisdom of Hildegard of Bingen. Compiled by Fiona Bowie. Grand Rapids, MI: William B. Eerdmans Publishing Co., 1997.

Brande, Dorothea. *Becoming a Writer.* 1934. Reprint. Los Angeles: Jeremy P. Tarcher, 1981.

Borg, Marcus J. *Meeting Jesus Again for the First Time.* New York: HarperSanFrancisco, 1995.

Cady, Susan, Marian Ronan, and Hal Taussig. *Wisdom's Feast: Sophia in Study and Celebration.* San Francisco: Harper & Row, 1989.

Cameron, Julia. *The Artist's Way: A Spiritual Path to Higher Creativity.* New York: Jeremy P. Tarcher, 1992.

Capacchione, Lucia. *Visioning: Ten Steps to Designing the Life of Your Dreams.* New York: Jeremy P. Tarcher, 2000.

Carnes, Patrick. *Don't Call It Love: Recovery from Sexual Addiction.* New York: Bantam Books, 1991.

Carty, Charles Mortimer. *Padre Pio, The Stigmatist.* Rockford, IL: Tan Books, 1973.

Cassou, Michell, and Stewart Cubley. *Life, Paint and Passion: Reclaiming the Magic of Spontaneous Expression.* New York: Jeremy P. Tarcher, 1995.

Chopra, Deepak. *How to Know God.* New York: Harmony Books, 2000.

Cope, Stephen. *Yoga and the Quest for the True Self.* New York: Bantam Books, 2000.

Cuneen, Sally. *In Search of Mary.* New York: Ballantine Books, 1996.

Daniel, Alma, Timothy Wyllie, and Andrew Ramer. *Ask Your Angels.* New York: Ballantine Publishing Group, 1992.

Das, Lama Surya. *Awakening the Buddha Within.* New York: Broadway Books, 1997.

Diaz, Adriana. *Freeing the Creative Spirit: Drawing on the Power of Art to Tap the Magic and Wisdom Within.* New York: HarperSanFrancisco, 1992.

Duerk, Judith. *Circle of Stones: Woman's Journey to Herself.* San Diego: Luramedia, 1989.

Edwards, Betty. *Drawing on the Right Side of the Brain.* Los Angeles: Jeremy P. Tarcher, 1979.

Edwards, Tilden. *Living in the Presence.* San Francisco: Harper & Row, 1987.

Estes, Clarissa Pinkola. *Women Who Run with the Wolves.* New York: Ballantine Books, 1992.

Farraday, Anne. *Dream Power.* New York: Coward, McCann & Geoghegan. 1972.

Ferder, Fran and John Heagle. *Your Sexual Self.* Notre Dame, IN: Ave Maria Press, 1992.

Field, Joanna. *A Life of One's Own.* Los Angeles: J. P. Tarcher, 1981.

Finley, James. *The Awakening Call.* Notre Dame, IN: Ave Maria Press, 1984.

Fisher, Kathleen. *Autumn Gospel: Women in the Second Half of Life.* New York: Integration Books, 1995.

————. *Women at the Well: Feminist Perspectives on Spiritual Direction.* New York: Paulist Press, 1988.

Fowler, James W. *Stages of Faith.* San Francisco: Harper & Row, 1981.

Galland, China. *Longing for Darkness: Tara and the Black Madonna.* New York: Viking Penguin, 1990.

Gawain, Shakti. *Creative Visualization.* Mill Valley, CA: Whatever Publishing Co., 1986.

————. *Living in the Light.* Mill Valley, CA: Whatever Publishing Co., 1986.

Gendlin, Eugene. *Let Your Body Interpret Your Dreams.* Wilmette, IL: Chiron Publications, 1986.

Gold, Aviva. *Painting from the Source: Awakening the Artist's Soul in Everyone.* New York: Harper Perennial, 1998.

Harris, Maria. *Jubilee Time: Celebrating Women, Spirit and the Advent of Age.* New York: Bantam Books, 1996.

Harvey, Andrew, and Anne Baring. *The Divine Feminine.* Berkeley, CA: Conari Press, 1996.

Haskins, Susan. *Mary Magdalene: Myth and Metaphor.* New York: Harcourt Brace, 1994.

James, William. *The Varieties of Religious Experience.* New York: Collier Books, 1967.

John of the Cross. *The Collected Works of St. John of the Cross.* Translated by Kieran Kavanaugh and Otilio Rodriguez. Washington, DC: ICS Publications, 1973.

Johnson, Robert A. *Inner Work.* San Francisco: Harper & Row, 1986.

Jung, Carl Gustav. *Memories, Dreams and Reflections.* New York: Pantheon Books, 1963.

Keating, Thomas. *Open Mind, Open Heart.* Rockport, MA: Element Inc., 1986.

Kelsey, Morton. *God, Dreams and Revelation.* Minneapolis: Augsburg, 1974.

———. *Adventure Inward, Christian Growth through Personal Journal Writing.* Minneapolis: Augsburg, 1980.

Koff-Chapin, Deborah. *Drawing Out Your Soul: The Touch Drawing Handbook.* Langley, WA: The Center for Touch Drawing, 1999.

Larranaga, Ignacio. *Sensing Your Hidden Presence.* New York: Image Books, 1987.

Mellick, Jill. *The Natural Artistry of Dreams.* Berkeley: Conari Press, 1996.

Moore, Thomas. *Care of the Soul.* New York: HarperCollins Publishers, 1992.

Moss, Richard. *How Shall I Live? Transforming Surgery or Any Health Crisis into Greater Aliveness.* Berkeley, CA: Celestial Arts, 1985.

Naparstek, Belleruth. *Your Sixth Sense.* New York: HarperSanFrancisco, 1997.

O'Carroll, Michael. *Medjugorje, Facts, Documents, Theology.* Dublin: Veritas Publications, 1988.

Orloff, Judith. *Second Sight.* New York: Warner Books, Inc., 1996.

Pagels, Elaine. *The Gnostic Gospels.* New York: Random House, 1979.

Peck, M. Scott. *The Road Less Traveled.* New York: Simon and Schuster, 1978.

Progoff, Ira. *At A Journal Workshop.* New York: Dialogue House Library, 1975.

Robinson, Lynn A. *Divine Intuition.* New York: Dorling Kindersley, 2001.

Ryan, Regina Sara. *The Woman Awake: Feminine Wisdom for Spiritual Life.* Prescott, AZ: Hohm Press, 1998.

Sanford, John A. *Dreams: God's Forgotten Language*. New York: Lippincott, 1968.

Savary, Louis M., Patricia H. Berne, and Strephon Kaplan Williams. *Dreams and Spiritual Growth: A Judeo-Christian Way of Dreamwork*. New York: Paulist Press, 1984.

Schulz, Mona Lisa. *Awakening Intuition*. New York: Harmony Books, 1998.

Signell, Karen A. *Wisdom of the Heart: Working with Women's Dreams*. New York: Bantam Books, 1990.

Stone, Merlin. *When God Was a Woman*. New York: Harvest/HBJ Book, 1976.

Teresa of Avila. *The Interior Castle*. New York: Paulist Press, 1979.

Timmerman, Joan. *The Mardi Gras Syndrome: Rethinking Christian Sexuality*. New York: Crossroads, 1985.

———. *Sexuality and Spiritual Growth*. New York: Crossroads, 1993.

Ueland, Brenda. *If You Want to Write*. St. Paul: Graywolf Press, 1987.

Underhill, Evelyn. *Mysticism*. Oxford, NY: One World Publications, 1993.

Vaughn, Frances E. *Awakening Intuition*. New York: Anchor Books, 1979.

———. *Shadows of the Sacred*. Wheaton, IL: Quest Books, 1995.

Virtue, Doreen. *Divine Guidance*. Los Angeles: Renaissance Books, 1998.

Warner, Marina. *Alone of All Her Sex: The Myth and the Cult of the Virgin Mary*. New York: Vintage Books, 1983.

Welch, John. *Spiritual Pilgrims: Carl Jung and Teresa of Avila*. New York: Paulist Press, 1982.

Williams, Strephon Kaplan. *Jungian-Senoi Dreamwork Manual*. Berkeley: Journey Press, 1980.

Winter, Miriam Therese. *The Gospel According to Mary*. New York: Crossroads, 1993.

The Cloud of Unknowing. Translated by Clifton Wolters. New York: Penguin Books, 1978.

Woodman, Marion, and Elinor Dickson. *Dancing in the Flames: The Dark Goddess in the Transformation of Consciousness.* Boston: Shambhala, 1996.

Zukav, Gary. *The Seat of the Soul.* New York: Fireside Book, Simon and Schuster, 1990.

ABOUT THE AUTHOR

Shirley Cunningham was born in Wisconsin and has been a high school English and Journalism teacher, a college and university lecturer, as well as a social service administrator. Currently, she is a spiritual director and counselor in private practice. Shirley has long been on her own spiritual quest and assists others through her workshops and retreats.

With two degrees in English, one from Viterbo College, La Crosse, Wis. which she earned magna cum laude, the other from Ohio State University, Columbus, Ohio, Shirley also has a Masters of Social Work from Arizona State University. She trained as a spiritual director at the Shalem Institute, Washington, DC and has been a long-time student of spirituality, psychology, journaling, dreams, intuition, imagery, and creativity and their interconnections. She has kept journals and written poetry from childhood. *Chasing God* is her first book.

Shirley lives in Scottsdale, Arizona, is married and has one son.

CONTACT INFORMATION

M s. Cunningham welcomes your letters and invitations to give seminars and retreats. Her topics include:

- Chasing God: A Workshop Based on the Book
- Listening to Wisdom's Voice: Journaling, Dreamwork and Intuition Development
- Journaling for Personal and Spiritual Growth
- Becoming Makers of Love: Integrating Spirituality and Sexuality
- The Quest for Wisdom: Midlife Woman's Journey to Maturity
- Writing Your Spiritual Autobiography;
- Enhance Your Romance: What to do Before You Say I Do

- The Circle of Women: How the Mother-Daughter Relationship Influences You
- The Sacred Journey: Life Stages
- Singles Retreat
- Spirituality and Work, in the Same Breath? Yes!
- New Life after Loss
- A Time for Us: Mothers and Daughters (age 7-10)
- Art in the Pines: Creative Spirituality
- Prayer Rising Like Incense
- Marriage Enhancement
- What's God Up To in Your Life?

Seminars and retreats can be customized for your group as to content, format and length. For further information, please write Amoranita Publishing Co., Box 15563, Scottsdale, AZ, 85267-5563, or call 480-998-3081. You can also visit our web site: www.amoranita.com

ORDER FORM FOR
AMORANITA PUBLISHING CO.

Name _____ Phone(_____) _____

Address _____

City _____ State _____ Zip Code _____

BOOK TITLE:	QTY.	PRICE	TOTAL PRICE

CHASING GOD

by Shirley Cunningham _____ X $19.95 = _____

    Shipping and Handling _____

  Arizona residents add 7.7 % ($1.54) sales tax _____

      TOTAL _____

SHIPPING AND HANDLING: U.S. Mail Priority - 1st item $4.00
          Each additional item add $ .50

METHOD OF PAYMENT: Check or money order payable to
          Amoranita Publishing Co.
          For credit cards, call 1-866-654-7268
          during business hours.

AMORANITA PUBLISHING CO.
* Box 15563 * Scottsdale, Az. 85267-5563
Phone: 480-998-3081 or 1-800-917-0220
www.amoranita.com

ORDER FORM FOR
AMORANITA PUBLISHING CO.

Name_____ Phone(_____)_____

Address_____

City_____ State_____ Zip Code_____

BOOK TITLE:	QTY.	PRICE	TOTAL PRICE
CHASING GOD			
by Shirley Cunningham	_____	X $19.95	= _____
Shipping and Handling			_____
Arizona residents add 7.7 % ($1.54) sales tax			_____
		TOTAL	_____

SHIPPING AND HANDLING: U.S. Mail Priority - 1st item $4.00
Each additional item add $ .50

METHOD OF PAYMENT: Check or money order payable to
Amoranita Publishing Co.
For credit cards, call 1-866-654-7268
during business hours.

AMORANITA PUBLISHING CO.
* Box 15563 * Scottsdale, Az. 85267-5563
Phone: 480-998-3081 or 1-800-917-0220
www.amoranita.com

ORDER FORM FOR
AMORANITA PUBLISHING CO.

Name_____ Phone(_____)_____

Address_____

City_____ State_____ Zip Code_____

BOOK TITLE: QTY.   PRICE   TOTAL PRICE

CHASING GOD

by Shirley Cunningham   _____   X $19.95   = _____

   Shipping and Handling   _____

  Arizona residents add 7.7 % ($1.54) sales tax   _____

       TOTAL   _____

SHIPPING AND HANDLING: U.S. Mail Priority - 1st item $4.00
        Each additional item add $ .50

METHOD OF PAYMENT: Check or money order payable to
        Amoranita Publishing Co.
        For credit cards, call 1-866-654-7268
        during business hours.

AMORANITA PUBLISHING CO.
* Box 15563 * Scottsdale, Az. 85267-5563
Phone: 480-998-3081 or 1-800-917-0220
www.amoranita.com